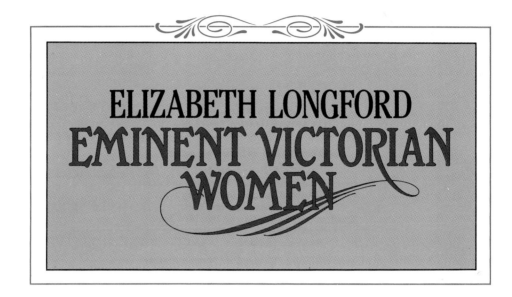

ELIZABETH LONGFORD
EMINENT VICTORIAN WOMEN

Alfred A. Knopf
New York 1981

The Queen is most anxious to enlist everyone to join in checking this mad, wicked folly of Women's Rights, with all its attendant horrors.... Woman would become the most hateful, heartless and disgusting of human beings were she allowed to unsex herself; and where would be the protection which man was intended to give the weaker sex? *Queen Victoria*

Queen Victoria

between Anglo-Saxon w
side. But after the Conqu
Church or wealthy wid
opportunity: many of the
Crimean War gave Flore
gave women the vote.

Of course there was t
some amends to wome
Uncumber in Westmins
uncumber women of the

Boccaccio matched F
Mulieribus (c. 1356) of 1(
martial women; but mo
at reports of Solomon's
wisdom lightly'. Then
which was more fitted
kept, just as she most ha
As for the Delphic Sybi
hours well, can gain wit
men be thinking of, wh

To overthrow the tra
divine order would be
Marriage was publishe(
unknown author warn
circumstances must she
Nature is given unto hii

Mrs Mary Wollstone
the birth of her daughte
ideas, so that Charles
petticoats') published h
the Terror. In the book
and their social trainin
should undergo natior
taught to earn their livii
were better organized
their husbands instead
or inconstancy, and if t
professions rather than
of being a governess'.

In his illuminating l
Lawrence Stone traces
family together by 'sub

‛THE SEX’

‛**T**he Sex’ was how members of Parliament would refer to women. The words were spoken archly and generally followed by loud laughter. One had to laugh off the fact that Victorian women were becoming discontented, unwomanly and a political problem. It was better to make ‛The Sex’ sound funny.

Needless to say, it was not among the things that amused Queen Victoria. When Lady Amberley (Bertrand Russell's mother) expressed advanced views in 1870, Queen Victoria denounced ‛this mad wicked folly of "Women's Rights" with all its attendant horrors, on which her poor feeble sex is bent, forgetting every sense of womanly feeling and propriety. Lady Amberley ought to get a *good whipping*.'

However misguided her conclusions, the Queen's gift for expressing popular sentiments in brisk language was never more apparent than in this famous diatribe. As we shall see, words like ‛mad', ‛wicked', ‛feeble', ‛propriety' and even ‛whipped' were all highly relevant to the question. Not that Queen Victoria hesitated to contradict herself when necessary on many of the issues. She supported women's right to become doctors, at least in India; the tendency of even the best men, even dearest Albert, to treat women as ‛playthings' was deplored; there was too much marrying, she felt, and too many children (though Mr Bradlaugh's suggestions for preventing their conception could be referred to only under her breath in the most general terms as ‛horrid things').

Never questioning her own ability to rule the greatest empire the world had ever seen, she might have smiled had she read John Stuart Mill's celebrated *Subjection of Women*, published the year before her own attack on Lady Amberley. For Mill believed that Queen Victoria and her predecessor Queen Elizabeth had played their sovereign parts well. Nevertheless Queen Victoria said that women's rights were ‛mad', and Queen Victoria was an eminent woman.

She was supported in her opinion by no less an authority than William Cobbett, the radical Tory guru, who had delighted the country with his *Rural Rides* and in 1829 offered *Advice to Young Men and (Incidentally) to Young Women*. He warned young men against falling in love, since women made their lovers forget duty, work and reason, and drove them into becoming, like the women themselves, ‛a little maddish'. But if a youth insisted on this maddish act he

should look out for chasti
long duration towards . . .
the *teeth*', which correspo
quick at work.' Queen Vi
all the plates removed befo

Besides admiring Her N
fickle and subject to 'n
'maddish'? True, he put i
proper education but ove
how could the domestic
the housework if women

The '*good whipping*' wh
and who should administe
in J. S Mill's views on th
subjection, argued Mill, w
stronger than women, an
grown up. The true differ
this force-based superiori
educational opportunities
into 'an academy for train

Whether or not Mill wa
there is no doubt that tl
necessary to many Victo
climax. To strike a man l
bring him down, symbo
him impotent, lame or de
blindness has a good myth
Testament and the classi
Romney Leigh in Elizabe
in fires caused by incendi
they become helpless. Re
see Jane.

The further one delve
Victoria seems to have fo
Rose Macaulay called wo
tion', while Virginia Wo
her own introduction to
stand . . . I looked up "W
of bluestockings in the la
for women. 'The men
women in their infancy
well ordered as they desi
household slaves, wome

Looking back beyon
Woman in History, 1957)

Under the Puritans and during the Restoration, the will of children no longer needed to be so ruthlessly broken by constant whippings, and women could be married for other qualities than desirable connections and doweries.

During the eighteenth century, however, a growing sense of social and political crisis brought back many of the rigidities. The beliefs of Methodists and evangelical churchmen in paternal authority and sexual repression were gathering strength among the middle-classes. But Stone sees the mysterious tide turn again about 1860, with a trend towards permissiveness spreading from the middle-classes to the elite in the 1890s.

Thus we may go on to note that the supreme confidence of the mid-Victorians coincided with increasing permissiveness, an interesting thought. There had been movements in that direction for some time. As early as 1832 in fact *The Laws of Women's Rights* in regard to property and marriage was published anonymously. Wrongs were admitted, but the author believed that redress could only be achieved through 'patience' and 'Parliament'. A newly discovered novel by Benjamin Disraeli and his sister Sarah, dated 1834 and entitled *A Year at Hartlebury*, shows that they, too, were pushing the women's cause. A group of 'petticoats' is standing around after the election result has been declared:

'I wish I had a vote', said Dame Harrald.
'The women have no votes', said Mrs Collins mournfully.
'The more's the shame', said gossip Faddle.
'In this world the men have it all their own way', remarked Dame Harrald pensively.

The case of Caroline Norton, however, is the most recognizable starting-point of the nineteenth-century struggle for women's rights. As a result of legal proceedings begun by her husband in 1836, Mrs Norton lost not only the custody of her children but also a legacy from her mother and even her own literary earnings – lost them all to her ex-husband whose chattels they were. Thanks largely to Caroline Norton's agitation, including a telling letter to Queen Victoria in 1855, the first of many successive Married Women's Property Acts was passed by Parliament in 1857.

'I do not ask for my rights', said Caroline Norton bitterly. 'I have no rights. I have only wrongs.' From this memorable epigram were to stem many others, some serious, some flippant. 'I have all the rights I want', says pretty Alice in Harriet Beecher Stowe's *Oldtown Folks*. George Eliot, though no devotee of women's rights, nevertheless wrote to congratulate Lady Amberley on her lecture entitled, 'The Claims of Women', with its protest against the common position of '*I* see nothing amiss in the world: *I* am very comfortable in it.' George Eliot may have been thinking of the 'Double-Duchess' (first of Manchester then of Devonshire) who perpetrated the notorious solecism, 'I hear much of women's rights but I only know that I have no wrongs.' It was a fraction less bad than the witticism, 'women's rights are men's lefts'.

Before a woman could press her right to keep her earnings, she had to have acquired the ability to earn. Writers of genius like the Brontës or Christina Rossetti could receive most of their literary training and encouragement from a creative family circle. Not every woman, however, would or could earn with her pen. The learned professions, responsible for qualified teachers and doctors, should have been an alternative. But how could a woman enter a profession without an education? The professions were a male closed shop, and so was male education – or male ignorance, for that matter, as George Eliot pointed out in *Middlemarch*: 'A man's mind – what there is of it – has always the advantage of being masculine ... and, even his ignorance is of a sounder quality.' In such adverse circumstances it might seem foolhardy of women to think of the professions at all. 'Why do you want to be a doctor rather than a nurse?' Elizabeth Garrett was once asked. 'Because a nurse can earn £20 a year', she replied, 'and a doctor £1,000.'

The continued barring of the professions against women seemed to have one valid excuse, particularly during the first post-war generation of the 1830s and 1840s. It was an uncomfortable time with fears of unemployment. J. C. Hudson took it upon himself in 1842 to write *The Parent's Handbook*. It was for the parents of boys only, and it emphasized the sad degree of unemployment which faced their sons. But they should take heart, he advised, and follow 'new paths' and successful lines, like the manufacture of soda-water, ginger-beer and shoe-blacking. Better still, there were two professions which Mr Hudson could always recommend. Lawyers and doctors would never have their work taken over by machines.

A *Punch* cartoon ridiculing women for being so 'unwomanly' as to put career before family, but suggesting they would only be concerned with 'female' issues.

THE PARLIAMENTARY FEMALE.

Father of the Family. "COME, DEAR; WE SO SELDOM GO OUT TOGETHER NOW—CAN'T YOU TAKE US ALL TO THE PLAY TO-NIGHT?"
Mistress of the House, and M.P. "HOW YOU TALK, CHARLES! DON'T YOU SEE THAT I AM TOO BUSY. I HAVE A COMMITTEE TO-MORROW MORNING, AND I HAVE MY SPEECH ON THE GREAT CROCHET QUESTION TO PREPARE FOR THE EVENING."

But what if it was taken over by women? Of course such a hideous possibility did not feature in the *Handbook*. Nevertheless Dr Elizabeth Blackwell was to qualify in New York (1849) and reach the British Medical Register seventeen years after the *Handbook* came out; and in 1876 Dr Elizabeth Garrett, after qualifying in Paris, became the first British woman doctor. Nothing of this sort was in Shirley Keeldar's mind – Shirley being the most 'advanced' of Charlotte Brontë's women – when she argued fiercely for women's education with her male guardian:

Keep your girls' minds narrow and fettered – they will still be a plague and a care. . . . Cultivate them – give them scope and work – they will be your gayest companions in health; your tenderest nurses in sickness; your most faithful prop in age.

This was the classic argument for women's general education. Even George Eliot, even Mary Wollstonecraft seem to have thought that the strongest argument was the one which proposed educated rather than uneducated 'friends' to husbands, 'companions' to fathers, mothers to children. Towards the end of the century an intelligent woman could still sum up her daughter's school speech-day and gymnastic display with the happy remark, 'There go the mothers of the future.' That all women – unmarried women, childless women, semi-attached women, lone women – should demand education for their own benefit was an idea of slow growth.

With whatever ultimate object, the movement for women's education advanced from the middle of the century. Miss Buss founded the North London Collegiate school in 1850, for delicately nurtured 'women of my own class', to save them from the misery of girls 'brought up to be married and taken care of, but left alone in the world destitute', a predicament which inspired much popular verse:

> But soon from indifference, caprice or what not
> She's turned on the world by her keeper forgot.

In 1858 Miss Beale was appointed Principal of Cheltenham Ladies' College. The two ladies jointly captured the public imagination, both for the flat-footed sound of their names (like the tramp of two policemen) and the belief that ladies who voluntarily gave their lives to girls' schools must be either 'men's lefts' or 'Cupid's lefts'.

> Miss Buss and Miss Beale
> Cupid's darts do not feel.
> How different from us,
> Miss Beale and Miss Buss.

Two years earlier than the North London Collegiate, Queen's College had been founded in Harley Street by the Governesses' Benevolent Institution – a boon for that saddest of all blots on women's world, the governess.

Florence Farr the Victorian actress gave George Bernard Shaw an epigram which he admired and disseminated: 'Home is the girl's prison and the woman's workhouse.' Someone else's home was too often the governess's prison and workhouse combined, where she worked longer hours and with less thanks than a galley-slave. After reading Anne Brontë's novel *Agnes Grey* for the first time, Lady Amberley said that every family with a governess ought to do the same, and she herself would re-read it 'to remind me to be human'.

Some employers, however, were human without having read *Agnes Grey*; and even more small girls were devoted to their governesses as to dedicated mother-substitutes. Princess Victoria adored her governess the Baroness Lehzen; Baroness Burdett-Coutts, the banking heiress and philanthropist, chose to live with her governess Mrs Meredith for most of her life; and Elizabeth Barrett Browning never lost touch with her beloved governess Mrs Orme.

Even at its worst the home-teacher's position was not an insult to womanhood specifically. Mr Crimsworth in Charlotte Brontë's first novel, *The Professor*, compares his own abasement by his brother to that of a tutor in a bad home. 'I looked weary, solitary, kept down, like some desolate tutor or governess. . . .' It was not the sex but the situation that caused the misery. And without the job of governess to fall back upon, many Victorian women would have been even worse off than they were. Lord Byron's unfortunate reject, Claire Clairmont, spent many dignified years as an English governess much prized on the Continent, getting some satisfaction, one gathers, from holding her young ladies with her 'glittering eye' on the night before she quitted a post and telling them the story of her 'fall'.

The governess's galley was not without its escape-hatch. The great Mary Carpenter who reformed the treatment of young delinquents and was received by Queen Victoria, had begun her career as a governess. Two of the Polidori sisters were governesses; one became the mother of the brilliant Rossettis, the other escaped into an Anglican convent. But it is true that the typical governess belonged to the same amateurish home-world as the Gamp (midwife). Both were amateurs in the home and both had to go. Perhaps Emily Eden in her novel *The Semi-detached House* has given the best satirical picture of the Gamp and her lady-successor, hospital-trained no doubt by Florence Nightingale: 'That rustling disturbed sort of quiet which is the result of a regular nurse's exertion' – but less irritating than 'the finished quiet of a ladylike attendant'.

If hospital training transformed the nurse, college training changed the governess. And in this sphere a whole galaxy of eminent Victorian women appeared, to lighten the century's later years. George Eliot's friends Emily Davies and Barbara Leigh-Smith (Bodichon) helped to found Girton College, Cambridge, while Elizabeth Wordsworth, daughter of a bishop and great-niece of the poet, founded both Lady Margaret Hall and St Hugh's College, Oxford.

The two ancient universities lagged behind London, America and many Continental countries in their welcome to women. Always on the look-out for 'impropriety', the dons and local inhabitants of both Oxford and Cambridge had to be propitiated by the meticulously ladylike deportment of college girls. Miss Wordsworth insisted on her young pioneers wearing gloves in the streets and hats in the garden. At lectures they required chaperons. When the sister of an undergraduate asked permission to have tea with a male family friend

on abolishing the lady than in getting her educated. How he hated her ambience! 'The drawing-room, with its feeble manners and effects of curtains and embroidery, gives the tone to our lives nowadays.'

Out-and-out Marxists went much further than woolly, handsome Carpenter. They opposed feminism as 'bourgeois liberal deviationism'. Clara Zetkin declared in 1896 that 'women's petty interests' were not worth fighting for; 'our task is to enrol the modern proletarian woman in the class struggle.'

Elizabeth Barrett Browning wanted a new world for women, but not the new world of the Fabians. The 'aunt' she described ironically in *Aurora Leigh* led

> A sort of cage-bird life, born in a cage,
> Accounting that to leap from perch to perch
> Was act and joy enough for any bird.

But what the Fabians offered was surely no better? Mrs Browning's hero Romney Leigh says:

> 'Ay, materialist the age's name is.
> ... We talk by aggregates.
> And think by systems ...'

Aurora his lover agrees there are too many statistics:

> 'If we pray at all,
> We pray no longer for our daily bread,
> But next centenary's harvest. If we give,
> Our cup of water is not tendered till
> We lay down pipes and found a Company.'

There was a more profound query that lay beneath many nineteenth-century differences of interest or emphasis. What was a woman? A clash of views was re-emerging from the immemorial past, which often involved morality. There were those who saw women as less moral than men; others who saw them as better. At St Mary's Hospital, Sir Almroth Wright stated the first view most baldly. 'There are no good women but only women who have lived under the influence of a good man.' Women, poor dears, had no innate moral sense. Though the great Darwin did believe that women possessed more intuition than civilized men, so did the 'lower races'. As a rationalist, T. E. Huxley found the average woman inferior to the average man in every respect. 'Even in physical beauty man is superior.' Her inferiority in brains went without question. John Blackwood the Victorian publisher believed that 'a female pen' could not avoid grammatical errors. Lord Grenville, a mid-Victorian Cabinet Minister, looked for nothing superior in women. 'A ladylike, sensible, useful, housekeeper sort of wife – after all the least palling sort.'

The other side was equally dogmatic in the opposite sense. J. S. Mill argued that women's self-sacrificing goodness might be learnt by men if marriage were 'a true partnership'. The great Italian patriot Mazzini wrote that women were 'better than men, more accessible to compassion and less calculating'. Mrs Humphrey Ward, who was against women's rights, wrote in her novel *Marcella*, 'Women are made for charity.' And indeed the loving charitableness of women was widely acclaimed. 'I can give and give', wrote Ellen Terry to G. B. Shaw, 'and that's what we women, I think, want most to do.'

To Shaw himself, two African travellers Mary Kingsley and H. M. Stanley epitomized woman's unselfish love and goodness versus man's selfish hate:

Compare the brave woman with her commonsense and goodwill, with the wild-beast man, with his elephant rifle, and his atmosphere of dread and murder, breaking his way by mad selfish assassination out of the difficulties created by his own cowardice.

As by-products of natural goodness, the nineteenth century saw in women special qualities like delicacy, modesty and quietness. Cobbett held conjugal infidelity to be worse in a woman than a man 'because here is a total want of *delicacy* . . . here is grossness and filthiness of mind. . . .'

Mrs Gladstone's idea of delicacy showed up the generation gap towards the end of the century. 'I was amused', wrote young Esther Bright after driving with the Liberal leader's wife at Cannes, 'at Mrs Gladstone's horror when she saw young girls riding bicycles in knickers. She threw up her hands and said "Horrible, horrible!"'

Anthony Trollope builds up a picture of the good Victorian girl – the one who did not want to vote: 'in talking, she would listen much and say but little. She . . . had at her command a great fund of laughter, which would illumine her whole face without producing a sound from her mouth.'

If that was the true woman, how could the suffragists, let alone the suffragettes, hope to get by? Mrs Lynn Linton called them the 'Shrieking Sisterhood', and Florence Nightingale wished they would keep quiet. 'The more chattering and noise there is about Women's Missions', she complained in 1865, 'the less efficient women can we find.' Nevertheless Mrs Josephine Butler, most ladylike of militant women, chose the noisy title of *Storm-Bell* for her magazine. An active cause could not fail to produce some chattering and noise. When her young grandson wrote about 'Granny's Caws', Mrs Butler was delighted.

One aspect of Victorian female delicacy was frail health. Many of our eminent women realized that potentially weak hearts or lungs would not prevent them from doing the things they really wanted to do, like lecturing or drafting reports. Meanwhile, they could make something useful and pleasant out of the spiritual 'delicacy' that was thrust upon them by their men. At least they could get an hour or two to themselves on the sofa. A friend visiting Miss Martineau produced a splendidly ambiguous report of her health: 'I found her confined to a sofa, dangerously ill, I believe, though not in immediate danger; for the rest, brisk, alert, invincible as ever.'

Spirituality in a religious sense was yet another force that was present either positively or negatively, as something active or something lost, in Victorian women's lives. There was a point after 1859, the publication date of Darwin's *Origin of Species*, when all advanced women would be found discussing 'the Darwinian Theory and Women's Rights', as Mrs Stowe noticed. The Darwinian theory might have helped some of them to slough off their religion, but it is surprising how many got it back, even if in esoteric forms. Indeed there was a continual drain of both men and women from rationalism to spiritual beliefs, as well as vice versa. Annie Besant left God for Mammon and Mammon for Krishnamurti; Elizabeth Barrett Browning and Harriet Beecher Stowe had a common interest in spiritualism. The Fabians lost Frank Podmore, who invented their name, to psychical research; the suffragettes lost one of their champions, Lawrence Oliphant, to a religious community; while the established religion remained the 'knot of agony and intensity' in the centre of Christina Rossetti's life (to quote Virginia Woolf), as it was the over-riding interest of Miss Wordsworth's and the nucleus of Mrs Gaskell's. Christina's mystical love-poetry showed how unhappy she would have been if she had married either of her two inadequate young men, Collinson and Cayley:

> You scratch my surface with your pin,
> You stroke me smooth with hushing breath:
> Nay pierce, nay probe, nay dig within,
> Probe my quick core and sound my depth.

To be sure, Lytton Strachey characteristically deprived his eminent Victorian, Florence Nightingale, of any mystical relationship, writing that God appeared to her as 'a glorified sanitary engineer'. But the brilliant Strachey was allowing his own rationalism, combined with verbal temptation, to run away with him. His concept of the 'glorified sanitary engineer', in no way suggests the 'agony and intensity' of Florence Nightingale listening for the Voice.

Apart from a continuing obsession with religion or its opposites, the New Woman of the Victorian age was generally thought to have broken with tradition. No longer delicate or beautiful, she seemed to have become untidy if not positively ugly, her strong-mindedness making her difficult to get on with. It was said that one terrified lady jumped out of a window rather than meet Miss Martineau – that allegedly appalling creation of the new age, a female Frankenstein's monster. In fact, throughout the ages, women who have achieved something new have been regarded as unfeminine. A group of seventeenth-century nuns, led by Mary Ward, were later to found a new teaching order but were nicknamed 'Apostolic Viragoes' or 'Galloping Girls'.

Unconventional some of the Victorians were. A pen-and-ink portrait by Edith Somerville of the Somerville-and-Ross female partnership, shows a lady exhaling from a cigarette in a long holder, a Japanese fan in the other hand and her feet crossed high up on the hob, displaying a noble pair of button boots. Madame Mohl, a celebrated French bluestocking, was both untidy and unconventional. She rode in an omnibus when visiting England dressed anyhow and talked for hours with her feet on the fender.

The typically English 'strong-minded' woman has been defined for us by Shaw with his 'Mrs Clandon' in *You Never Can Tell*, supposed to be based on George Eliot. Author of 'Twentieth Century Treatises' – T.C. Cooking, T.C. Creeds, T.C. Clothing, T.C. Conduct, T.C. Children, T.C. Parents – Mrs Clandon marches in the van of her own period (1860–80) and asserts character and intellect rather than the affections, being humanitarian rather than human.

Her dress is businesslike but avoids masculine waistcoats, collars or watch-chains; and since she is an agnostic, she will not affect Quaker styles. She makes no attempt whatever at 'sex attraction' through her clothes. She is a veteran of the Old Guard of the women's rights movement whose Bible, says Shaw, was J. S. Mill's *The Subjection of Women*. Later he sums her up as 'dignified but dogged, ladylike but implacable'.

'Implacable' is perhaps the most important word in this portrait. One thinks thankfully of the men who escaped from being eaten up by 'implacable' women: Jowett from Florence Nightingale and John Cross from George Eliot; and sadly of those who succumbed, like Sidney Herbert and Arthur Hugh Clough, who died in Florence Nightingale's service. But whose fault was it? Victorian women were still the 'weaker sex', and a man was ashamed to fail in an endurance test that these 'delicate' creatures could pass so magnificently.

Towards the end of the century there was a fairly widespread change in ideas of 'womanliness'. The *Gentlewoman* newspaper, for instance, introduced a feature called 'Our Victoria Wreath', to be bestowed on any woman for 'some worthy womanly achievement'. The wreath was awarded to Miss Philippa Fawcett for defeating the Senior Wrangler (mathematician) in the Cambridge final examinations; to Miss M. M. Dowie for crossing the Carpathian Mountains alone; and to Miss Hunt for saving the life of her father, an officer in barracks, from a burglar. These splendid achievements would hardly have been considered 'womanly' during the early Victorian age.

Ideas of 'man' and 'woman' could be mixed together even by such genuinely Victorian ladies as Mrs Josephine Butler, who was not at all surprised when the male students at Keble College asked her to explain to them the prostitution problem. 'They want some thoroughly truthful and manly instruction on this

**Illustration of an advanced woman for *The Silver Fox*
by Edith Oenone Somerville.**

question', she wrote to the puzzled Warden, 'and they claim that they can best get it by writing to a woman.'

Womanhood had been expanding and diversifying since the mid–nineteenth century. 'The motherliness of God' was an expression used by Hannah Pearsall Smith, American grandmother of Ray Strachey, author of *The Cause*. Both the Oxford Movement and the Pre-Raphaelites made cults of the mother without a husband. And Mary Shelley (Mary Wollstonecraft's daughter) showed in *Frankenstein* that a being created by a man alone could only be a monster.

The Victorians recognized their own 'woman problem' but did not solve it. One would like to know what they would have thought of Professor Joanna Bunker Rohrbaugh's solution, presented tentatively in her *Women: Psychology's Puzzle*. After a re-examination of all the assumptions, this American professor suggests that what women want is 'personal and social *acceptance* of those masculine qualities they already have'—not the acquisition of more. Androgynous individuals, she thinks, may be the happiest; those who are able to be 'both highly masculine and highly feminine'. Meanwhile, in the words of Ellen Moers, author of *Literary Women,* women are still no less than in the nineteenth century, 'that burning topic of the day'.

My team of eleven represent only a fraction of the genius available. Women did exceptionally well in an age that had not yet yielded even their elementary rights. Every woman described briefly in this first chapter deserves a chapter of her own. Some have not yet had a mention. Instead of the great explorer, Mary Kingsley, I might have chosen that remarkable traveller and letter-writer Isabella Bird. She recalls in *A Lady's Life in the Rocky Mountains* her exploits alone and unarmed on horseback, climbing peaks in North Colorado, heading off stampeding cattle ('as much use as another man') or being wooed by the mysterious 'Mountain Jim'; and always wearing her half-male 'Hawaiian costume' (invented when in Hawaii) consisting of bloomers under a skirt. Yet this lady did not wish to be a man, only to escape into the freedom of adventure. In Colorado she merely needed a log cabin, 'But elsewhere one must have a house and servants, and worries', the world of '. . . uselessly conventional life'.

Some readers may have expected to find a chapter on the three Pankhursts or Lady Constance Lytton. But the suffragettes, with their well-cut skirts and jackets, smart hats and wasp waists, their use of force and the use of force-feeding against them, are all part of the run-up to the Great War. They are essentially Edwardian.

There are no 'immoralists' among my eleven. Yet Catherine Walters ('Skittles') was eminent at least in the sense of standing out. As the last of the *poules de luxe* or courtesans, she had chosen 'the oldest profession of all', which her grace, wit and equestrian skill turned into a fabulous success. Yet even 'little Skitsy' was ditched by the future Duke of Devonshire. (He later married the 'Double-Duchess', she who boasted of having no wrongs.) There was a

Henry Peach Robinson's photograph 'Fading Away' *top* **and Augustus Egg's painting 'Past and Present No. 1' show two aspects of the Victorians' fantasy of womanhood.**

motherliness about Skittles which prompted the Prince of Wales to sign himself, 'ton petit Bébé'. It is a reflection on Victorian motherhood that Skittles, of all people, should have stood in, if only on paper, for Queen Victoria.

I regret more the absence of a Victorian woman painter and quote the feelings of Tillie Olsen (Silences) as she walked through the National Gallery: 'We have been left out.' I accept the explanation of Germaine Greer in The Obstacle Race, that it is 'the relative roles of men and women' that have stopped women hitherto from being great painters. Artistic daughters were meant to support their painter-fathers not rival them. And it is impossible to paint in secret; turpentine is not odourless, and a canvas and easel cannot be quickly snapped shut, like Jane Austen's notebook, when the drawing-room door opens. Nevertheless, Lady Butler, sister of the poet Alice Meynell, became an RA and there were illustrators like Beatrix Potter and Marianne North.

Working-class wives occupy an eminence of their own. Burdened with sick children, drunken husbands and poverty, these anonymous heroines none the less found time to fill up questionnaires about their conditions, and generally support the reformers. Often mere survival was a mark of high distinction. Honour is also due to the women like Margaret Llewellyn Davies and Margery Spring-Rice who devised, distributed and edited those questionnaires.

The huge Victorian class of female servants had a shadowy below-stairs existence that never achieved eminence. Eminent Victorian women could not get on without them, yet they were an additional problem to the 'sad blot' that was women. Alice Meynell lamented her fate with servants in the early 1880s. Her house was charming and she herself gentle and considerate, but in one year and ten months she had had nine cooks, five housemaids and three nurses.

Women servants in great mansions often lost their taste for freedom, like animals in captivity. Miss Harriet Rogers, housekeeper at Errdig Hall, received a bitter note from her friend J. C. Maddocks in 1871:

Dear Miss Rogers,
If I say I was pleased to receive your letter I should say what I did not feel.
So often have we looked forward to the pleasure of your visit but as often as we have looked we have been disappointed and for what reason? First because Miss Rogers had not the courage to ask Mrs Yorke [her employer] for a week's leave.

J. C. Maddocks' last cogent paragraph might well be addressed to a wider audience of women:

All things seem impossible, until an effort is made, and as we said when we were speaking about this subject, the longer you remain satisfied with so little liberty the longer you shall be.

'Today women have a sense of themselves', says Tillie Olsen. What she calls the Silences in women's creativity may soon be broken. If so, they must not cease to thank the vision and energy, above all energy, of the Victorian pioneers.

F. M. Brown's portrait of Dame Millicent Fawcett and her blind husband Henry Fawcett MP has echoes in fictional relationships created by Victorian women writers. *Overleaf:* 'The Poor Teacher' by Richard Redgrave shows the governess's isolation.

⇒ THE BRONTËS ⇐

CHARLOTTE 1816–1855, EMILY 1818–1848, ANNE 1820–1849

From the pages of the Brontë novels a quite unexpected type of hero and heroine sprang into the Victorian world. Both were in a sense anti-heroic figures. For the woman was a governess and the man a 'black swan', darkly outlandish if not black-hearted. The governesses were born of the Brontë sisters' own experience. But the black hero-villains emerged from a very odd brew, into which Charlotte and Emily had stirred memories of actual men they knew, characters they had read about in romance and history, and creatures of their secret imagination. It was partly the misery of their lives as governesses that evoked the compensatory passion of their dreams.

As we shall see, all three surviving sisters made grim attempts to earn a living as teachers. Charlotte and Anne transmuted their frustrations into four of their novels: *Jane Eyre, Agnes Grey, Villette* and *The Professor,* in order of publication. Emily, whose six months as a teacher at Law Hill Charlotte called 'slavery', was

Branwell Brontë's portrait of his sisters Anne, Charlotte and Emily.

29

to banish all trace of this experience from her only novel, *Wuthering Heights*. Teaching was utterly against her whole nature. As she wrote:

> I'll walk where my own nature would be leading;
> It vexes me to choose another guide;
> Where the grey flocks in ferny glens are feeding;
> Where the wild wind blows on the mountain side.

It is possible, however, that the wind and mountains of Wuthering Heights were wilder and freer than they would have been if Emily Brontë had not slaved from six in the morning until eleven at night, cooped up in the Patchett's school.

Charlotte and Anne were different. Each gave the career of Victorian governess a fair trial, starting out with prejudices in favour of the life. 'How delightful it would be to be a governess!' says Anne's heroine Agnes Grey; 'To go out into the world; to enter into a new life; to act for myself; to exercise my unused faculties; to try my unknown powers. . . .' The more sophisticated Charlotte at first had similar illusions: 'the stir of grand folks' society' she thought would be her exciting milieu. Instead, she discovered that a governess had 'no existence'. Or worse, the harsh life of a 'dependent', whose chief virtue was to 'endure'. Charlotte seems to have found the teaching itself and the domestic drudgery attendant on it equally repulsive. She wrote of 'a terrible fag in Geographical Problems' and another fag in mending 'Ellen Lister's clothes'.

Many of the governess's tasks, such as clearing up the children's mess of eggshells deliberately ground into the carpet, which the servants refused to touch (*Agnes Grey*), were downright menial. For a governess, though inexorably 'genteel', was rarely treated as a member of the family; rather a social hermaphrodite halfway between the family and the servants. The Brontës had hit off a period in educational practice when Rousseau's theories of 'the noble savage' encouraged some parents to let their offspring behave as little savages. The Victorian triumph of repressed governesses *and* repressed children was yet to come. Anne Brontë was expected to cope with what her sister called 'an unruly, violent family of *modern children*', whose parents would not back up her authority. In desperation Anne once tied two little Inghams of Blake Hall to a table-leg. She was sacked.

Childish cruelty was encouraged as manly. A boy whose father allowed him to dismember fledglings would naturally turn to 'tormenting the governess' if no better sport was available. A girl-pupil was wildly exhilarated by the screams of a hare as her dog tore it to pieces. Charlotte was stoned by a small Sidgwick of Stonegappe Hall. Nevertheless, her influence over this child was to develop satisfactorily until he burst out at dinner that he loved her; whereupon Mrs Sidgwick barked, 'Love the *governess*, my dear!'

Held in open contempt, governesses had to be self-effacing to the point of annihilation. 'I sat with an assumption of smiling indifference', says Agnes Grey, when the man she loves (a local curate named the Rev. Edward Weston) is publicly discussed. Jane Eyre conceals herself on the window-seat during Mr Rochester's house-party. Indeed, Jane's creator, Charlotte Brontë, is at pains to show that adored Mr Rochester himself at first holds the usual, dismissive opinion of governesses. Who is this girl who comes to his rescue after he has been thrown from his horse? 'I am the governess', explains Jane. 'Ah, the governess! Deuce take me, if I had not forgotten! The governess.'

That ludicrous caricature of a vulgar aristocrat, the Hon. Blanche Ingram, dots the i's and crosses the t's for Mr Rochester. She and her sister have had a dozen governesses in their day, she says, 'half of them detestable and the rest ridiculous, and all incubi – were they not, mama?' To which Lady Ingram her mama replies, 'My dearest, don't mention governesses; the word makes me nervous. I have suffered a martyrdom from their incompetence and caprice; I thank Heaven I have now done with them!' Jane hears it all.

In Charlotte's later novel, *Shirley*, the degradation of governesses is forcefully stated. For *Shirley*, being a story of the Luddite riots in West Yorkshire, is concerned with the rights of women as well as property and labour. 'While I live', says Mr Helstone to his niece, 'you shall not turn out as a governess, Caroline. I will not have it said that my niece is a governess. . . . I will purchase an annuity'. (Emily, who had the practical capacity among the Brontës, once began working out such a scheme for herself and her sisters.) Caroline Helstone's cousin, Shirley Keeldar, is more vehement still. 'What an idea! Be a governess! Better be a slave at once. Where is the necessity? Why should you dream of such a painful step?' One can almost hear Emily Brontë urging her sister Charlotte, in the same words, to drop all that humiliating governess business. The New Woman, Shirley Keeldar, was modelled on Emily Brontë, the story having been developed and finished while Emily was dying and after she was dead. 'The Major' was Emily's nickname and 'Captain Keeldar' was Shirley's, Emily was followed by her bulldog Keeper and Shirley by Tartar.

A fair summary of the ideal governess was eventually furnished by Charlotte. 'I am miserable when I allow myself to dwell on the necessity of spending my life as a governess', she wrote. 'The chief requisite for that station seems to me to be the power of taking things easily as they come . . . a quality in which all Brontës are deficient.'

All the Brontës were poets and all had feelings of the utmost intensity. None could take life easy. It is time to see how this astonishing family came into being.

Their mother Maria Branwell died of cancer in 1821 aged thirty-eight, after giving birth to six children in seven years. She 'fades out of sight', according to Mrs Gaskell, Charlotte's dedicated biographer and herself an eminent Victorian. Most of what Mrs Gaskell wrote about the mother of the extraordinary Brontës was in a low key. Meek, retiring and devout, very elegant, talented and well balanced, she was a reader of amiable books and the author of one pious essay intended for publication: 'The Advantages of Poverty in Religious Concerns.' If Haworth Parsonage, where she died, was a 'religious concern', Maria Brontë had every opportunity to know the advantages of poverty; the income of her husband the Rev. Patrick Brontë was £200 a year. But Mrs Brontë deserves a profile in somewhat higher relief than Mrs Gaskell allows.

Maria Branwell was born into a prominent Cornish family. Her parents combined artistic elegance and money-making with ardent Methodism. It is safe to say that their Brontë grandchildren inherited far more than piety from Penzance: Charlotte owed to the Branwells her precise italic handwriting; to them she and her brother Branwell owed their gift for drawing and painting, Emily her good head for business, and all of them a second strand of Celtic imagination to offset the Irishness of the Brontës. From one of Maria Branwell's love-letters to Patrick Brontë it seems that she also had a sense of humour. It began 'My dear saucy Pat'. When Charlotte read the letters twenty-nine years later she wrote: 'it was strange now to peruse, for the first time, the records of a mind whence my own sprang, and . . . at once sad and sweet to find that mind of a truly fine, pure, and elevated order. . . . There is . . . a gentleness about them indescribable. I wish she had lived. . . .'

Handsome, red-headed Patrick Brontë was raised on a farm in County Down, Northern Ireland, his father Hugh having been born in the south but brought to Ulster where he married and fathered ten children. The family name was Brunty or Branty, but Patrick changed it to the distinguished 'Brontë' at Cambridge University, where, by sheer pertinacity and love of learning, he planted himself. The Napoleonic wars were raging inside Patrick's head as well as throughout Europe, and Lord Nelson was Duke of Brontë not Brunty. Patrick saw himself as 'great at heart as a Titan – "Admiral Horatio Viscount Nelson, and Duke of Bronti"' (*Shirley*).

After taking Holy Orders, Patrick moved from curacy to curacy in England until he reached Hartshead near Huddersfield, where he met Maria Branwell in 1811. They were married on 29 December 1812, and Patrick wrote 'a nice little hymn for her'. Early in 1814 their eldest daughter Maria was born, followed next year by Elizabeth. They moved to Thornton near Bradford, a small friendly town where four more babies were born in quick succession: Charlotte (1816), Patrick Branwell their only son (1817), Emily Jane (1818) and Anne (1820). In 1821 when Mrs Brontë already had an internal cancer the family moved again. They travelled in seven wagons to wind-swept Haworth Parsonage, high on the Yorkshire moors, where Patrick became 'Perpetual Curate'.

Haworth was the focal point of the Brontës' imaginative life. No home has ever played a more integral part in nursing genius. The Parsonage occupies a bleak spot in the parish of Bradford, at the top of a steep narrow street, with the church and its graveyard threatening it from the side and the moors menacing it from above. A visitor on a 'wild and chill' day in 1850 described the churchyard as 'a dreary, dreary place, *literally paved* with rain-blackened tombstones'; Mrs Gaskell found it 'terribly full of upright gravestones'; Margaret Lane, another distinguished Brontë biographer writing some hundred years later, noted that graves 'crowd and bristle and conceal the turf; and when it rains, the slab surfaces appal the eye with their unbroken gleam'. The outside of the house was destitute of colour. 'No flowers or shrubs will grow there', observed one of Charlotte Brontë's acquaintances, and inside there had not been a coat of paint for thirty years.

Perhaps because of the trepidation aroused by this gloomy concensus, the modern visitor may find Haworth less sombre than he expected. There was no 'wuthering' – the sound of wind laden with snow – on the moors when I first saw them. They seemed rather to lie in that exquisite peace evoked by Emily Brontë's requiem over the graves of Catherine, Heathcliff and Edgar Linton:

I lingered round them, under that benign sky: watched the moths fluttering among the heath and harebells, listened to the soft wind breathing through the grass, and wondered how anyone could ever imagine unquiet slumbers for the sleepers in that quiet earth.

Indeed the Brontës themselves did not always see their home as gloomy. True, Charlotte told her publisher it was 'a strange, uncivilized little place'; but she modified that in *Jane Eyre* to a 'breezy mountain nook in the healthy heart of England'. Anne called herself 'a joyous, mountain-child'; Emily found the

Maria Brontë, who died after bearing six children in seven years.

moors a stage for comedy as well as high drama – she loved to act as Puck, leading the nervous Charlotte astray. And in the village there was warmth and colour in the firelight, crimson furnishings and polished glasses at the Black Bull, all of it fatally magnetic to Branwell.

His sisters did not complain of the curious domestic arrangements at the Parsonage. Owing to digestive troubles, Mr Brontë had decided to dine alone even before his wife's death; and the children's Aunt Branwell, who now lived permanently with them, was often glad to do likewise. So they were able to enjoy the kitchen humour of 'Tabby', their beloved maid-of-all-work, revelling in her bizarre Yorkshire dialect even when it meant helping her to 'pilloputate' (peel a potato). They must also have heard traditional ballads from Tabby or the younger servants, for in *Wuthering Heights* Nelly Dean sings ballads to Hareton Earnshaw, and the nurse Bessie sings them in *Jane Eyre*.

The Rev. Patrick Brontë's eccentricities did not seem terrifying to his children either, though Mrs Gaskell, misunderstanding his procedures, has made them terrifying to posterity. His habit of firing off pistols out of the back door every morning, to unload them, was not a sign of his being a 'half-mad' Irishman, but of measures to protect his isolated family, which he considered necessary after the Luddite riots of 1811 and subsequent agricultural disturbances. (The heroine of *Shirley* did the same.) It must be added that the head of the Brontë household adored guns, invented new types of weaponry whose blueprints he sent to the Duke of Wellington and in fact would have made a better soldier than parson. As Charlotte Brontë says of Mr Helstone in *Shirley*, 'The evil simply was – he had missed his vocation: he should have been a soldier, and circumstances had made him a priest.'

This vein of violence was to have a powerful influence on the young Brontës' imagination. Patrick Brontë did not, however, saw up his wife's chair-backs in his rages, or burn her silk dresses; he only cut off the puff sleeves of one cotton dress. As he admitted to Mrs Gaskell after her first edition, he was certainly eccentric; but had he been *con*centric, calm and sedate, he would 'in all probability never have had such children'. Until his eldest was ten, he entertained these children, of whom he came to be so pathetically proud, with family legends and ghost stories that made them 'shrink and shudder', and taught them English history revolving around Nelson and Wellington. The fact that Charlotte wrote 'indifferently', while her sisters sewed 'very badly' (school register) did not worry him. Alas, when Maria Brontë was ten, she, Elizabeth, Charlotte and Emily were removed from this stimulating atmosphere and sent to Cowan Bridge School for the daughters of the clergy, a semi-charitable institution.

The school had one advantage: its fees were nominal; but then so was the feeding. A cook whose wages were no doubt also rock-bottom, served up abominable messes which the four delicate little Brontës often could not touch. A stench of rancid fat pervaded the establishment. The milk was often 'bingy', a perfect breeding-ground for tubercular germs. The big girls grabbed the better morsels from the small children, undeterred by hell-fire sermons from the proprietor, the Rev. Carus Wilson. The cold was intense and chilblains an agony. Low fevers swept the school while the Brontës were boarders, and there were a number of deaths. Suddenly the school authorities realized that Maria's 'cold' and 'hollow cough' (at first the remains of whooping-cough) were the last stages of consumption. Their father brought all four girls home in the same year, too late for Maria and Elizabeth, who died in 1825.

Charlotte was to take her revenge on Cowan Bridge School twenty-two years later, when Maria reappeared as the clever long-suffering little saint, Helen Burns, in *Jane Eyre*. The school she called 'Lowood', the name of Napoleon's prison-house on St Helena.

The Parsonage, overlooking Haworth's gloomy and crowded churchyard.

The deaths of their two eldest sisters had a desolating effect on the remaining children. It also made them cling together, Charlotte and Emily sharing a tiny slip of a bedroom over the hall. All four children used it as a nursery and playroom after lessons and light housework were finished. In this historic little room began the communal story-telling that was to develop into the great Brontë novels – the most original of all Victorian literature.

In 1826 when Charlotte was ten, Patrick Brontë brought a rush of excitement into the quiet nursery. He presented Branwell with a box of twelve wooden soldiers. The 'Twelves' were to unlock the doors of fancy and to lead lives even more adventurous than the famous tin soldier of Grimm's fairy tale or R. L. Stevenson's toy armies in 'The Land of Counterpane'.

Recognizing the seminal nature of her father's gift, Charlotte described the event three years later, calling it 'the origin of our plays':

First, 'Young Men'. Papa brought Branwell some wooden soldiers at Leeds . . . so next morning Branwell came to our door with a box of soldiers. Emily and I jumped out of bed, and I snatched up one and exclaimed, 'This is the Duke of Wellington! This shall be the Duke!'

Branwell took the second best name, 'Buonaparte', while Emily and Anne had to make do with 'Gravey' (because Emily's was 'a grave-looking fellow') and 'Waiting-boy' (because he was 'a queer little thing' like Anne). After 'Young Men', came the play-games called 'Our Fellows' taken from Aesops Fables, followed by the 'Islanders' (from the Arabian Nights), out of which grew the Glass Town stories.

These were dominated by four Genii who founded the shining city of Glass Town and were responsible for the four leaders, who had now become the Duke of Wellington's elder son Lord Douro (Charlotte), the explorers Parry and Ross (Emily and Anne) and a personage named Alexander Rogue (Branwell). The Genii represented cosmic forces capable of either maintaining or destroying the balance of nature – 'by their magic might they can reduce the world to a desert, the purest water to streams of livid poison. . . .'

As the children grew older, their plays, mimes and games became serial stories, written down in minute italic handwriting to resemble print. These 'Little Magazines' or miniature thrillers are the key to the Brontës' eminence, making it both more intelligible and more mysterious. Charlotte wrote in 1829, 'All our plays are very strange ones.'

A further source of their strangeness lay in contemporary stories on which the children fed their hungry imaginations. The novels and poems of Scott, narrative poems of Byron and tales of Hoffman set the 'gothic' tone, while *Blackwood's* magazine, lent by a local doctor, ran a spooky series by James Hogg, the 'Ettrick Shepherd'. Charlotte was particularly impressed that a shepherd should be in such close touch with the supernatural.

Another 'gothic' influence was the romantic artist John Martin, whose engravings were introduced into the Parsonage by the Rev. Patrick Brontë and suggested the physical aspects of the Brontës' Glass Town. Martin's wild and beautiful pictures combined the atmosphere of Haworth moor in a storm with actual Byronic subjects, such as 'Manfred' and 'The Deluge'. In *Shirley* Caroline Helstone makes this elemental linkage between Martin, Byron and Haworth quite plain. She is describing a 'livid' sky, 'with brassy edges to the clouds, and here and there a white gleam more ghastly than the lurid tinge'. She continues: 'I have seen such storms in hilly districts in Yorkshire ... while the sky was all cataract, the earth all flood, I have remembered the Deluge.'

Once having tasted these perilous sweets, the children's inventive powers could never rest content with reality. The girls could create the extra dimension out of their own interior lives; Branwell was to need drugs.

Towards the end of 1827 another mysterious development took place when Charlotte and Emily established what they called their 'bed plays' (written at bed-time), to be followed by Branwell and Anne with their own 'bed plays' next spring. 'Bed plays mean secret plays', wrote Charlotte. This first pattern of pairing, however, did not survive; for in time we find that Charlotte and Branwell are co-operating as joint authors, with Emily and Anne striking out on their own in 1831.

In the works of these two final and long-enduring partnerships the Brontë genius first became defined, and in Emily's case continued to express itself up to the last. She and Anne poured themselves into the Gondal sagas, Gondal being allegedly an island in the north Pacific, though its scenery was pure Haworth. The masculine element was provided by Emily. She found Gondal utterly satisfying, putting her most beautiful poetry into the mouths of Gondal characters. 'Deep in the ground', for instance, is not a lament over some lost human love of her own but for Julius Brenzaida, King of Gondal.

Charlotte's and Branwell's 'Angrian' stories were set in a wider world. Their Angria had little connection with Haworth. It was an imaginary African country seized from an Ashantee chief by British heroes. Charlotte's mouthpieces and narrators were still the two sons of Wellington, Lord Douro and Lord Charles 'Florian' Wellesley, the elder becoming King of Angria and Duke of Zamorna. Their father had adopted a black Ashantee orphan, just as the real Duke of Wellington adopted an Indian orphan during his wars. The Ashantee orphan, however, was the first of several Brontë waifs whose origins were unusual, the next being Emily's Heathcliff and the last being Emma in Charlotte's unfinished fragment. Polly in *Villette* also has a touch of the waif.

The recurrence of the waif-theme could have more than one explanation. The idea of the child Heathcliff, a little dark boy brought from Liverpool by old Mr Earnshaw, may have come into Emily's head from tales of the black-haired Irish driven on to the shores of England by the potato famine. Or more specifically from the tale of their great-great-grandfather Hugh Brunty's adoption of a black-haired foundling from the Liverpool packet, whom he called Welsh, and who in turn adopted their red-headed grandfather, the younger Hugh. And the Brontë girls may themselves have felt like orphans washed up at Cowan Bridge School.

Emily in particular was 'different' and may have felt so. As a child, she alone had dark hair among her light-haired siblings. The servants considered her the prettiest of the children. She outgrew all the Brontë children including Branwell, who in manhood resented his mere 5 feet 3 inches. Both Charlotte and Anne sighed for the elusive beauty that graced their friends. 'It is foolish to wish for beauty', says Agnes Grey; nevertheless Agnes would prefer a pair of vacant large black eyes to her ordinary grey ones. Emily would have none of it. She wished to be 'as God made her'.

No less significant than the orphans was the emergence in Charlotte's earliest writings of the typical Brontë hero. At about eighteen she pictured the heroic eye of an Angrian emitting 'a gleam, scarcely human, dark and fiend-like'. At only fifteen she opened her delightful story, 'The Search for Happiness', with a characteristic sketch:

Not many years ago there lived in a certain city a person of the name of Henry O Donell, in figure he was tall of a dark complexion and searching black eye, his mind was strong and unbending, his disposition unsociable and though respected by many he was loved by few.

But when a lady did love this type of hero, Charlotte knew that she would love to distraction. An Angrian heroine loved the masterful Douro with 'burning intensity' and insisted she would continue to do so 'if he were torturing me'. She might have said, *because* he was torturing her.

Charlotte wrote her last Angrian story, 'Henry Hastings', at the age of twenty-three. It described a brother-sister relationship in which the brother went to the bad. The Angrian bond between Charlotte and Branwell had been dissolved. Emily and Anne, however, continued their Gondal saga at least till they were twenty-seven and twenty-six respectively. 'The Gondals still flourish bright as ever', reported Emily in 1845 only three years before her death; though Anne in the same year considered the Gondals 'not in first-rate playing condition'. Meanwhile all four Brontës had been making one attempt after another to forget their own 'playing condition' and achieve a 'living condition' that, if not first-rate, would be somewhere near the average for parsonage children.

Charlotte had had to try school again before she turned fifteen. This time it was a not inhuman institution named Roe Head, near Mirfield, Yorkshire, run by Miss Wooler, an amiable spinster. Two schoolgirls of about Charlotte's own age became her friends, Ellen Nussey, her chief confidante and the preserver of her letters, and Mary Taylor (a future businesswoman of renown), the bewitching daughter of a radical family of feminists and outspoken brothers. Ellen gave Charlotte ballast while Mary encouraged her to take off. The advice Charlotte gave to Ellen on reading is worth noting: no novels but Scott; all Byron and Shakespeare except *Don Juan* and the Shakespearean comedies because of their bawdiness. Charlotte could no longer take part in the family literary forum at Haworth. She kept her hand in by telling horror-stories in the dormitory, until one girl had a heart attack.

The perfect neatness of Charlotte's clothes only emphasized their outmoded and dowdy style. 'She looked like a little old woman', said her friend Mary, remembering how the half-frozen Charlotte stumbled out of the covered

Emily Brontë's 'diary paper' with a sketch of herself and Keeper *above*, and *left* her drawing of a bearded man. *Below*: one of the tiny books the Brontë children wrote.

wagon that had brought her the twenty miles from Haworth, 'so short-sighted that she always appeared to be seeking something, and moving her head from side to side to catch sight of it. She was very shy and nervous, and spoke with a strong Irish accent.' Mary, the candid friend, had to tell Charlotte she was 'very ugly', a brutality for which she later apologized. 'You did me a great deal of good, Polly, so don't repent of it', said Charlotte. She meant moral good, of course, and forthwith decided she was not only small but 'stunted'. It also 'did good' to her art. Handsome Byronic heroes were after all not unknown; but an inconspicuous plain Jane heroine packed with brains and personality, instead of the doe-eyed houri who usually went with the Byronic package was something quite new for the reading public.

But plain little Charlotte could not exist alone. She needed a Byronic hero, imaginary or real, to compensate for her inadequacies. Once at Roe Head she was to see a vision of the beloved Angrian Duke of Zamorna leaning against an obelisk. 'I was quite gone.' By the end of summer 1832 the ailing child had gone home, to stay there for another three years. Her father gave the girls' education as much time as he could spare from his parish duties and teaching Branwell. Branwell should have been sent to school; but Patrick could not forgo the presence of his golden boy.

In 1835 another milestone was reached. 'We are about to divide, break up, separate', wrote Charlotte to Ellen Nussey that July. She used those three different verbs to emphasize the enormity of separation. Emily, now seventeen, was sent to Roe Head; Charlotte rejoined the school but on the staff; Branwell was to launch himself in London as an art student. Both Emily and Branwell failed utterly to make the grade, Branwell losing his nerve so completely that when he returned home he had not presented even one of his introductions, and Emily pining until she too was sent home. Nevertheless she had something to show for her three months of intense homesickness. Visions, the first of her mystic experiences, began appearing to her:

> He comes with western winds, with evening's wandering airs,
> With that clear dusk of heaven that brings the thickest stars,
> Winds take a pensive tone, and stars a tender fire,
> And visions rise, and change, that kill me with desire.

Emily's place at Roe Head was taken by Anne. Already fifteen, Anne was having her first experience of school. She looked forward to it. When illness struck, however, Anne had nothing better to fortify her than Aunt Branwell's ferocious religious teaching: an uncompromising belief in the damnation of all sinners.

The rigours of Miss Wooler's school (it was moved in 1836 from Roe Head to Dewsbury Moor) caused Anne to develop a cold that Charlotte recognized as incipient consumption. However, before Anne was sent home, she too discovered something of value. A Moravian bishop from Mirfield paid her a sick-visit and broke to her the good news of heavenly love and forgiveness. During the brief sad years that lay ahead, religion was to be a melancholy pleasure, and not the hell-dominated nightmare that it became for Branwell.

Charlotte was shaken by a clamorous urge to write. 'I am just going to write', she entered in her Roe Head journal for 1836, 'because I cannot help it'. She longed to be at home where everyone was free to write and discuss. If she shut her eyes she could see Haworth Parsonage and hear the moorland wind. 'There is a voice, there is an impulse that wakens up that dormant power which in its torpidity I sometimes think dead.' It was the drudgery of Roe Head that damaged her creative power, and the restorative voice was both the physical wind and the wind of inspiration. Branwell and Emily could hear it and would think of her and Anne. It awakened in Charlotte a desire to '*do*', as in Byron's epic, *Childe Harold*. Visions possessed her as soon as the day's toil was over: 'This moment of divine leisure has acted on me like opium, and was coiling about me a disturbed but fascinating spell. . . .'

Next year Miss Brontë was writing to Robert Southey, the Poet Laureate and biographer of Nelson, Duke of 'Bronti', on how to '*do*' something in the literary world. Southey replied: 'Literature cannot be the business of a woman's life, and it ought not to be.' At once poor Charlotte swung away from ambition towards duty, assuring the great man that she had tried to carry out 'all the duties a woman ought to fulfil'. In Charlotte there was a perpetual conflict between the moral 'ought' and the artistic 'must'; whereas in Emily there was no such dichotomy. Emily simply walked where her own nature led.

Shortly before she was nineteen Emily wrote a 'diary paper' with Anne that vividly expresses her refusal to recognize any world but Haworth. The date is 26 June 1837: Branwell is reading 'Eugene Aram' aloud to Charlotte, while she sews in Aunt's room; Emily and Anne are in the drawing-room with their paper and pens. Where will they all be in four years time? Anne the enterprising guesses, 'We shall all be gone somewhere together comfortable.' Emily guesses, 'We shall all be in this drawing-room comfortable.'

Yet in the very next year Emily was a teacher at Law Hill – uncomfortable. She told her class that the only living thing she liked at Law Hill was the house dog. Nevertheless her visions were now coming thick and fast and they liberated her; though the returns to normal were as painful for Emily as they are for all mystics:

> Oh! dreadful is the check – intense the agony –
> When the ear begins to hear, and the eye begins to see . . .

For a short time in 1838 the family were all at home again, Emily receiving her mystic visitant and Charlotte working ever more professionally at the Angrian tales, since the school doctor had sent her home from Dewsbury ill and depressed. She wore 'that look of wan emaciation which anxiety or low spirits often communicate to a thoughtful, thin face' – a look which Charlotte was later to see on her heroine's face in *The Professor*. Branwell was failing to get commissions in Bradford as a portrait painter, though in constant demand at the Black Bull, as a wit, brilliant raconteur and genial drinking companion. Unfortunately he had none of his sisters' shyness.

Then Charlotte and Anne had to return to the treadmill. They tried out a new way of fulfilling their duties as women: the way of a governess. No epithets could be too black in Charlotte's opinion for the Sidgwick-Benson family of Stonegappe Hall. She never got five minutes' talk with her employer, except to be scolded. 'I could like to work in a mill', she wrote to Emily from Stonegappe. 'I could like to feel some mental liberty.' In eight years time Mrs Sidgwick was to become Mrs Reed in *Jane Eyre*, whose deathbed non-repentance for defrauding her niece Jane of a fortune has all the macabre improbability of Victorian melodrama. The Sidgwicks and their Benson relatives were soon to become famous Victorian families of the very best vintage, and it could be that Charlotte exaggerated. However, she was not incapable of appreciating kindness when she met it. The White children whom she taught in 1841 were 'wild and unbroken, but apparently well disposed'. Here the main trouble was parsimony: a salary of £20 a year with £4 deducted for laundry. Anne's experiences at Blake Hall were hardly less traumatic and when she was dismissed at Christmas 1839 she had developed a stammer.

It had been a bad year. The disappointed but still charming and gifted Branwell was now buying sixpennyworths of opium over the counter, as one might buy aspirins today – so cheap and prevalent was the drug as a household painkiller. Charlotte had to cope with two proposals of marriage from clerics (virtually the only young men she met) which brought home to her the gulf between her imagination and drab reality. She turned down the Rev. Henry Nussey, her 'dear dear' Ellen's brother, for significant reasons: she was not 'cool-headed' enough for him, she told Ellen, being 'a wild romantic enthusiast', and sometimes 'a shattered wretch', while the Nusseys had 'calm and even' temperaments. The truth was that Charlotte needed to feel 'adoration' for a husband, and could never feel it for someone of a calm mind. And Henry, like St John in *Jane Eyre*, only wanted Charlotte to help him in his work.

The next two years, 1840–41, saw the familiar pattern of family partings and reunions. Anne though still delicate advertised and finally took a job as governess with the Robinsons of Thorp Green Hall near York; she was passionately but secretly in love with her father's irresistible curate, the Rev. William Weightman, a 'white swan' if ever there was one, whose willing sympathy could control even Branwell. They nicknamed Willie Celia-Amelia for his pretty face. He had made eyes at Anne, as at many others, but died of cholera in 1842 before he could declare whatever love he felt.

Branwell's artistic promise had been jettisoned in favour of a job as a railway clerk, from which he was sacked that March. Negligence caused by heavy drinking led him to overlook a subordinate's removal of some £11 from the till. Anne, thinking to save her precious brother, obtained for him the post of tutor with the Robinsons. At Rawton, with the Whites, Charlotte received a letter from her friend Mary Taylor in Brussels describing the novelty of life abroad. Immediately Charlotte felt 'such a strong wish for wings' that 'rebellious and absurd emotions' welled up. 'I quelled them in five minutes', but it was painful.

A few months later both Charlotte and Emily acquired wings. What with the anxiety over Anne's health and Emily's pining, the whole Brontë family, Papa

Monsieur and Madame Heger, the owners of the Pensionnat Heger in Brussels, who were Charlotte Brontë's models for Paul Emmanuel and the hard Madame Beck in *Villette*.

and Aunt included, decided the solution was a school of their own at Haworth Parsonage. For this Charlotte and Emily needed 'languages'. (Emily used to read a German book while kneading the dough, just as her father had, as a young man in Ireland, kept a book open while weaving at his loom.) On 8 February 1842 the two sisters went to Brussels. These Brussels years were more than another milestone. If Charlotte had thought there was no Zamorna to be met with in her workaday world, she was mistaken. She recognized him in 'Paul Emmanuel' (*Villette*) alias Constantin Heger, professor at the boys' college and teacher at the Pensionnat Heger where the two Brontës boarded. The Pensionnat was run by Madame Zoë Heger, his wife. Emily did not 'draw well' with Monsieur Heger, wrote Charlotte, as if her sister were an intractable horse; and indeed the long-legged Emily would probably have preferred to be a horse rather than Constantin Heger's pupil. He on the other hand detected her remarkable qualities, saying she should have been a man and would have made a great navigator, inflexible of purpose.

Charlotte was deeply in love with him. After the sisters came home in November following the death of Aunt Branwell, Charlotte returned alone to Brussels in January 1843 for another year. Her excruciating loneliness at the Pensionnat after the whole Heger family and all their pupils had gone away for their summer holidays swung the balance in Charlotte from ecstasy to misery. Even then she clung to her beloved 'master' until January 1844, when she left at the Hegers' suggestion, accompanied by a kind promise to send one of their children to the future Parsonage school. For two more years Charlotte bombarded M. Heger at intervals with anguished love-letters that received no answers. This 'cruelty' she put down to Mme Heger (the sinister Mme Beck of *Villette*) who of course had realized from the start what was going on, though M. Heger apparently did not. It was she who brought to an end the English lessons which Charlotte was giving to M. Heger. Charlotte returned her hostility with interest: 'The people here are no go whatsoever', she had written to Branwell. 'The phlegm that thickens their blood is too gluey to boil.' But not too gluey to take brisk action when necessary.

What was it that M. Heger had which the two clerics had not? Charlotte described him early on to Mary Taylor in terms so violent that one's suspicions are aroused. He was sometimes like 'an insane tom-cat', sometimes like 'a delirious hyena' – spitting, laughing and making grimaces. M. Heger did indeed let fly, lashing himself into passions, as a preliminary to periods of ineffable sweetness. He believed in a 'love-hate' method of teaching and according to his obituary had a 'magnetic' attraction for children. And not only children. For Charlotte he was the ideal 'black swan', tempestuous, exciting and masterful. Like Douro he was loved even while he tortured.

And what did Charlotte hope for? Winifred Gérin, another of the Brontës' biographers, thinks that Charlotte and M. Heger might have built up an enduring friendship had not Mme Heger interfered. Mrs Gaskell seems to have found Charlotte's passion for M. Heger too dangerous even to be mentioned, naively suggesting that his wife's animosity was due to her hurt feelings as a devout Roman Catholic, whose rituals were called 'mummeries' by the evangelical Charlotte. What Charlotte probably wanted was an *amitié amoureuse*. But this was impossible in the early Victorian age between parsonage and pensionnat.

The Brontës' proposed school at Haworth Parsonage might have taken Charlotte's mind off M. Heger, had it ever opened. The sisters planned to take five or six boarders. 'We had prospectuses printed . . . and did our little all; but it was found no go', wrote Emily in her frank way. Schemes to convert some of the Parsonage rooms were wisely held over.

Not a single application was received. Charlotte put their failure down to Haworth's bleak and isolated 'situation', which might not seem suitable for children. But there was probably also a surplus of governesses. The formidable Harriet Martineau, later to become well acquainted with Charlotte, was too deaf to teach orally and so in 1827 had advertised a 'Correspondence Course for young ladies on Religion, Philosophy, Political Economy and Literature.' She too had no applications whatever.

Emily no doubt bore the disappointment with equanimity, for the prospect of sharing her moors and the 'little glittering spirits' of her visions with a crocodile of young ladies cannot have been altogether agreeable. A far more cruel blow fell the following year. In July 1845 Mr Robinson dismissed Branwell from his position as tutor at Thorp Green Hall for adultery with Mrs

**Thomas Davidson's illustration of the episode when Mr Rochester first sees Jane Eyre.
Overleaf: 'Manfred on the Jungfrau' by John Martin, whose dramatic paintings appealed strongly to the wild imaginations of the young Brontës.**

Robinson. Branwell arrived home in a state of collapse. His shattered dream could be put together again, it seemed, only at the Black Bull or with opium. 'I shall never be able to realize the too sanguine hopes of my friends', he lamented, 'for at twenty-eight I am a thoroughly *old man*'. Charlotte wrote to Ellen on 17 July, 'He thought of nothing but stunning or drowning his distress of mind. No one in the house could have rest.'

It is doubtful whether Branwell had in fact been Lydia Robinson's lover – he never made this claim – but he had certainly loved her passionately for just over a year, fully assured that she would marry him as soon as her ailing husband died. Charlotte, however, believed the worst and as a result Mrs Gaskell in her *Life* referred to Branwell's 'deadly crime'. Poor old Patrick Brontë, convinced that his cherished son had been led astray by an abandoned woman, received the distraught sinner with the tenderest care. Emily too seems to have taken what may be called a 'masculine' view of the delinquent. She and Anne never referred to his sins in their 'diary papers' and the tall Emily would unbar the front door to the crumpled little figure of her brother when he staggered home late at night and carry him in her arms up to bed.

Criticism of Charlotte's attitude has been severe. Her disapproval of Branwell took the form of two years' silence towards him, writing him off in her journal as 'hopeless'. Mrs Gaskell admitted to 'the slight astringency' of Charlotte's character, which she thought would have been cured by marriage. Various explanations have been offered for the difference between Charlotte's reaction and Emily's, a difference that stands out spectacularly in Emily's diary paper for 30 July 1845, her birthday and the month of her brother's disaster: 'I am quite contented for myself, not as idle as formerly, altogether as hearty. . . .' If everyone could be as 'comfortable' as she was, she continued, 'then we should have a very tolerable world of it'.

The elder sister was a conscientious moralist, the younger a detached mystic. Following up this clue, Winifred Gérin points out that Charlotte blamed her brother for failing to resist the temptation that she herself believed she had overcome in regard to M. Heger. Such morality would not be attractive if it stood alone. A more sympathetic explanation may be found in the case of Charlotte's close friend Mary Taylor. This lovely girl had been admired by Branwell until she unwisely told him that his love was returned. The spoilt boy forthwith lost interest in Mary, who never loved another and emigrated to New Zealand in 1845, the very year of Branwell's disgrace.

That Branwell could prefer Mrs Robinson to the talented Mary must have seemed utterly perverse, especially as the wealthy Mrs Robinson broke her alleged promise to marry Branwell on becoming a widow. (When Branwell received the news at the Black Bull in May 1846 he dropped to the floor in a fit 'bleating like a calf'. Mrs Robinson became Lady Scott instead of Mrs Brontë.) From then on Branwell's disintegration was a truly fearsome burden upon the Parsonage family. Having been cheated of wife and fortune, Branwell ran into

Charlotte Brontë's watercolour of Glass Town, her imaginary city.

debt, from which his sisters bailed him out. 'It is not agreeable to lose money, time after time, in this way', wrote Charlotte; 'but where is the use of dwelling on such subjects. It will make him no better.'

Ironically, it was money and Branwell between them that gave the impetus to his sisters' triumph. After the death of Aunt Branwell in 1842 each child had inherited something like £350, her capital having already paid for the expeditions to Brussels. With a little money in hand, Charlotte was on the look out for useful ways of spending it before Branwell drained it all away. And she was in bitter need of some positive success to offset his failure. One day she came across Emily's visionary poems, most of them written since 1837 (some part of Gondal). Charlotte was a poet also but she felt astonished and thrilled by her sister's talent: 'terse, condensed and vigorous and genuine . . . wild, melancholy and elevating.' The old dream of authorship was revived, wrote Charlotte; 'it took the character of a resolve' – Charlotte's resolve not Emily's – to publish. Emily and Anne reacted to Charlotte's excited praise in opposite ways. Indignation swept over Emily at this violation of her privacy; Anne timidly produced her own poems for Charlotte's inspection. To Charlotte they had 'a sweet sincere pathos'. Perhaps she was thinking of Anne's threnody to Willie Weightman:

> Life seems more sweet that thou didst live,
> And men more true that thou wert one;
> Nothing is lost that thou didst give,
> Nothing destroyed that thou hast done.

The upshot was that Emily's wrath subsided. She must have some 'latent spark of honourable ambition' urged Charlotte, appealing to the Wellingtonian traditions in which their father had brought up his family. A selection of poems was made, a publisher at last found in Aylott & Jones of Paternoster Row, a publication date fixed – May 1846 – and pseudonyms devised, because 'we had a vague impression', wrote Charlotte Brontë afterwards, 'that authoresses are liable to be looked on with prejudice'. They would be Currer, Ellis and Acton Bell: the same initials but sexless names. That seemed to be playing fair with the public. *The Critic* perceptively saw 'more genius' in the Bells' poems than was generally apparent in what it called 'this utilitarian age'. Ellis Bell was praised in the *Athenaeum* for a fine quaint spirit and an evident 'power of wing'. But despite Ellis's wings the public bought only two copies altogether.

That might have been an end to the Bells' adventure, particularly as they had paid for it. Indeed Charlotte called the book 'a drug'. But the 'dreams of authorship', once revived, were not to be easily renounced. In any case all three sisters had half-finished novels on the stocks, and a month before the poems were published had written to Mr Aylott about *The Professor, Wuthering Heights* and *Agnes Grey*. As a mainly religious publisher, Mr Aylott did not touch novels, but he sent Miss Brontë (who was acting on behalf of the Bells) some names. After going the rounds for eighteen months, *Wuthering Heights* and *Agnes Grey* were accepted by Thomas Newby who, however, rejected Charlotte's *Professor* as undersized. Almost in despair, she sent it to Messrs Smith, Elder on 15 July 1847. George Smith also found *The Professor* too short (it did not find a publisher until 1857, after Charlotte's death); but if Currer Bell would write a full-scale, three-volume novel for them, he would be most interested. As it happened, while Patrick Brontë was recovering from a successful cataract operation in Manchester the previous summer, Charlotte had both looked after him and begun *Jane Eyre*. It had been finished in five months and the fair copy was posted to Smith, Elder on 24 August 1847. Within seven weeks, on 16 October, it was out.

Jane Eyre was an instant success. Like her favourite Lord Byron, Charlotte might have said, 'I awoke one morning to find myself famous' – except that no one knew who Currer Bell was, not even which sex. Harriet Martineau indeed said the author must be a woman because of the way Grace Poole, mad Bertha's wardress, sewed the rings on to new curtains. From today's vantage-point the author seems obviously a woman and a Victorian woman at that. The ambience of *Jane Eyre* is ladylike, Mr Rochester being every stocky inch a 'gentleman' and Jane very 'genteel'. But whereas the elegant Victorian cage in which they perform was made for a pair of sexless canaries, it happens to contain two merlin hawks (Emily had a merlin once, called Hero) intent upon the full rigours of the courting ritual. The libraries gulped down *Jane Eyre*, though with an occasional hiccup, for as Margaret Lane says, 'the erotic Byronic landscape rightly made contemporary puritans uneasy'.

Presenting Jane as the archetypal governess, plain, exploited and 'Quakerish', Charlotte suddenly has this demure little person sitting on her employer's knee listening to a description of his past mistresses. Though Jane refuses to become Mr Rochester's mistress herself, she also declines to marry the Rev. St John Rivers because he does not love her physically and only wants her as a co-worker in the Indian missions. 'He prizes me as a soldier would a good weapon', thinks Jane; 'and that is all.' What distinguishes Jane from other Victorian governesses is not her plight but her passion. She will not wear Mr Rochester's jewels when he offers them. Her strength lies in remaining both Quakerish and hot-blooded. It is the story of King Cophetua and the Beggar Maid, or Cinderella, with Blanche Ingram as the ugly sister; but this Cinderella triumphs through her burning love not her looks.

The pulse of passion in the story caused some critics to call it 'coarse'. Charlotte was shocked and asked Harriet Martineau what they meant. It would be better to lose all her power of invention than write what was 'unfitting', she told Mrs Gaskell. Miss Martineau gave an evasive answer: 'I told her that love was treated with unusual breadth and that the kind of intercourse was uncommon, and uncommonly described, but that I did *not* consider the book a coarse one, though I could not answer for it that there were no traits which on a second leisurely reading, I might not dislike on that ground.' On being asked later to review *Villette* for the *Daily News*, Miss Martineau got her second chance and roundly accused Miss Brontë of depicting all her female characters as obsessed with 'one thought – love. . . . It is not thus in real life', continued Miss Martineau severely; women's lives were not introspective nor self-conscious but enjoyed a 'repose' due to their many other 'substantial interests' beside that 'one passion'. Sheltering behind dummy women who had better things to do than make love, the advanced Miss Martineau showed herself to be on the reactionary side.

Charlotte's reply is worthy of her; indeed, with its echo of St Paul's Epistle to the Corinthians, it is the finest defence of love ever written by a Victorian:

I know what *love* is as I understand it; and if man or woman should be ashamed of feeling such love, then is there nothing right, noble, faithful, truthful, unselfish in this earth, as I comprehend rectitude, nobleness, fidelity, truth, and disinterestedness.

The character of Mr Rochester is far less original than Jane's. A Childe Harold lifted out of a story by Mrs Inchbald on to the Yorkshire moors, Mr Rochester made the fresh impact of a poetic hero in a realistic prose narrative. Many characteristic traits helped him to be romantic: an ugly overall impression that was yet handsome; a swarthy complexion, grim stern mouth, chin and jaw. He was heroic-looking but ground his teeth. 'He was proud, sardonic, harsh ... moody, too.' Harriet Beecher Stowe complained that his courtship of Jane was like 'the breaking of a horse'. Yet he told Jane that he was meant by nature to be a good man. Mr Rochester is loved for his faults, Jane for her virtues.

Jane's virtues, however, are not static. The suggestion of meek submission soon gives place to a character as positive and forceful as Mr Rochester's own, but based on solid interior strength rather than a series of reactions to external buffets. From the child whose 'turbulent impulses' compelled her to answer back, Jane develops into a girl who defeats both Rochester and Rivers by argument. Jane was in fact the 'strong-minded woman' that George Eliot was later to become. With each wooer Jane gradually came to feel an equality. 'I was with an equal', she said of her confrontation with Rivers. And to Rochester: 'I am not talking to you now through the medium of custom, conventionalities. . . . It is my spirit that addresses your spirit; just as if both had passed through the grave, and we stood at God's feet, equal – as we are!'

The fact that Jane passionately needed Rochester to remain her 'master' may appear a contradiction; important though it is, however, it amounts in the end to an idiosyncrasy of Charlotte Brontë's temperament. The New Woman in Jane was independent of that need. In any case the 'masterhood' was reciprocal, for Mr Rochester says, 'Jane, you please me and you master me. . . .' There are plenty of touches to show that Charlotte put herself into Jane with increasing self-confidence. Her pitiable smallness becomes an asset, in contrast to 'big' Bertha and even more to massive Miss Ingram. Charlotte soon has Mr Rochester laughing at Miss Ingram's voluptuous proportions. She's 'a hefty armful', 'a strapper – a real strapper, Jane: big, brown and buxom'. (Charlotte was 'undeveloped', wrote Mrs Gaskell, probably meaning flat-chested.) The final message to Victorian England is 'governess makes good' – despite the housekeeper's warning to Jane Eyre: 'Try and keep Mr Rochester at a distance: distrust yourself as well as him. Gentlemen in his station are not accustomed to marry their governesses.' The critic in the *Edinburgh Review,* though he praised

Jane Eyre, missed its real point, for he wrote, 'From out of the depths of a sorrowing experience here is a voice speaking to the experience of thousands.' Yes; but ultimately speaking in defiance not sorrow.

Neither *Agnes Grey* nor *Wuthering Heights* made the immediate impact of *Jane Eyre* (which Queen Victoria found 'powerfully and admirably written'). The former was too quiet – a quality which has always damaged its popularity – while the latter seemed at first too strange and wild.

With *Wuthering Heights* the Victorians felt themselves to be struggling in deep waters. Passion is again the theme, but it is a passion that transcends human love and may be interpreted as nature mysticism, with Christianity and paganism sharing the controls; or as a morality play in which Good and Evil contend for the soul; or as a violent melodrama which is none the less human, since the cruelty of Heathcliff to Isabella Linton and their consumptive son has clearly been caused by the bullying he himself received as a difficult waif, whose indulgent adoptive father has died.

The elemental passion of Heathcliff and Catherine Earnshaw must be taken as the sole undivided pivot of the action. They are indeed one in their love as Catherine so dramatically declares: 'My love for Heathcliff resembles the eternal rocks beneath – a source of little visible delight, but necessary. Nellie, I *am* Heathcliff! – He's always, always in my mind – not as a pleasure, any more than I am always a pleasure to myself – but as my own being. . . .' Their unity however is not that of equally wicked spirits riding the storm on a broomstick made for two. Heathcliff has become completely satanic while in Catherine storm and sunshine are mingled, as Nellie Dean points out. 'A wild, wicked slip she was – but she had the bonniest eye, the sweetest smile, the lightest foot in the parish.' Hindley Earnshaw calls Heathcliff 'an imp of satan', dark-skinned, black-haired and morose. His eyes are 'a couple of black fiends . . . like devil's spies'.

Nevertheless there was a time when Heathcliff had been a heart-broken child, joining little Catherine Earnshaw in passionate tears over the death of her father: 'No parson in the world ever pictured Heaven so beautifully as they did in their innocent talk', says Nellie Dean. As a deprived and persecuted boy of twelve, Heathcliff deliberately blackens himself in contrast to the fair Edgar Linton (a 'white swan'): 'I shall be as dirty as I please, and I like to be dirty, and I will be dirty.' Yet a little later on Heathcliff is pleading, 'Nellie, make me decent, I'm going to be good.'

The tragedy turns on the pull of this dark earth on two souls destined for heaven. (It is impossible that Emily should have believed in hell and damnation, any more than Anne did.) 'Let me in!' is the story's heart-cry: into this world; into the earth; into heaven. First it is the ghost of Catherine trying to get through Mr Lockwood's window, but an earth-bound ghost, since her wrist bleeds when sawed on the broken glass by the terrified Lockwood. Then there is the demoniac Heathcliff echoing Cathy's 'Let me in!' to the quivering Isabella, in order that his blackness may ruin her colourless purity. 'Isabella, let me in or I'll make you repent!'

'Let me out' is the reverse side of the same compulsion. Catherine's dream of heaven culminates in her being let out of a premature bliss, where she was separated from Heathcliff, and hurled down like Satan into the secret places of earth.

... heaven did not seem to be my home; and I broke my heart with weeping to come back to earth; and the angels were so angry that they flung me out, into the middle of the heath on the top of Wuthering Heights, where I woke sobbing for joy.

After Catherine's death, however, neither she nor Heathcliff can endure this same earth without the other, her body lying in it but her spirit haunting him; he willing his own destruction after he has seen her ghost. Emily Brontë achieved the same macabre, improbable effect through Heathcliff's willed death by self-starvation as Dickens was to bring off in *Bleak House* with 'spontaneous combustion'. It is only when the quiet earth has taken in both Catherine and Heathcliff that they can rest in peace, body and soul.

Wuthering Heights is an isolated masterpiece shot through with poetry. As such it cannot be completely explained in any analytical sense. What might be called the 'let me in' theme in the actual Brontë household, may, for instance, have subtly affected Emily: Branwell imagining the return of the spirit of his beloved sister Maria and Emily literally letting in the wild-eyed, opium-bemused ghost of the old Branwell. Whatever came from the real Haworth world into the world of *Wuthering Heights* was heightened on the way. Even the real dogs, Grasper and Keeper, became Skulker and Throttler. *Wuthering Heights* must be felt; and very possibly it is felt more truly in this century than ever it was by the Victorians. Charlotte Brontë herself considered it 'immature'.

Because of the Bells' anonymity and *Jane Eyre*'s vast popularity (Charlotte made £500 from it) the unscrupulous publishers of Ellis and Acton Bell pretended all the Bells were one, and that one was Currer. In fairness to Messrs Smith, Elder, Charlotte took Anne with her to London on Friday 7 July 1848 to show George Smith and his colleagues that the Bells were at least two. (Emily saw no reason to go.) The sisters walked to Keighley in a storm of thunder and snow, reached London after a night journey, and arrived unheralded at George Smith's Cornhill office, to show him that Currer and Acton Bell were not the two men he had been corresponding with, but 'two young ladies in black'.

After being whirled to the opera, to church, to the Academy, to the National Gallery and to dinner with the Smiths, they returned home, Charlotte a 'jaded wretch'. Meeting strangers always produced in her sickness and headache, but this time it seems to have been worse, 'my face looking grey and very old, with strange deep lines ploughed in it. . . .' Nevertheless this testing adventure was to pave the way for personal meetings with literary lions, some of whom were already her admirers. Thackeray praised *Jane Eyre* as the first English novel he had been able to read for years. George Henry Lewes, of the *Cornhill*, drew from Charlotte one of her best letters on authorship. Having been implored by Lewes

The moors where Emily Brontë found the solitude and drama her spirit needed.

to write something 'less melodramatic' than *Jane Eyre* next time, Charlotte promised to be, if possible, more like Jane Austen – though authors wrote best, she added, when 'an influence seems to waken in them, which becomes their master – which will have its own way'.

Of greater importance to Charlotte was the support of her publishers. The disabilities under which 'authoresses' suffered made male publishers their special guardians. What George Smith did for Charlotte Brontë, John Blackwood was to do for George Eliot. In a sense, however, the shy frail Charlotte had more literary stamina than George Eliot. Perhaps because of the family conclaves involving outspoken criticism, Charlotte could stand up to reviews. Unlike George Eliot she insisted on seeing them all, even bad ones. She had known ever since childhood that she could tell a story and tell it well.

By the summer of 1848 Anne Brontë had another novel ready, *The Tenant of Wildfell Hall*. Charlotte disapproved of its theme – the ruin of young men through vice – at least in the hands of her delicate sister. Anne, however, had firm moral aims: to warn golden youth and to assuage her own guilt at having introduced Branwell to Mrs Robinson. Anne's painful exercise failed to make the flesh creep, though she has a good scene where Lord Lowborough, a reformed drunkard, succumbs to the bottle again in his club, 'amid a tempest of applause'. She also makes valuable points on women's rights: her heroine Helen Huntingdon earns her own living as a painter rather than accept her husband's plea for a double-standard in sex. 'It is a woman's nature to be constant', urges Arthur Huntingdon, 'but you must have some consideration *for us*, Helen; you must give us a little more licence.'

Charlotte and Anne agreed on one point at least. That brothers (as well as sisters) should be taught to avoid vice, instead of being a privileged sex, allowed to go to the devil their own way. In the protests of Anne's hero-villain to his wife, one can hear poor Branwell's whine to his sisters: 'Oh, hang it! Don't torment me with your preachments now, unless you want to kill me outright. I can't stand it, I tell you. I'm suffering enough without that.'

Reproaches were in any case too late. Branwell was rushing downhill and had nearly reached the bottom. He had long lost his faith and was rapidly losing his reason. He threatened to blow out his brains. One day he set fire to the bed-curtains when dead drunk. Anne discovered the blaze and Emily carried him bodily to safety. 'Don't tell Papa.' (Mr Brontë had such a phobia of fire that he never allowed window-curtains, only shutters, at the Parsonage.)

The end came on 24 September 1848. Branwell died of tuberculosis that opium had exacerbated instead of quelling as he had hoped. During the last few days of his life he had allowed his broken-hearted father to say prayers for the dying, to which Branwell responded with Amen. He died in Mr Brontë's arms, *not* standing up, as Mrs Gaskell was wrongly informed, with his pockets full of Lydia's love-letters.

The effect on the sisters was catastrophic. Charlotte was prostrated for a week in bed. Anne was visibly failing. Emily's 'cold and cough' that had already given Charlotte anxiety rapidly became worse. Within weeks she too was dying. 'I *do* wish I knew her state of mind', wrote Charlotte. In an attempt to amuse her, Charlotte read aloud a review in which Ellis Bell was described as 'dogged, brutal and morose'. The fragile villain 'smiled half amused and half in scorn as he listened'. Up to the eleventh hour Emily maintained her impenetrable reserve, refusing to see a doctor or to allow anyone even to feed the dogs for her. 'No coward soul is mine' was rightly the first line of her last poem.

> No coward soul is mine,
> No trembler in the world's storm-troubled sphere:
> I see Heaven's glories shine,
> And faith shines equal, arming me from fear.

On 19 December she came downstairs as usual and took up her needlework. But her eyes were glazing. She said, 'If you will send for a doctor, I will see him now.' That afternoon she died on the dining-room sofa. The 'little lamp' that she had kept burning so straight and clear to guide her mystical 'Strange Power' had ended by bringing only the besotted Branwell to her window. Now he too was gone and the light was out.

All the servants were convinced that Emily had died of sorrow for the loss of her brother. Winifred Gérin, however, believes that her will to live was sapped by the failure of her mystic visions after the publication of the poems. Publication had angered Emily; she was more angry still when Charlotte revealed the Bells' identity to George Smith: there may have been a rift.

Emily's private life was invaded and she left the world. Those are facts. But whether the two were connected must remain doubtful. It is known that Emily had discussed a second novel with Thomas Newby and that she kept five reviews of *Wuthering Heights*. Perhaps Charlotte's own words taken from the new story she was trying to work on, *Shirley*, may bring us as close to the truth as we can get: 'People never die of love or grief alone; though some may of inherent maladies, which the tortures of those passions prematurely force into destructive action.' In that sense Charlotte was to write of her sister, 'She was torn panting, conscious, reluctant though resolute out of a happy life.'

Winter passed miserably with Keeper moaning at Emily's door and the wind sobbing round the house. Spring brought no consolation. Anne's doctor found that both her lungs were tubercular. She could not recover. Charlotte took her to Scarborough which she loved. She died there on 28 May and was buried in the churchyard where Mr Weston had proposed to Agnes Grey. Her last poem also was brave and expressed religious resignation: 'I hoped that with the brave and strong/My portioned task might lie.'

Her bereaved father was understandably concerned for Charlotte's future. He suggested a companion for her. But Charlotte said, 'My work is my best companion.' She had been writing *Shirley* during and after the past terrible months. It was published in October 1849 and celebrated the Emancipated Woman in the portrait of Shirley, as well as being a tribute to Emily Brontë. Shirley was stoical, cauterizing her arm after it was bitten by a dog, just as Emily might have been bitten by Keeper when she dragged him off the white bedspread and punished him savagely with her fist in his face. Shirley could be disdainful and half-insulting even to her lover: 'pride, temper, derision blent in her large eye, that had, just now, the look of a merlin's' – Emily's merlin. Louis Moore loved this touch of abrasiveness in Shirley, and Charlotte wrote of Emily, 'I think a certain harshness in her powerful and peculiar character only makes me cling to her more.' Charlotte was to say of Emily, most memorably, 'Stronger than a man, simpler than a child, her nature stood alone.' Of Shirley she wrote: 'She is a strange being ... not a man-like woman at all – not an Amazon, and yet lifting her head above both help and sympathy.'

But there for a moment the likeness ends. 'Perfect health was Shirley's enviable portion'; and Charlotte clearly thought that the New Woman could operate efficiently only from a basis of good health. Moreover, Shirley unlike Emily was to choose a man to dominate her: her cousin's tutor, Louis Moore, who had taught her French as a girl – 'My master', in both senses.

In *Villette*, Charlotte's second masterpiece, she at last got that irascible darling 'little man', Constantin Heger, out of her system. Both her father and publisher begged her to have a happy ending with Lucy Snowe marrying Paul Emmanuel. But the most Charlotte could concede was a faintly ambiguous end to the storm at sea, in which Paul's body is not specifically washed up. Charlotte had to suffer the loss of M. Heger for the last time, and to drown Paul as inexorably as George Eliot was to drown Tom Tulliver.

Miss Martineau and Mrs Gaskell both detected 'coarseness' in *Villette*, shrinking from the mixture of cold puritanism and passion in Lucy Snowe. As for Matthew Arnold, son of one of Lytton Strachey's eminent Victorians, he found *Villette* a 'hideous, undelightful, convulsed, restricted, novel'. But we must remember that Matthew's father had once written, 'I fear that our countrymen who live abroad are not in the best possible moral state. ...' And Charlotte Brontë had lived abroad. Even G. H. Lewes reviewed *Villette* as 'Female Literature' i.e. as a book written by a woman and therefore to be judged by special standards of propriety instead of on its own merits. 'God defend me from my friends', wrote the angry author. Better friends, however, were found among her ordinary women readers. M. Paul was vastly popular with them, Lady Harriet Erskine vowing she would not marry until she met a Professor Emmanuel. (She married Hans Münster, the German ambassador who at any rate was a foreigner.)

Charlotte had worked up to the completion of *Villette* in November 1852 through months of grief and loneliness, in the 'hush and gloom' of the Parsonage. Expeditions to London and visits to literary friends, like Harriet Martineau at Ambleside and the Gaskells in Manchester, broke the monotony but did not find her the human lover she craved. True, one of her publishers, James Taylor, did propose to her. But though he was 'a little man' and suitably 'despotic', she was allergic to him physically. His long nose which he poked into her face, 'struck iron into my soul' – the wrong kind of iron.

It was exciting to see Wellington, her idol ('He was a real grand old man') and to meet Thackeray, the novelist she most admired. He acutely guessed that Miss

Arthur Bell Nicholls

Brontë 'wants some Tomkins or another to love her and be in love'. There was an absurd scandal that Thackeray, because his wife was mad, had been Charlotte's Tomkins – or rather, Mr Rochester.

By the end of 1849 everyone in the literary world knew who the mysterious 'Bells' were. The sensation was immense. Charlotte was lionized. This astonishing little person calling herself 'Currer' had written 'a naughty novel' (Lewes) whose heroine was 'rather a brazen minx' (J. G. Lockhart on Jane). Charlotte resisted the lionizing as far as possible. Her best dress was inconspicuous and on her head she wore a brown satin ribbon instead of the fashionable plait of false hair that Ellen had bought her. When the great educationist, Sir James Kay-Shuttleworth, took her for a drive she longed to jump out of the carriage and hide in the fields – but such 'erratic and vagrant instincts' would only draw attention to 'the "lioness"'. It was love she needed not lionizing.

There had been gossip in 1846 that Miss Brontë was going to marry her father's curate, the Rev. Arthur Bell Nicholls. 'A cold far-away sort of civility', wrote Charlotte crossly to Ellen, 'are the only terms on which I have ever been with Mr Nicholls.' Six years later on 15 December 1852 he proposed to her. The Rev. Patrick Brontë flew into a rage forcing Charlotte to refuse him in harsh terms. Marriage would kill her, he knew. She had already suffered from ominous pains in her chest; and marriage meant child-bearing, as fatal to consumptives as opium. Nevertheless, her father's insensate fury against Mr Nicholls was counter-productive. When Nicholls broke down at the altar rails while preparing to administer the sacrament to Charlotte and Mr Brontë called him 'an unmanly driveller', Charlotte began to feel sorry for him. When she found him in a passion of tears outside the Parsonage door, she began to love him. He had resigned his curacy in the face of Mr Brontë's wrath and now Mr Brontë could not get on without him. Mr Nicholls returned to Haworth with permission to see Charlotte. The story ended in Mr Brontë putting humanity before his sombre presentiments and giving permission for the marriage.

Arthur Bell Nicholls, whose middle name had given the sisters their pen name, was no Mr Rochester. But he had a degree of sternness which seemed to make Charlotte's conquest valuable, and he was a 'very stiff' Highchurchman, as M. Heger had been an uncompromising Catholic. If Charlotte could take the one she could take the other. Indeed she laughed gently at Arthur's bigotry: to find himself at tea with a Dissenter 'would unhinge him for a week'. And she laughed at his ordering Ellen Nussey to burn her letters from Charlotte.

Charlotte was married on 29 June 1854, wearing a black satin dress, white bridal mantle and white bonnet trimmed with green leaves. She had prepared for her wedding with 'happiness of the soberest order', and her trousseau was of the soberest order also. The chemisettes had to be child's size: 'the full woman's size don't fit me.' They spent the honeymoon in Ireland. (Nicholls had been born on Tully Farm, County Antrim, in 1818.) Charlotte was enchanted with everything: Arthur's Irish relations now living near Birr, the beauty of the South, the wild majesty of the West. When they returned to live in the Parsonage her health remained surprisingly good. No more burning pains or sick headaches. She loved and was loved.

Well before Christmas their brief joy faltered. Charlotte was persuaded by her husband to walk across the moors to see a swollen waterfall. Her thin shoes let in the rain and she was soon shivering with a chill. Spasms of violent nausea developed. In January the doctor pronounced her pregnant. Consumption laid her waste with horrifying speed, as it had Emily. Neither sister 'lingered'. Charlotte lay in the great bed opening her mouth for food like a tiny bird's beak, said the servants. (How touching that Mr Rochester should have compared Jane Eyre to a linnet perching on his foot; and Mrs Gaskell had likened Charlotte's handshake to a small trembling bird lying in her palm.) When Arthur Nicholls prayed by her bedside she asked, 'Oh, I am not going to die, am I? He will not separate us – we have been so happy.' She died on 31 March 1855.

In her obituary notice Harriet Martineau again had to scold Charlotte for creating Jane Eyre and Lucy Snowe; Miss Martineau wanted to see in literature 'a different kind of woman' – a woman emancipated from sex as well as slavery.

Yet the Brontës' heroines, passionate as men, *were* women of a very different kind from any who had hitherto appeared on the Victorian stage. Jane Eyre, in particular, struck a blow for the future of the ordinary plain little woman that Mary Garth repeated in *Middlemarch* and that still resounds today.

GEORGE ELIOT
1819–1880

Mary Anne Evans, the noblest of Victorian novelists, was born almost exactly six months after Queen Victoria on 22 November 1819. With the temperament of a frustrated genius, Mary Anne tried to establish what she called her 'unfolding self' by changing her given name to Marianne, then to Mary Ann, reverting to Mary Anne and finally becoming Marian. She also tried to conceal her identity rather than establish it, for the conditions of her time never encouraged her to write as Miss Evans. Her best selling novels all appeared under the name of George Eliot.

Her astonishing life story will show how she emerged from a series of formidable morasses, in which first her family and then society bogged her down, to climb from social ostracism to quasi-royal adulation.

Her father Robert Evans was agent to the Newdigate family of Arbury Hall in Warwickshire, and Mary Anne was born at South Farm on their estate. All her early novels have the charm of Warwickshire, and country images give a sensuous richness to her similes. To describe the union of squire Arthur and dairy-maid Hetty in *Adam Bede* she wrote: 'such young unfurrowed souls roll to meet each other like two velvet peaches that touch gently and are at rest.' (In deference to Victorian readers the sensuous simile was applied to the souls.) Dogs, of which George Eliot was extremely fond, have a carefully observed life of their own, notably 'Pug' in the same novel. 'On a cushion a little removed sat Pug, with the air of a maiden lady' – just tolerating the gambols of someone else's boisterous puppies.

There was also a hardness in country folk which George Eliot half admired, half feared. Adam Bede himself is the archetypal man, the idealized peasant-artisan based on her father in his youth. She glories in Adam's bare muscular arms and 'thick firm black hair tossed about like meadow-grass' whenever he takes off his carpenter's paper cap. But Adam is as hard as his own nails – until his sweetheart Hetty causes the death of her illegitimate baby by Squire Donnithorne, when Adam accompanies her into the court with the words, 'I'll never be hard again.'

George Eliot also feared her own passions, and even after she had channelled them into her writing they still gave trouble. 'My own books scourge me.' Her youth was shaken by the demands her genius made upon her conventional family. Her chief demand was devastatingly simple. She had to be needed and loved utterly and entirely by one human being. Yet she did not remain first, unquestionably first, with any of those available to love her. Mrs Evans preferred her prettier, elder daughter Chrissey who in turn married and, unlike Mary Anne, became a prolific mother herself. (Although George Eliot was generous to her nieces and nephews, she probably felt at times like Miss 'Pug' with the puppies.) In any case her mother died in 1835 when Mary Anne was sixteen. She became the conventional home-bound daughter looking after the widower, her father.

This was the fate of many Victorian women, but Mary Anne lost the religious faith that sustained most domesticated daughters. She temporarily lost her father's love as a consequence, having declined to attend church services in which she did not believe. True, she soon came to see that some people needed an established faith in order to live good lives, just as she required the right to question, doubt and search after truth; her anti-church gesture had done no good to anyone and she revoked it. Although she later willingly undertook the Victorian sacrament of nursing her father in his last illness, things could never be quite the same between them.

It was, however, a more intimate male relationship that caused Mary Anne's chief misery. This was a passionate devotion to Isaac Evans her brother, which must be approached from two angles: Mary Anne's temperament and the limitations of Victorian social life. She was often to make it quite clear that women did not please her as much as men. At the same time the only member of the opposite sex whom a Victorian girl knew well was her brother. Mary Anne was a plain little girl; but at least she always had her brother – or it must have seemed like 'always' – to love and be loved by. She threw herself into Isaac's country pursuits, preferring a fishing expedition with him to any amount of reading. Only when he went to school and grew beyond her companionship did she turn to books as a substitute.

Unfortunately, when she too had gone to school she had a sharp attack of teenage Calvinism. Her well-meant attempt to 'save' Isaac in the holidays only drove him further from her. When he married in 1841, Mary Ann and her father left the family home at Griff for Foleshill, a part of Coventry. Their new home was a handsome semi-detached house named Bird Grove.

It was in Coventry that Mary Ann met two young married couples, the Brays and Hennells, who were to be a long-lasting influence in her life. Cara Bray came of a Unitarian family, typically combining dissenting beliefs with good works. Her young husband Charles had lately graduated via dissent to free thought, attaching himself to some kind of determinism. Sara Hennell, Cara's sister-in-law, was to become one of George Eliot's closest friends in the feminist world. The other was to be Florence Nightingale's cousin Barbara Leigh-Smith (Bodichon), who opened a school and was later a co-founder of Girton, the first Cambridge college for women.

The Brays' stimulating attitudes came to the parched Mary Ann like dew in the desert. Her intellect responded, while the religious side of her nature was kept alive by the endless philosophical discussions in which Unitarian and Catholic friends alike might join. These discussions ultimately led to Mary Ann's rejection of Christianity, her creed becoming the Comtean 'Philosophy of Humanity'. She was to reject it as a writer, however, since her artistic aim was not to present human relations as ideas, but to make ideas 'incarnate'.

Rosehill, the Brays' substantial house, was also the setting for musical evenings, when Mary Ann and Cara would play duets. Music was a passion with Mary Ann and probably soaked up some of her now unchannelled religious emotions. In the first of her short stories 'Amos Barton', it is music that comes to console Milly Barton on her deathbed: a scene that Victorian readers found irresistible. 'Music – music – didn't you hear it?' says the dying Mrs Barton. A Victorian Christian would have called it 'angel voices'; and no doubt George Eliot's enraptured readers interpreted it thus.

By 1843 Mary Ann was again going to church with her father, but despite this concession Isaac Evans felt far from satisfied with his 'little sister'. Cara is our authority for Isaac's criticism when Mary Ann was twenty-four: 'It seems that brother Isaac with real fraternal kindness thinks that his sister has no chance of getting the one thing needful – i.e. a husband and a settlement – unless she mixes more in society. . . .' Only Chartists and radicals and such riff-raff would fall in love with her, Isaac thought, if she went on mixing with people like the Brays and Hennells instead of belonging to the church.

Here we see a soul-searing dilemma being prepared for the sensitive Mary Ann. Church had become an annexe to the marriage-market. But if she refused to enter, she would become a burden on her brother and her sister Chrissey, who had a bankrupt husband and many children. Isaac succeeded in setting up within Mary Ann a new private torture-chamber filled with the cruel instruments of self-distrust and despair.

Around the time of her twenty-fourth birthday she narrowly escaped a liaison with someone much worse than a young Chartist or radical. She had been bridesmaid to her friend Rufa, daughter of Robert Herbert Brabant. After the wedding Dr Brabant swept Mary Ann off to Cornwall, where his guileless guest was to take the place of the daughter he had lost. In fact she was unwittingly taking the place of his blind wife who, in Professor Gordon Haight's apt phrase, 'though blind, knew quite well what was going on'. The ingenuous Mary Ann was sent packing, Dr Brabant later saddling her with all the blame.

With a bogus reputation for learning, the sixty-two-year-old doctor may have been a prototype of Mr Casaubon in *Middlemarch*. Dorothea Brooke fell for Casaubon much as Mary Ann fell for Brabant. Both at first described the two imposters, fictional and real, as 'archangels'. From the point of view of Mary Ann's own story, the interest lies in her precipitancy and innocence. In the case of Dorothea, George Eliot called this spirit 'ardent'. It was an ambivalent state, which could produce either positive greatness or deluded enthusiasm. As a novelist who was to become famous for her psychological acumen, George Eliot exhibited in youth considerable naiveté and ignorance of men. Her behaviour in subsequent affairs of the heart was to be almost, if not quite, as naive as in the episode with the 'archangelic' doctor.

But first Mary Ann was to find herself immersed in the world of German scholarship. At twenty-five, on the Hennells' suggestion, she began translating David Friedrich Strauss's *Leben-Jesu*. In 1845 a young picture-restorer proposed to her, was accepted and then within a few days turned down. Cara Bray considered his profession neither lucrative enough for her brilliant friend nor 'over-honourable'. Mary Ann, however, blamed herself for *'Precipitancy'* and declared her only present attachments to be 'intellectual and religious loves'.

The rejection of the nameless picture-restorer left Mary Ann with punishing headaches, which she tackled by applications of those 'sweet little creatures', leeches, and tours of the Walter Scott country. Then on 15 June 1846 her translation of the *Life of Jesus* was published anonymously. For her part in this iconoclastic volume she was paid just £20. But her horizons were beginning to widen. With the Brays in 1848 she met the American sage, Ralph Waldo Emerson – 'the first *man* I have ever seen'. And a year later her father died – 'the one deep strong love I have ever known'. The decks were cleared; but for what? Without her father's restraining influence, she had a terrifying vision of herself becoming 'earthly sensual and devilish'. As a child she had suffered from night fears. Now her fear spilt over into the day.

Yet to become 'earthly sensual and devilish' was in a sense too high a hope. The new necessity to earn her living made it more likely that she would become a governess, and governesses were anaemic, cerebral and genteel. Gwendolen

Illustration of Hetty Sorrel after the death of her child (*Adam Bede*).
Overleaf left: **Patty Townsend's watercolour of Griff House.**
Overleaf right: **interiors of Rosehill, the Brays' house, where Mary Ann Evans first found friends and intellectual stimulus.**

1887. Patty Townsend

Harleth in *Daniel Deronda* preferred to marry the revoltingly selfish Grand-court, rather than apply for the job of governess. And Miss Morgan the governess in *Middlemarch* was 'brown, dull, and resigned'.

A prolonged holiday abroad brought no solution to Mary Ann's problems. There were 'electric thrills' from reading Rousseau's *Confessions* in Geneva, and another change of name. She was now Marian, but no nearer to earning a living. At this stage she was an 'outsider' by temperament. To be a governess, however, was to be an outsider through economic necessity. By 1851 Marian had decided to write for a living in London. She had only to make this decision for two more highly unsuitable men to appear.

The first was Dr John Chapman, young, Byronic and not 'over-honourable', though in a different sense from the picture-restorer. Marian quickly found him to be even more of a complete *man* than Emerson. As the publisher of her Strauss translation, Chapman was known to her already. He lived at 142 Strand, with his wife Susannah, two small children and his mistress, Elizabeth Tilley. The children were later sent to Barbara Bodichon's Carlisle Street school, where everything was taught except religion.

Marian's first aim was to get freelance work through Chapman. When this did not materialize she became co-editor with him of that important periodical the *Westminster Review*. She moved into 142 Strand, whose top rooms Susannah let out. Chapman was quite prepared to make all three women happy but Susannah and Elizabeth ganged up against the newcomer, for Dr John had been seen holding her hand. Marian remained relatively secure at 142 Strand only because Chapman was incapable of editing the *Westminster* without her. Her intellect was put to other uses as well. She gave him German lessons 'for love'.

The bright side of her ambivalent position was shown in the number of other interesting men she met or corresponded with; William Empson, editor of the *Edinburgh Review*, understood that she was a man herself – a common misapprehension which Marian was soon to get used to, and indeed welcome. There was also a Mr Lewes, who, Marian agreed with Chapman, would do an excellent piece for the *Westminster* on 'Modern Novelists'. Chapman had been finally dealt with on 3 June 1851. He and Marian took a wet walk together, and as the rain pattered down made 'a solemn and holy vow' to do the right thing thenceforth. Though ardently in love, she would give up *'passionate enthusiasm'* in exchange for mere *'affection'*.

She had jumped out of the frying pan into the fire; except that her next *'man'* was far from fiery. Herbert Spencer was one of those 'advanced' Victorian writers who persuaded himself and his contemporaries of his outstanding merits, only to sink almost without trace in the following century. He became a self-centred hypochondriac who fussed and philosophized his way into a solitary bachelor's old age. When he met Marian she was about thirty and he five months younger. The next year, 1852, they were meeting every day and he described their relations as 'very intimate', but not intimate enough for Marian.

Dr Kimble making himself agreeable to his female patients (*Silas Marner*).

She wrote to him on 3 July the most desperate letter of her life. 'If you become attached to someone else, then I must die.... I do not ask you to sacrifice anything' – sacrifice was for women – 'I would be very good and cheerful and never annoy you.' Herbert refused her agonized plea; nevertheless she survived, bravely telling the Brays it was only a 'deliciously calm' friendship after all. 'We have agreed that we are not in love....' This overt reaction to what was a bitter blow to her certainly seems an advance in Marian's self-control. It was the result of being out in the world as a 'Free Woman' and out of the Victorian family cage. Another man who loved her, William Hale White ('Mark Rutherford') remembered her correcting proofs at 142 Stand with her feet over the arms of her chair, a feminine gesture of freedom.

Spencer blamed Marian's failure to arouse his passions on her lack of aesthetic appeal. There were indeed those who thought that the plain child had become a positively ugly woman. She had a strong jaw, and large mouth with a long upper lip: her nose was large and long (thought on the Continent to be characteristic of all English ladies and the cause of their looking both 'noble' and 'equine'), her cheeks pallid, her expression over-intense; the smallish deep-set eyes occasionally seemed blue but usually grey. Some of these features might have looked well in a man but not in a Victorian woman. She had been called 'awkward and three-cornered' as a girl. She was now 'strongly built' but not tall. Stocky? Ungainly? Bessie Parkes, however, the feminist mother of the Bellocs, detected remarkable suppleness in Marian's figure: 'at moments it had an almost serpentine grace.' Bessie was among those who thought the wise eyes were blue and sometimes 'filled with laughter'.

George Combe, who might be called the 'phrenologist-royal' for his popularity at Windsor, commented on Marian's huge head – $22\frac{1}{4}$ inches round – imagining its cast to be that of a man. Around this imposing cranium with its predominant bump of 'Intellect' and its precariously balanced 'Animal' and 'Moral' bumps, waved a mass of fine light brown hair with a crinkle in it where it lay on her forehead. Today her wide curving mouth would be envied, as would her 'finely formed' hands; and at no period could her sweet low voice have failed to please.

There was a strong masculine vein in her intensely feminine nature. But Victorians had to be one thing or the other. As she grew older more and more people were to comment on her masculinity. Her devoted publisher John Blackwood described her at forty as having 'a face like a man. But a good expression', meaning a womanly expression. Despite the massive skull, Combe called her 'extremely feminine', while Spencer, though susceptible to her 'womanly manner', was the first to notice her masculinity. Marian herself was feminine in her clothes-consciousness. She wore plain black velvet, a rare style for an unmarried lady, and refused to attend two balls because she did not possess an adequate ball-gown. 'It would be a crucifixion of my own taste', she wrote, 'as well as other people's to appear like a withered cabbage in a flower garden.' When the handsome Chapman lectured the withered cabbage on 'the mystery and witchery of beauty', Marian burst into bitter tears.

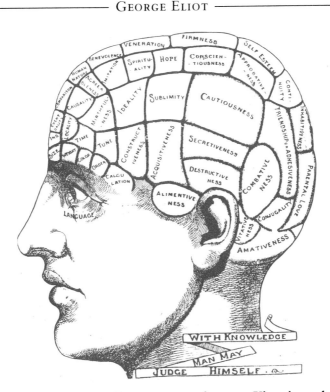

A phrenologist's head. George Eliot was among the many Victorians who believed it was possible to identify character traits by the size and shape of bumps on the skull.

A lady of such hysterical sensitivity needed support. For 'hysterical' was a word that George Eliot applied both to herself and her heroines. At nineteen she had been to a dance whose noise and stamping fell short of true *'Protestant'* character. Mary Anne had reacted with 'that most wretched and unpitied of afflictions, hysteria'. In the early 1850s her friends had decided she was 'not fitted to live alone'; she herself yearned for one human being to lean upon, to take care of her, to devote to her every single particle of his fervent love.

It was a tall order. Nevertheless there was a man ready to fulfil it. George Henry Lewes, himself deprived of love by the unfaithfulness of his beautiful wife Agnes, was to take the place of every relationship, human and divine, in which the world had hitherto failed Marian. Father, brother, lover he would become, even God the creator – for the supernatural God whom Marian had lost was to return in the shape of George Lewes, creator of George Eliot.

It seems that Agnes and George had included an unwritten 'freethinkers' clause in their marriage by which neither was pledged to fidelity. In such cases, the woman usually suffered most, but with the Leweses it was Agnes who had the advantage. After giving George three children she had four more by Thornton Leigh Hunt, son of the writer. George quixotically paid for all seven, since Thornton had ten legitimate children by his own wife. The making of money was never Lewes's forte, though he was a versatile writer, natural scientist and a dazzlingly amusing talker. He had also been a theatre critic and actor, playing Shylock as an unconventionally sympathetic character in 1849, long before Sir Henry Irving thought of doing the same. In George Eliot Lewes discovered a goldmine. And if her marvellously productive vein was neither in existence nor suspected when they 'married', it became the lynch-pin of their material existence, which explains her unexpectedly keen attitude towards sales, advances and royalties. She was the bread-winner.

They met in a London bookshop and were introduced by Chapman. Though Marian's first impression of Lewes was unfavourable (another example of her fallible judgment) she was soon seeing a great deal of him, and seeing him with new eyes: '... Lewes, as always genial and amusing. He has quite won my liking, in spite of myself.' By September 1853 she had moved to lodgings off Hyde Park Square where Lewes became her lover. She was translating the German humanist Feuerbach, who held that 'Love is God himself ... not a visionary, imaginary love – no! a real love, a love which has flesh and blood ...' Marian found that piece easy to translate: God is Lewes.

'At thirty-four', writes Gordon Haight in his biography, 'her deeply passionate nature had at last found a wholly satisfying love that responded keenly to Lewes's more experienced sexuality.' As the couple had decided not to bring more illegitimate children into the world, Lewes practised some kind of birth control, or so said Barbara Bodichon. Marian had told Barbara that Lewes was 'unsensual, extremely considerate'.

Their natures complemented one another; his sparkling, hers profound. Even their looks were in a sense complementary, for Lewes's notoriously ugly, shaggy head dwindled down to a small fragile frame. His feminine vein complemented Marian's masculine one. To this 'marriage of true minds' – and bodies – there were no impediments that needed to be admitted. They could never be legally married – even when Marian could well afford to buy her 'husband' an expensive divorce, his having once condoned Agnes's adultery ruled out this solution – but the fact that Lewes was beyond the conventional pale probably added to his attraction for Marian. They felt free to elope together, free from all chains except those of love. For this time Lewes's relationship was not to be 'free love'. He had learnt his lesson. They were both committed, Marian specifically calling their union moral and a sacred bond. They were a married couple, husband and wife, in all but law; in June 1854 they left England for the Continent as Mr and Mrs Lewes.

While they were abroad, imbibing the highbrow nostalgia of Goethe's Weimar, reports of the elopement began to reach Marian's friends and family. The kindest criticism made of her was Carlyle's – that she was a 'strong-minded woman'; the worst Thomas Woolner's – that she and Lewes were 'stink pots of humanity', 'Mormonites', 'hideous satyrs and smirking moralists'. The phrenologist-royal wondered whether he had missed one of Miss Evans's bumps: the bump of Insanity. Professor Ruby Redinger (author of a revealing study of George Eliot entitled *The Emergent Self*) points out that the Victorians showed 'a strange mixture of indignation and jealousy' in their reactions to the elopement. Marian could laugh off the malice of a deaf bluestocking like Harriet

Isaac Evans

John Chapman

Herbert Spencer

George Henry Lewes in 1840. When Charlotte Brontë met Lewes she wrote that his face 'almost moved me to tears – it is so like Emily's. . . .'

Martineau: 'She is sure to caricature any information for the amusement of the next person to whom she turns her ear-trumpet.' But Cara Bray's lengthy silence after one shocked letter was hard to bear. Marian protested that 'Women who are satisfied with such ties [light and easily broken] . . . obtain what they desire and are still invited to dinner.'

The social ostracism of herself and Lewes at least gave Marian time to lick her wounds and plan for survival. She refused to recapture the 'smile of the world', as she put it in *Daniel Deronda*, by compromising. But there was a potential wound that her remaining friends must refrain from inflicting. They must address her not as Miss Evans but as 'Mrs Lewes'. Her feminist admirers were the worst offenders. It was becoming clear that Marian's breaking of the moral code was only partially in line with feminist ideology. She never publicly supported the women's rights movement because, she said, her peculiar social position would have damaged the cause. But a more potent reason was her own doubt. She wrote to Emily Davies, another champion of Girton College: 'It [the women's rights movement] seems to me to overhang abysses of which even prostitution is not the worst.'

Mr and Mrs Lewes settled in Richmond, working at their twin desks like Queen Victoria and Prince Albert at Osborne – except that the scratching of George's pen irritated Marian, while any sound from dearest Albert was venerated by Victoria. In constricted quarters the Leweses were earning a very modest living, but Marian was deeply happy to be helping a beloved man with his work. Then came a seaside holiday at Tenby, South Wales, in 1855 which was to prove the first milestone on the road to her own literary success. Marian had often dreamt of writing a story, but her feelings of guilt and despondency always caused her aspirations to wilt. In Germany George had encouraged her to no avail. At Tenby he started again. 'You must try and write a story . . .' This time it worked. Marian awoke one morning with an idea for a story about the evangelicals in the industrial Midlands. She told Lewes that it would be called: 'The Sad Fortunes of the Reverend Amos Barton.' George said, 'O what a capital title!' Even if the title was not all that 'capital', it was always George's duty to boost Marian's morale. He became the man-midwife to *Scenes of Clerical Life* (1856); and Tenby, in Haight's words, the birthplace of George Eliot.

While George Lewes was escorting his two elder boys to their progressive school in Switzerland, Marian had a wisdom tooth dealt with and polished off for the *Westminster Review* an article on 'Silly Novels by Lady Novelists'. Why did not the lady writer of snobbish Church fiction, she demanded, ever write about religion among the Negroes like Mrs Beecher Stowe? Or about the 'real drama' of evangelicalism among the middle and lower classes? Eleven days after sending her piece to Chapman, the anonymous author began 'Amos Barton'. It seems a paradox that George Eliot the unbeliever should write her first and last novels about religion. The paradox, however, is only skin-deep, for religion or its denial still had every Victorian by the throat.

The faithful Lewes despatched 'Amos Barton' to his friend John Blackwood, editor of '*Maga*' (*Blackwood's Magazine*) boldly comparing this new writer – a *he*

– to Jane Austen, but explaining that because of *his* 'shy, shrinking, ambitious' nature he preferred to conceal his identity. (If it had been known that the author was one half of that 'Mormanite' couple, the Leweses, and the female half at that, 'Amos Barton' would have been still-born.) The delighted Blackwood accepted 'Amos': 'Your friend's reminiscences of Clerical Life will do ...', he said; 'very pleasant reading ... I beg to congratulate him ...' 'Mr Gilfil's Love Story' and 'Janet's Repentance' triumphantly followed 'Amos' in *Blackwood's* later the same year, 1857, making up the trio called *Scenes of Clerical Life*. And Marian now had a pen name, a ruse for securing her incognito. She called herself George after Lewes and chose Eliot as 'a good mouth-filling, easily-pronounced word'. (Eliot could also stand for 'To L – I owe it'.) She signed a letter to John Blackwood, 'Yours very truly (incognito apart) George Eliot.' Her incognito was not generally broken until *The Mill on the Floss* was published, when the revelation of George Eliot's identity adversely affected the book's sales, but by then George Eliot's persona was too powerful to be permanently damaged by Mrs Lewes. Dickens was one of the few writers to guess from the start that the author of the *Scenes* was a woman. He wrote in 1858 to congratulate 'George Eliot, Esq.' on his unique art in 'making himself mentally so like a woman'. Her editor John Blackwood was not so percipient. He addressed Marian as 'My dear Sir' until *Adam Bede* was on the way, when he discovered with shame that it was

A *Punch* caricature of a typical Victorian prejudice that a female novelist would inevitably write of matters too improper for other women to read.

A NOVEL FACT.

Old-fashioned Party (with old-fashioned prejudices). "AH! VERY CLEVER, I DARE SAY. BUT I SEE IT'S WRITTEN BY A LADY, AND I WANT A BOOK THAT MY DAUGHTERS MAY READ. GIVE ME SOMETHING ELSE!"

a woman to whom he had used 'some easy expressions'. His grandson was to make the opposite mistake with E. M. Forster, addressing him as 'Dear Madam'.

The pen name brought trouble as well as security. A truly male rascal named Joseph Liggins claimed to be the author of the *Scenes*. But money troubles at least had vanished. 'We ate our turkey together', wrote Marian happily on Christmas Day 1857. Before publication of the *Scenes* she and George had sometimes been down to plain bread and butter, suffering indigestion from under-nourishment. Another heart-rending trouble was to remain.

It was while writing 'Janet's Repentance' that Marian took a brave decision. She must tell Isaac and her family that she was living with Lewes. Not 'Janet's' repentance, however, turned out to be required, but Marian's. Isaac would not accept her confession, refused to answer her letter, communicated only through a solicitor and even prevented the family from communicating. Marian's ostracism was complete. She never set eyes on her idolized tyrant again and might rarely have heard her family pet-name, Polly, but for George's having adopted it. Nevertheless 1857 had been a wonderful year: 'The long sad years of youth were worth living', she felt, 'for the sake of middle age. . . .' She wrote in her diary on New Year's Eve, 1858, 'The dear old year is gone with all its *Weben* and *Streben*' (weaving and striving).

For the next eighteen years or so George Eliot faced a double, inter-related challenge. First, the eternal *Streben* with her own genius, and the depressions, the acute miseries and even the bouts of ill-health that were the price she had to pay. Second, there was her external position with Lewes. Without Lewes she could not have written at all. He was the guardian angel who always made a point of praising her latest book the most and keeping all reviews out of her sight except the very best. Yet with Lewes there was the perpetual challenge of their ostracism. Marian had always craved admiration. In childhood she had fancied the gypsies because they would revere her as a little lady.

George Eliot had many personal memories and griefs to work off in her first novels. *Adam Bede* (1859) is a moving celebration of love. So stirring, not to say disturbing was it to some Victorians that Mr Gladstone, for instance, had to scourge himself after reading it. The unctuous Herbert Spencer, however, who had never felt the pangs of love, wrote, 'I feel greatly the better for having read it.' Seth, Adam's brother, having been turned down by Dinah Morris the charming young Methodist preacher, suggests to Adam that she is above falling in love, being better than ordinary women. 'But if she's better than they are in other things', objects Adam, 'I canna' think she'll fall short of 'em in loving.' That, not any lonely exaltation of the intellect, was George Eliot's creed. There is a paean for Lewes too. First love has 'spring charm', she writes, while maturer love 'yields a richer, deeper music'. Both her heroines, Dinah and Hetty, are beautiful and there is no George Eliot novel in which a woman's beauty does not feature.

Sympathy is a keynote of *Adam Bede*, as it was to be of all her work, until she reached Grandcourt in *Daniel Deronda*. Even Arthur Donnithorne the gay seducer is presented as a good fellow at heart. In her own voice, George Eliot tells her readers how pain changes into sympathy – 'the one poor word which includes all our best insight and our best love'. In her hand sympathy was transformed from a 'poor word' into the divining rod of her genius. Sympathy with the poor, with 'common coarse people', with 'commonplace things' was raised to a mystical experience in *Adam Bede*.

The Mill on the Floss (1860) has been called by A. S. Byatt the last of George Eliot's early 'natural histories', in which she lovingly recorded the 'particularities' of the physical and human landscapes she knew. In *The Mill* George Eliot worked off, for instance, some pungent feelings about respectability. Mrs Pullet, one of Maggie Tulliver's three aunts who are based on George Eliot's own relatives, expresses the Victorian ethos of sorrow and joy in all its absurdity: 'She had leisure and money to carry her crying and everything else to the highest pitch of respectability.'

One of George Eliot's alleged artistic failures is Stephen Best in *The Mill*. Critics have believed that a girl like Maggie could never have fallen passionately in love with such a superficial character. However, George Eliot might have pointed to her own humiliating personal experiences. At least Best had more decency than Brabant and more sexuality than Spencer.

The ever-remembered sufferings of George Eliot herself give a special poignancy to Maggie Tulliver's starved young life: her 'analytic mind', love of music, divided nature and resentment at being 'only' a girl. Its profoundly felt feminism has led Ellen Moers in her *Literary Women* to call Maggie's secret retreat, the Red Deeps, a typically female landscape of mounds and hollows. Tom and Maggie are made to act out the brother-and-sister tragedy of Isaac and Polly. The self-sacrifice of Maggie and her consequent drowning in Tom's arms seem on the surface a starker tragedy than the real-life separation from Isaac. Yet the tragedy was in a sense a triumph. After it was written George Eliot was released from some after-effects of her thralldom. The unhappy Issac and Mary Anne were held under the water by George Eliot until they drowned. Or nearly drowned. Nine years later she could still feel that her 'root of piety' lay in her 'kith and kin, though they reject *me.*'

Silas Marner (1861), with its emphasis on money, reminds us again of George Eliot's own compulsions in that direction. She was once to throw over her loyal publisher John Blackwood, when George Smith offered her £7,000 to publish *Romola* with the *Cornhill*. It was not a success. Later, John Blackwood magnanimously took back his most illustrious author.

Romola (1862–63) is an interesting failure. The *Saturday Review* criticized it for 'instructive antiquarianism', for Romola, though she bears the 'ardent and sympathetic' stigmata of a great George Eliot heroine, unluckily lives in the Florence of Savonarola instead of the English Midlands, and she walks in streets that exist in George Eliot's quarry of reference books rather than in her creative memory. The character of Savonarola, however, does shed light on the way George Eliot's mind had moved. Savonarola's 'glorious vision of achievement' is doomed to sink into nothingness, making George Eliot's sombre point against over-ardent idealism. To Romola, Savonarola's glance conveyed a sense of 'interest in her and care for her apart from any personal feeling . . . a gaze in which simple human fellowship expressed itself in a strongly-felt bond'. This is remarkably like the tribute paid to George Eliot herself by the brilliant young Edith Simcox, who was in love with her. Indeed the impact made by Savonarola resembled that which George Eliot was soon to make on her circle of ardent friends and disciples. Tennyson later said George Eliot's face resembled Savonarola's. One feels that a gracious, impersonal affection was consciously developed by the lionized George Eliot, as the right persona for a woman of extreme eminence.

In *Felix Holt the Radical* (1866) George Eliot is concerned with social change in England and again passes judgment on extreme idealism. A phrenologist discovers that Felix has a 'large bump of ideality, which prevents him from finding anything perfect enough to be venerated'. He changes during the novel into the most moderate of radicals. There are also wry sketches of woman's dilemma. While Dissenters' womenfolk are generally content to occupy their leisure with 'biographies of devout women and that amount of ornamental knitting which is not inconsistent with Nonconformist seriousness', Esther Lyon, the dissenting minister's beautiful daughter, is half-prepared to raise her stakes. When Felix Holt tells her that women, unless they are Saint Teresas or Elizabeth Frys, generally think Radical reform is 'madness', Esther retorts: 'A woman can hardly ever choose in that way; she is dependent on what happens to her. She must take meaner things because only meaner things are within reach.' But in due course Esther takes Felix; and the voice of George Eliot comments, 'To be right in great moments, is perhaps the thing we most desire for ourselves.' By the date of *Felix Holt*, George Eliot was unshakably sure that she herself had been right in her greatest moment.

Yet she never deceived herself into thinking that her relationship with Lewes was easy. 'A supreme love', she wrote in *Felix Holt*, 'fulfils the soul's highest needs'; but the soul 'must often tread where it is hard to tread, and feel the chill air, and watch through darkness. It is not true that love makes all things easy. It makes us choose what is difficult.'

As George Eliot's fame grew, Lewes succeeded in attracting to their house great aristocrats and notables, especially those of a feminist mind. Queen Victoria had given *Adam Bede* her royal imprimatur as 'a true picture' of what happened when the squire admired the dairy maid; and after the death of her literary adviser, Sir Arthur Helps, she asked his daughter to send her the twin signatures of Marian and Lewes from their letter of condolence. Two of the Queen's daughters, the Princess Royal and Princess Louise, met both the Leweses personally. As for Mary Ponsonby, wife of the Queen's private secretary, she found herself treating the great George Eliot in 1873 as if she actually were the Queen: 'Certainly no Emperor or King in my Court days', recalls Lady Ponsonby, 'had ever been approached with such awe; it makes me laugh now to think of the involuntary deep curtsy I greeted her with. . . .' It is possible that the extreme excellence of George Eliot's last two novels was a function not only of her increased literary skill but also of her being at last an 'insider'. *Middlemarch* came out in parts from 1871 to 1872 and *Daniel Deronda* appeared in 1876.

Middlemarch is a complete world in itself, created with all George Eliot's subtle psychology, mature characterization, depth of background and four interwoven plots to give the story length and breadth. Virginia Woolf described it as one of the few English novels written for grown-up people. The autobiographical touches are there, but none is used for a purpose outside the novel. George Eliot has entire mastery over all her characters, so that she is able to make us care. We are genuinely alarmed lest Dorothea and Will Ladislaw should miss their 'great moment' and finally and fatally bungle their love affair by outmanoeuvring one another once too often.

The aspiring Dorothea Brooke and Dr Lydgate are both egotist-idealists who enthusiastically cut loose from the anchor of real life, with all its variety and 'particularity'. Dorothea learns through suffering that idealism is not enough. Her warmth and beauty have won devotees from the beginning. But it is only today, when the centenary of George Eliot's death has come round, that a young assessor of her characterization can write: 'I like Mr Casaubon' – *like* that cold prig whose phantom work of scholarship was a reflection of his hollow marital love? It says much for George Eliot's power to create living persons rather than cardboard figures, that there can be two opinions of Edward Casaubon.

It is Dorothea, however, of all George Eliot's characters, who carries in her 'maternal' hands the possibility of a brave new world. Like other high-minded men and women in the novels, Dorothea looks out of a window when her spiritual vision of the world is about to expand. It happens first on a snowy morning when she gazes upon the 'still, white enclosure' of the garden and realizes that despite marriage her life continues to suffer from 'the stifling oppression of that gentlewoman's world' into which she had been born. Both Dinah Morris in *Adam Bede* and Mordecai in *Daniel Deronda* draw inspiration from a 'peaceful' or 'large' view from a window. But the final landscape that Dorothea unveils when she opens her curtains at dawn has a deeper and more complex symbolism. It enables her to 'clutch her own pain, and compel it to silence', as she ponders over the sufferings of Will, Rosamund and Lydgate:

On the road there was a man with a bundle on his back and a woman carrying her baby; in the field she could see figures moving – perhaps the shepherd with his dog.

Each figure is in some way burdened or responsible for others.

Far off in the bending sky was the pearly light; and she felt the largeness of the world and the manifold wakings of men to labour and enduring. She was part of that involuntary life, and could neither look out on it from her luxurious shelter as a spectator, nor hide her eyes in selfish complaining.

If Dorothea is the crown of George Eliot's feminine achievement, all the women in *Middlemarch* (which is Coventry) have their indispensable parts to play in this consummate orchestration of Victorian England: from Mary Garth's simple perfection to the superficial insights of the spoilt Rosamund and the conventional woman's wisdom of Dorothea's sister Celia. 'Brothers are so unpleasant' says Rosamund, touching the epicentre of George Eliot's deepest shock as casually as if she were discussing unpleasant weather. 'And, of course men know best about everything', says Celia, 'except, when women know better.' There is no end in *Middlemarch* to what Henry James called 'masterly pictures of the manifold life of man'.

It was compulsively readable to contemporaries. William Trent, the Protestant archbishop of Dublin, was seen apparently listening to a speech but actually with George Eliot's novel open inside his top hat. After reading *Middlemarch* people could understand Herbert Spencer's tribute to her genius: 'The female Shakespeare, so to speak.' Lord Acton was to call her works 'the high-water mark of feminine achievement' – balanced one must admit by Ruskin's reference to 'the sweepings of a Pentonville omnibus'.

To some critics it is disappointing that George Eliot's great *oeuvre* should have ended with *Daniel Deronda* (1876), described by Professor Quentin Anderson as 'about the most splendid failure among English novels'. It is true that some aspects of the second, Jewish plot seem strained, especially the brother-sister relationship of Mordecai and Mirah. And the odious Grandcourt, in the first plot, has no redeeming features, breaking George Eliot's rule to depict only 'mixed human beings in such a way as to call forth tolerant judgment, pity, and sympathy'. On the other hand, Mordecai is convincing as the Jewish visionary and the novel achieves what George Eliot intended for Judaism:

There is nothing I should care more to do [she wrote to Mrs Stowe], if it were possible, than to rouse the imagination of men and women to a vision of human claims in those races of their fellow-men who most differ from them in customs and beliefs.

From the feminist angle there are poignant insights. 'You are not a woman', says Daniel Deronda's Jewish mother to her son. 'You may try but you can never imagine what it is to have a man's force of genius in you, and yet to suffer the slavery of being a girl.' George Eliot knew. The petulant but touching words of the spoilt Gwendolen Harleth on women's passive role are as good as anything in *Middlemarch*:

'We women can't go in search of adventures; to find out the North-west Passage or the source of the Nile, or to hunt tigers in the East. We must stay where we grow, or where the gardeners like to transplant us. We are brought up like the flowers, to look as pretty as we can, and be dull without complaining.'

It was partly because George Eliot had never been a pretty flower that she neither stayed where she grew nor allowed gardener Isaac to transplant her by marriage, into another conventional habitat.

Towards the end of her twenty-four happy years with Lewes, life for George Eliot had become undeniably good. In 1863 she had been able to afford an enchanting London house and garden called The Priory, on the Regents Canal. The house cost her £2,000 (she had earned £16,000 as a novelist by the following year) and was beautifully decorated for the Leweses by their distinguished friend Owen Jones.

All their regulars, including John Walter Cross a young banker who looked after their finances, attended their Sunday evenings, and also many of the famous like Robert Browning, T. H. Huxley, the Burne-Joneses and Lord and Lady Amberley. Henry James the young American novelist visited The Priory and promptly fell in love with Marian whom he called Lewes's 'great horse-faced blue-stocking', perceiving that 'in this vast ugliness, resides a most powerful beauty'. He had found his way into a Victorian secular ashram run by a charming lady guru. Part of her pleasure in social life came from feeling that she was doing people good.

There were constant holidays abroad and at the seaside, and in 1878 the Leweses acquired through Johnnie Cross a real country-house of their own: Witley Heights, in Surrey. It even had a tennis court, where they 'perspired freely'. But the days of their mutual happiness were numbered. Marian's first agonizing attacks of kidney-stone (her father had suffered in the same way) occurred in 1874. Four years later it was George who was on the danger list. Marian had long dreaded his death, as she showed in a letter thanking Arthur Helps for a copy of the Queen's *Leaves from the Journal of Our Life in the Highlands*: '. . . I am a woman of about the same age, and also have my personal happiness bound up in a dear husband whose loss would render my life simply a series of social duties and private memories.' Her reaction to George's actual death on 30 November 1878 seems also to have resembled the reaction of Victoria to Albert's. The Queen gave a 'bitter agonizing cry', while Marian became hysterical, '. . . her screams heard through the house'. She afterwards used writing paper with a thick black border.

Not quite eleven months later, however (16 October 1879), Marian had surprisingly come out of her seclusion and written a letter that would have astonished Queen Victoria, for whom mourning was a life's work. 'Best loved and loving one' the letter began; '. . . the sun it shines so cold, so cold, when there are no eyes to look love on me.' She signed herself Beatrice, and her Dante was the forty-year-old Johnnie Cross. He had proposed three times and was 'third time lucky'.

Or was he lucky? Up till Lewes's death he had called himself their 'nephew' and George Eliot was his 'aunt'. Her clamant need to be looked after, however, finally convinced them both that she must become his wife. ('I was getting hard', she wrote to Lewes's eldest son Charles.) They were married on 6 May 1880 at St George's Church, Hanover Square, Charles Lewes giving her away. When Isaac Evans declared he had 'much pleasure' in breaking the 'long silence' to congratulate her, her cup of happiness was full; fuller in a sense than it had been since the break in 1857. As late as 1869 she had written a nostalgic sonnet-sequence called 'Brother and Sister', in which she still seemed to hanker after Isaac's love, remembering how he and she as children 'leaned soft cheeks together'. Johnnie, on the other hand, may have found that he had sipped at more elixir than he could swallow.

The tall, handsome, red–bearded banker J. W. Cross who married George Eliot.

On their honeymoon in Venice he suffered a sudden brief mental breakdown. And Henry James was to write that if George Eliot had not died when she did, her intellectual pace would have killed Cross. As it was he probably lived most fully with George Eliot after her death, while writing her *Life*.

The Crosses moved to 4 Cheyne Walk on 3 December 1880, seeking a climate milder than that of Surrey. They went to the *Agamemnon* on the 17th and to a concert on the 18th. The next day Marian had a sore throat, followed by acute pain in her kidneys. Nevertheless she began a letter to her friend Mrs Richard Strachey, condoling with her on a brother-in-law's death. It was interrupted, probably by Herbert Spencer, and was the last thing she wrote. She died on 22 December 1880, and was buried in Highgate Cemetery, a corner of her coffin touching Lewes's. Isaac, none other, was a chief mourner. Almost exactly a hundred years later, on Midsummer Day, 1980, a memorial tablet was unveiled to her in Westminster Abbey. Some critics found the Christian service 'scandalously inappropriate', while others, deeply moved, felt that George

Eliot's nobility rather than her agnosticism had been honoured and justice finally done.

Professor Leavis writes that the major novelists 'are significant in terms of the human awareness they promote; awareness of the possibilities of life'. George Eliot's genius removed many blinkers from her contemporaries; indeed it was a characteristic of great Victorians to be dazzled by life's 'possibilities', though Victorian women often saw the possibilities without being able to achieve them. George Eliot preached enthusiasm of a reverend, moderate and rational kind. Hers was the only fiction that Sir Leslie Stephen would admit to the shelves of the London Library. All the main characters in George Eliot's novels see 'the possibilities of life' and develop accordingly, each fictional self being as 'emergent' as her own.

On human relations she still widens our horizon. Her women characters in particular live, and we mind what happens to them. Women found her remarkably attractive (several were in love with her); and though she did not reciprocate the lesbian feelings that she excited, she breathed greater life into her women than into her men.

There were two relationships which from the beginning affected her writing; the loving one with her father and the traumatic one with her brother. All critics agree on the importance of these two. Nothing comparable has been written about George Eliot's relations with her mother. Mary Anne was 'deprived' of an important source of affection both by Mrs Evans's coldness and by her early death. The mother-principle remained none the less as a powerful force struggling to emerge in George Eliot's own life and in her novels. One of her differences with the feminists (to whose causes she generously contributed) was that they overlooked woman's special tenderness, expressed in maternal feelings.

The novels are full of references to 'Madonnas': Romola is mistaken by peasants for the Madonna herself; Janet might have renounced alcohol had she been a mother; Dorothea Brooke has 'powerful feminine, maternal hands'; Will's German friend Neumann calls her 'the most perfect young Madonna I ever saw,' and Lydgate thinks, 'This young creature has a heart large enough for the Virgin Mary.' Gwendolen Harleth's mother is the only person she can bear near her. Lewes called Marian 'Madonna'. His sons called her 'little Mutter'; others 'Mother' or 'Madre', and her love-sick female circle were her 'daughters'. She was clearly a mother-figure to Cross, with whom the seven-month marriage must have seemed a kind of incest and so broken his nerve.

In offering her a married man as her '*man*', fate seemed to have given her a second raw deal. The first had been to take away her own mother; the second, to take away the chance of marrying and becoming a mother herself. Nevertheless fate had been kinder to her than to Charlotte Brontë. With her unhealthy kidneys George Eliot also might have died during her first pregnancy. Instead she went on to fulfil the demands of her nature by becoming a 'fictional' mother as well as a 'fictional' wife. In doing so she wrote unique works of Victorian fiction in which intellect and passion are perfectly combined.

FLORENCE NIGHTINGALE

1820–1910

Few women become legends in their lifetime. We think at once of Florence Nightingale and Joan of Arc, with whom indeed Miss Nightingale compared herself (war generates instant legend) but who else? Florence Nightingale was the only woman among Lytton Strachey's four 'Eminent Victorians'. He succeeded in restoring, through a varnish of irony, the formidable character of a hitherto sentimentalized 'angel of mercy'. Her enemies were in a sense his enemies; for he was writing in 1918, at the end of a war which had witnessed blunders worthy of her own Crimea. When Strachey had done with Miss Nightingale she was both more impressive than before and at the same time diminished. Her occasional ladylike responses belong to the era which Strachey was out to satirize. When at eighty-seven she received the Order of Merit – the first woman so honoured – she had to be portrayed by Strachey murmuring, 'Too kind – too kind', no longer able to comprehend what was happening. Her words sound on Strachey's page a note of mild farce. He had a gift for making the illustrious departed look foolish:

Cardinal Manning leaving behind only a dusty red hat, Dr Arnold bequeathing nothing but 'athletics' and 'good form' to the public school system, General Gordon going 'a little off his head' and Florence Nightingale repeating in a whisper her senile gratitude.

Over thirty years after Strachey, in 1950, came Cecil Woodham-Smith's *Florence Nightingale* enriched with Miss Nightingale's diaries and 'private notes' which had been consigned by her family to the British Museum. The Nightingale story will never be told more readably, lucidly and comprehensively than in these six hundred pages. Among modern readers has appeared Sir George Pickering, a distinguished physician, who in his essays entitled *The Creative Malady* (1974) discovers a new dimension to Miss Nightingale's enthralling story, produced by psychoneurosis – the illness 'with a purpose'.

She was born on 12 May 1820, the same year as the novelist Anne Brontë. But whereas Anne lived to be only twenty-eight, spending less than three weeks on her deathbed, Florence took to her 'deathbed' at the age of thirty-seven, and remained there on and off – mostly on – for another fifty-three years. Delicacy was an ambiguous quality in Victorian women.

Florence was called after the Italian city where she was born; just as her elder sister Parthenope had been named for the city of her birth, Naples (Greek version). Perhaps if Parthe had been called plain 'Naples' she would have been cut down to size instead of becoming a maddening thorn in Florence's flesh.

Flo, as she was known to her family, was an outsider. She was not really like her clever dilettante father, William Edward Nightingale (always referred to as W.E.N.) in temperament, although she had his brains. Nor did she resemble her beautiful mother Fanny, whose highest ambition was to shine in society. Fanny's father and grandfather, however, were both political idealists, William Smith fighting for the abolition of slavery alongside Wilberforce, and Samuel Smith sympathizing with the Americans in the War of Independence. Flo was not like Parthe either. Less gifted and less pretty than Flo, Parthe always wanted a share of her sister's success, and the whole of her devotion. After Parthe had had a mental breakdown in 1852, Florence wrote: 'A physician once seriously told a sister

W. E. N. with his daughters. Parthe clings to her father, but Flo walks alone.

who was being Devoured that she must leave home in order that the Devourer might recover health. . . . That person was myself.' Parthe shared only one talent with her sister: the power to make herself ill when thwarted. She wished to enslave Florence, as Florence was later to enslave others. There was a love of power for its own sake running through the Nightingale women.

When Florence reached her teens she was educated by her father up to his own high standard in classics and philosophy. (Parthe had tried to share the lessons, but found them too boring.) This pupil-teacher relationship created the one wholly loving bond between Florence and her family. Then in January 1838 the parents took their two girls abroad, Florence being destined, it seemed, to answer the call of matrimony with spectacular success when she 'came out' the following year. Tall, willowy, with a pale skin, lively grey eyes and a crowning glory of abundant, wavy, light-chestnut hair, she would be a gift to any public man along his road to fame and fortune. Her mother's hopes, however, were doomed to disappointment. For Florence at sixteen had already heard a call, a call which was emphatically not that of matrimony.

According to her own recollection, she was only six when the pointlessness of her home life began to dawn. As a child she thought there must be something wrong with her. Was she a monster? She frightened her mother with strange reserves and outbursts. In adolescence she decided there was something wrong with her home. Did not life hold better things than house-parties? On 7 February 1837 the answer had come: 'God spoke to me and called me to His service.' (Florence's 'voice' had been as objective and external as Joan of Arc's 'voices'.) She felt confident He would speak again soon, telling her exactly what to do. Meanwhile she was prepared to enjoy her first visit abroad, especially Italy, the land of freedom-fighters for whom she felt passionate sympathy.

In Paris the Nightingales met Mary Clarke, an eccentric English lady with aristocratic connections and a wide circle of intellectual friends. She was to become Florence's lifelong confidante and adviser, her beloved 'Clarkey'. At this early date Mary had an intense *amitié amoureuse* with M. Claude Fauriel the French scholar. Later she married his great friend M. Julius Mohl. Florence conceived for Mary Clarke one of her 'passions' (previously lavished upon Aunt Mai Smith and Miss Christie, a governess). More important, Mary's famous friendship with Fauriel provided a model for Florence's later relationship with Sidney Herbert. Neither provoked a breath of scandal.

The Nightingales returned to England in April 1839, Florence acutely aware that amid the welter of Italian, French and Swiss voices the Divine Voice had not uttered again. There could be only one explanation. Gallivanting around Europe, she had become unworthy. Before leaving Paris for home she resolved to eradicate the temptation to 'shine in society'. Thus she and her family entered upon a collision course which was to last for fourteen years. Since her parents were unaware of Flo's secret decision, her refusal to marry seemed merely perverse. To make matters worse, Flo's cousin Henry Nicholson of Waverley in Surrey fell in love with her, while Flo herself developed a violent passion for his beautiful sister Marianne, who was being presented at the same time as the two Nightingales. Florence's season became a saturnalia of pleasure and guilt – guilt over Marianne, guilt over Henry whom she encouraged in order to keep close to his sister, and guilt over her general wickedness which prevented the Voice from revealing her vocation.

Next year Florence made a gallant attempt to improve. She and her Aunt Mai Smith assailed Fanny jointly with the argument that her gifted daughter needed some occupation beyond needlework and playing quadrilles on the piano; could she not learn mathematics from 'a clean middle aged respectable person' who was of course a married man? Fanny at first opposed the lessons; then cut them short after a year; but not before Florence had absorbed the mathematical disciplines which were later to make her a master of statistics.

As an available young lady in her early twenties, she was always being badgered to do 'Ladies' work'. She wrote complaining to another favourite girl cousin, Hilary Bonham Carter, in 1841: 'There are hundreds of human beings always crying after ladies. Ladies' work has always to be fitted in'; but where there was a man in the family, 'his business is the law'.

The misery of Britain's 'Hungry Forties' made her realize at least that her vocation lay somewhere among the poor and oppressed. That much was obvious from her visiting in the rural slums around her father's estates of Embley in Hampshire and Lea Hurst in Derbyshire. Fanny handed out soup and small silver, but she dreaded infection, and Florence was permitted to make only conventional visits of the 'Lady Bountiful' variety. She was forbidden to enter cottages when the need was greatest; whereupon she herself would fall ill, her family would relent and so the wretched cycle would begin again.

At the same time, a youthful habit of Florence's that she called 'dreaming' now became an alarming addiction. What were these 'trance-like' states into which she might easily fall while making conversation with one of her mother's socially imposing friends? There is something unusual about the trances, and the violent language with which Florence would condemn them. They were 'shameful visions', a 'shameful' secret that she shared with no one, a threat to her mental balance, 'my enemy', 'evil', 'sinful' – indeed perhaps a 'sin against the Holy Ghost'.

Spiritual pride is generally taken to be the sin against the Holy Ghost, and apparently Florence's 'visions' or 'dreams' were fantasies of self-exaltation in which she saw herself the centre of glorious deeds and sublime reputation. One significant point is that when she was actually doing a deed of some social value, such as nursing her young nephew Shore Smith, the dreams stopped.

If Florence had never indulged in these fantasies, would she have reached her goal sooner? It took her sixteen years to answer the first 'call'. Yet without the ambition that her fantasies revealed, she might never have got there at all; so varied and effective were the obstacles that a Victorian family could devise against the woman of action.

Florence's mother, for instance, fobbed her off for a time with organization of the still-room, pantry and linen-room at home. For a short while it worked, and Florence told Clarkey, 'I am very fond of housekeeping. In this too highly

Sidney Herbert

educated, too–little–active age, it is at least a practical application of our theories to something. . . .' When almost all outside careers were closed to ordinary women, housekeeping could be an elaborate art open to many classes, as Mrs Poyser showed in George Eliot's *Adam Bede*. Yet 'Can reasonable people want all this?' asked Florence, as she surveyed the beautiful complexity of her three-room domestic domain.

At the opposite pole, Hannah Nicholson, Marianne's maiden aunt and a religious mystic, offered Florence the alternative of union with God through absolute self-abnegation and submission. While grasping this method of banishing her 'dreams', Florence did not tell Aunt Hannah that God had called her for some *active* purpose.

It should be noted that a certain eligible man often featured in Florence's 'dreams', living with her in marriage and sharing the glamour of heroic deeds. This was Richard Monckton Milnes, later Lord Houghton; talented, devoted to humanitarian work, especially with young criminals, and at the threshold of a career in politics, he was in love with Florence. It is possible therefore that sexual love was an ingredient of her fantasies, in which Marianne also may have played a part. If so, the Victorian attitude to women and sex would account for Florence's use of strong adjectives like 'shameful' and 'sinful'. Alternatively, her daydreams may have seemed 'sinful' in a more straightforward sense. They were giving her a phantasmal glory of heroic achievement when in fact nothing had been done. In an autobiographical sketch called *Cassandra* (1852) her later attitude to 'day-dreams' became more sympathetic. She then believed that all middle- and upper-class women indulged in them. They were women's 'plans and visions', indeed their very 'life, without which they could not have lived'.

It was after her twenty-fourth birthday, probably in June 1844, that she had discovered her true vocation. Earlier that year she was still writing, 'Aunt Hannah, pray . . . that I may know for what to pray. . . .' By June she knew. For when the philanthropic American couple, Dr Ward Howe and his wife Julia came to stay at Embley in June, Florence put to the doctor a significant question: did he think it would be 'unsuitable and unbecoming' for her to adopt a career like the Catholic Sisters of Charity, namely nursing in hospitals? 'Do you think it would be a dreadful thing?' Dr Ward Howe replied like the go-ahead nineteenth-century American he was, 'Go forward . . . Choose, go on with it. . . .' His spirited wife was to write the famous 'Battle Hymn of the Republic'.

Nevertheless there were still nine more years to wait. The immense delay between 1844 and her actual nursing may be partly due to renewed uncertainties in Miss Nightingale's distracted psyche. It is true that she herself wrote in a 'private note' of 1857, 'Since I was twenty four . . . there never was any vagueness in my plans or ideas as to what God's work was for me'. But if we turn to earlier 'private notes', diaries and letters, doubt still invades her certainty, perplexity mingles with her self-knowledge, right up to 1851:

5 December 1845. 'God has something for me to do for Him – or He would have let me die some time ago. . . . Oh for some great thing to sweep this loathsome life into the past.'
24 September 1846. Letter to Hannah Nicholson. 'I feel my sympathies are with ignorance and poverty.'
24 December 1850. 'My God, I don't know myself. I cannot understand myself – How can I hope to make anyone else understand my case?'
1851. 'My God what am I to do? . . . Thou hast been teaching me all these 31 years what I am to do. . . . Where is the lesson? Let me read it. Oh where where is it?'
1851. 'Oh God! What am I?'

The truth was that Florence found herself forced by parental opposition to have two strings to her bow: nursing and teaching. Her story as a teacher is an interesting one, but not much emphasized. She spent six months at Rome in 1848, when her twin achievements were to meet Sidney Herbert – the future catalyst of her genius – and the saintly Madre Santa Colomba of the Convent of the Trinità de'Monti, whose brilliant teaching methods were copied by Florence in her girls' school near Lea Hurst. Florence received her second 'call' at the convent, this time to surrender her will to God's. She might have decided to teach permanently but for one fatal flaw: it was impossible to teach properly without training. In a letter to her father dated 26 October 1850 she wrote: 'Zealous to do good, I would say [to myself], "Don't, I advise you not [;] the higher your notion of what teaching is, the more you will be disgusted by what you do, unless you take pains to qualify yourself beforehand."' She had no opportunity to qualify herself and so denounced the ladylike 'home occupation' of teaching as a fraud.

Among the many distinguished friends she made during this period (Baron Bunsen the German ambassador, Lord Palmerston, Lord Shaftesbury, Elizabeth Barrett Browning, George Eliot) was the future Cardinal Manning, who saw in her for a time a possible Catholic convert. If she had become a Roman Catholic she might have got her teaching-training in the Church, whose organization she admired. But there were other contrary influences.

In any case education was not her first choice, as she had made clear in the 'private note' of 1851:

The thoughts and feelings that I have now I can remember since I was six years old . . . What are they? A profession, a trade, a necessary occupation, something to fill and employ all my faculties, I have always felt essential to me, I have always longed for consciously or not. During a middle portion of my life; college education acquirement – I longed for but that was temporary – the first thought I can remember and the last was nursing work and in the absence of this, education work, but more the education of the bad than of the young. . . . Still education I know is not my genius – though I could do it if I was taught – because it is my duty here.

The nursing prelude was a more stormy one, because it *was* Florence's 'genius' but not, according to her family, her 'duty here'. They had been horrified by her plan to train in Salisbury Royal Infirmary, and perhaps found her own Protestant nursing sisterhood. (Florence had discovered that to nurse even her grandmother and Gale her old nanny properly she needed professional knowledge.) Her parents violently objected, for hospital nurses at this date were drunken harridans and conditions in the wards so primitive that Flo would be assaulted by every kind of fever, if not by the lascivious doctors. Nevertheless she had begun stealthy preparations for a future that might not dawn, studying in 1845 the first batches of Blue Books on public health, and reading the *Kaiserswerth Year Book* sent to her by Baron Bunsen in 1846. Kaiserswerth was a charitable hospital and training institution run by Deaconesses.

Another, severer aspect of Florence's secret preparation was her decision to cut out human love. Marianne in any case had quarrelled because of Florence's treatment of her brother, and Hilary Bonham Carter was reluctantly given her congé. When Richard Monckton Milnes proposed in 1849 Florence refused him, though he was still haunting her at the end of the next year: 'I know that since I refused him not one day has passed without my thinking of him.' They adored one another, she wrote; he suited her 'passional' nature, but his social way of life was not hers.

In this analysis Florence was surely deceiving herself, for Monckton Milnes, as we saw, was far from being a drone, though his life was extremely sociable. (Thomas Carlyle once said that if Jesus Christ returned to earth the first thing to happen would be Monckton Milnes inviting him to breakfast.) One must conclude that Florence's 'passional' nature was not really satisfied by him. When she met him again at Lady Palmerston's after several years he merely remarked, 'The buzz to-night is like a manufactory.' Her vanity was wounded.

But he had never roused her as Marianne had, nor perhaps even Mrs Brace-bridge ('Sigma') a new friend who entered her 'dreams'.

The year 1850 saw the first breakthrough for Florence. On her way home from a tour of Egypt with the Bracebridges she was allowed to spend a fortnight at Kaiserswerth. As she passed through the hospital gates she left her lady's maid Trout outside, a major step for a Victorian. (Even Elizabeth Barrett took her lady's maid with her when fleeing from Wimpole Street to join Robert Browning.) Yet the discarding of Trout proved to be only temporary. The following year Florence swung in self-immolatory mood to enslaving herself body and soul to the hysterical Parthe. 'When I was 30 . . . my mother requested me to abstain for 6 months from doing *anything* my sister disliked and to give up that time entirely to her . . . I committed this act of insanity . . .' After the six months she felt suicidal and – a more positive reaction – deeply hostile to exaggerated ideas of family duty. Invective poured from her pen: '. . . I know nothing like the petty grinding tyranny of a good English family.' She wrote *Cassandra*, her bitter autobiographical sketch, in 1852. She was the doomed heroine; her family and indeed the whole of Victorian society with its pitiful round of little books, little drives, little sugary sentiments (because 'women have no passions, or so they say') were the villains.

Things went on better when Florence was again allowed to enter Kaiserswerth – in spite of Parthe's neurotic opposition – and train there for three months. But on W. E. N. falling ill she had to return home. By now she had taken the measure of all three Nightingales. Of her father she wrote: 'He had not enough to do'; he needed power, 'A factory under his superintendence . . .'; of her mother '. . . she has the genius of Order to make a place, to organize a Parish, to form Society . . . and has never felt the absence of power' (but she was unhappy over Parthe's and W. E. N.'s health and Flo's contrariness); and Parthe '. . . is in unison with her age, her position, her country . . . knowing nothing of human life but the drawing-room . . . nothing of want of power'. One Whit Sunday 1851, Florence wrote a 'private note': 'My life is more difficult than almost any other kind. My life is more suffering than almost any other kind. Is it not God?' Whit Sunday had brought out in her the gift of tongues – and also the gift for almost limitless emotional exaggeration; it may be the gift of genius.

At last in 1852–53 the prison walls really began to crumble. Through Manning, Florence made contact with the Sisters of Charity in Paris. Later she stayed with the Mohls, visiting institutions for the sick and deliriously happy to be leading a life that was no longer 'ladylike'.

Total breakthrough came in August 1853 when she was appointed Superintendent of what she called 'a Sanitarium for Sick Governesses run by a Committee of Fine Ladies.' It was situated at 1 Harley Street near Wimpole Street, and the post had been given to Florence through the good offices of the Hon. Sidney Herbert and her own 'reputation' – the very 'reputation' that God had asked her to forswear. She herself might be described as a Sick Fine Lady. But escape from Parthe and reform of the Sanitarium soon restored her to blooming health. Piped hot-water, a service-lift worked by a windlass, modern bells for the patients and an overhaul of the chaotic accounts were all demanded and achieved by the new Superintendent. The governesses adored their 'dear dear Miss Nightingale'. As for the object of their worship, she sympathized with them despite 'their unmanagable tempers' and despite the fact that three-quarters of their illnesses were 'Fancy'; this being the sad plight of 'educated women in England . . . or rather of half-educated women'. She had complained in the past that her family ranged all her own sufferings 'under the one comprehensive word: Fancy'.

Within six months the Harley Street nursing-home was running efficiently and so had become a mere 'mole-hill' in Florence's estimation. Something more substantial occupied her when cholera broke out in a red-light district of London and she was able to nurse prostitutes in the Middlesex Hospital. But she still awaited the real mountain, the 'great thing' to sweep her aloft.

Her friends already revered her, saying, 'She stands perfectly alone, half-way between God and His creatures.' To the comfortable, contented Mrs Gaskell she seemed almost too 'sublime' in her care for the race as against the individual, holding that every child ought to be reared in a crèche. Flo's mother told Mrs Gaskell tearfully, 'We are ducks who have hatched a wild swan.' 'But the poor lady was wrong', wrote Lytton Strachey at his best; 'it was not a swan that they had hatched; it was an eagle.'

That year the eagle got her 'great thing'. War was raging in the Crimea and, even more violently, cholera. There were no medical supplies for the wounded at the base hospital in Scutari despite official assurances of plenty. The hospital had been the Turkish barrack. Outside it was a fine building with golden domes at the four corners, but inside it was a whited sepulchre – or rather a blood-stained blackened sepulchre deep in dirt and slime. Only after Miss Nightingale arrived were the vermin killed and the walls whitened with lime-wash.

The British and French allies had just won the battle of the Alma against the Russians, but the French alone won the aftermath. Their wounded, as at Waterloo, had the advantage of *ambulances*, which the British had not; French soldiers had pre-fabricated huts (made in England) which the British government declined; the French wounded were nursed by Sisters of Charity while the British dying lay unattended in long lines on the bare boards.

Suddenly this disgraceful situation was revealed in all its horror to the British public by William Howard Russell, war correspondent of *The Times*. Public opinion exploded. The French success made their own government's failure even more galling. 'Why have we no Sisters of Charity?' demanded an infuriated reader of *The Times*. There was one member of the government, Sidney Herbert, who realized that they *did* have a superb Sister of Charity, in all but name. Other voices, however, asked why they had Sidney Herbert for Secretary at War when his mother was a *Russian*.

In spite of his alleged Russian sympathies, Sidney Herbert forthwith deployed his most powerful secret weapon against the enemy, posting Florence Nightingale and a band of thirty-eight nurses to Scutari, with *carte blanche* and *The Times* Crimea Fund to put things right. To send a young *woman* attended by *women* was revolutionary. It could not have caused a greater sensation if Queen Victoria herself had gone out – as no doubt she would have been only too glad to do. Meanwhile Florence Nightingale had made her friend Liz Herbert warn the British ambassador's wife not to expect the worst. 'This is not a Lady', drafted Florence for Liz, 'but a real Hospital Nurse....'

In fact, it was that very qualification – a real Hospital Nurse – which was to cause the most alarm. Dyed-in-the-wool officials, whether diplomatic, military or medical, would have accepted and shuffled off 'a Lady' with polite ease. But Florence Nightingale had an errand of propaganda as well as one of mercy. She was sent out as an administrator, charged by Herbert to break down the prejudices against female hospital nurses and to establish a precedent in nursing.

Florence allowed herself only four days in which to select her nurses, on whose high characters the whole experiment depended. Fourteen were professionals, fourteen were from Protestant religious houses, ten were from two Catholic convents. Manning had promptly assisted Florence with the latter. 'Reverend Mother Bermondsey' proved her best religious assistant, as Mrs Roberts of St Thomas's Hospital became her most valuable professional. No young women were allowed to join for fear of sexual adventures, and some of the elderly nurses turned out to be 'fat drunken old dames of fourteen stone', whose weight broke the gimcrack bedsteads. Charles Bracebridge, Sigma's husband, became Florence's Privy Purse and courier. It was not his fault that the first thing the nurses saw when they arrived in Scutari harbour on 4 November 1854 was the gigantically swollen body of a dead horse.

The dead horses of the Crimea were symbolic. 'It's no use flogging a dead horse', went the saying, and in Scutari Miss Nightingale had been sent out to flog a very dead horse indeed. Common sense and hope were as dead as the object in the harbour, or the cholera victims, or the amputation cases rolling on the decks of the Black Sea transports. Another dead horse was found to be acting as a filter for the whole water supply of the Barrack Hospital. And after the Charge of the Light Brigade it became known that even the noble animals which had survived the charge – 'Back from the mouth of Hell' – had afterwards died in their lines from starvation. The British, professional horse-lovers, could not lightly forgive such ingratitude.

Florence had brought with her three letters: two of good wishes and blessings from her mother and Manning, the third an ironic note from Richard Monckton Milnes. 'So you are going to the East.... You can undertake that, when you could not undertake me.'

Her undertaking was indeed awesome. As a born administrator she had the sense not to quarrel with the muddlers on the spot. She waited for them to approach her with an appeal. This meant facing quarrels with her nurses, who had to sew endless bags for pillows while the 'noble fellows' they longed to nurse were dying like flies. The appeal came when a new, overwhelming torrent of sick and wounded poured into Scutari after the battle of Inkerman, and there was still nothing to receive them: no invalid food, no clothing, no sanitation. Half-naked men dying of dysentery lay in floods of their own filth.

Miss Nightingale was known to have bought ample supplies on her way through Marseilles, rightly disbelieving the official assurances that there was already plenty of everything in the Crimea. Once the appeal was made to her, she treated the Barrack Hospital as veritable Augean stables to be swept out completely and totally renewed from floor to ceiling. Away went the 'kitchen' with its huge greasy cauldrons in which lumps of meat, gristle and bone were parboiled and dished out to sick men who could not swallow the nauseous stew; proper invalid food appeared from her store. Away went the so-called 'sanitary' arrangements, consisting of blocked privies, two chamber-pots between hundreds of patients and a few communal tubs which the hospital orderlies emptied as seldom as possible. The sick or wounded who had arrived from the battlefields with a chance of survival were murdered by 'Crimean fever' – what would have been called 'gaol fever' in the noisome cells of Newgate.

Away went the worst horror of all, the insane War Office system. It was bureaucracy run mad. No official would risk infringing one of the interlocking, antiquated rules for fear of dismissal, and so orders were never carried out promptly. Better seven thousand soldiers dead than seventy bureaucrats out of a job. According to these rules, the shiploads of stores which did arrive could not be unpacked and distributed until the appropriate 'Board' had 'sat on' them.

A rare satirical impression of Florence Nightingale in the Crimea.

Above: the battlefield at Balaclava
Right: the linen store at Scutari
Below: 'The Jug of the Nightingale'

FOMENTATION
EMBROCATIONS
CRUEL.

**Florence Nightingale's superhuman achievement in the
Crimea earned a torrent of sentimental adulation.
Immortalized as 'The Lady of the Lamp'** *right*, **she received a
brooch inscribed 'Blessed are the Merciful' from Prince
Albert. In fact she was a ruthless but brilliant administrator,
and the reorganization of the Turkish Barrack Hospital** *above right*
was only the start of her activities.

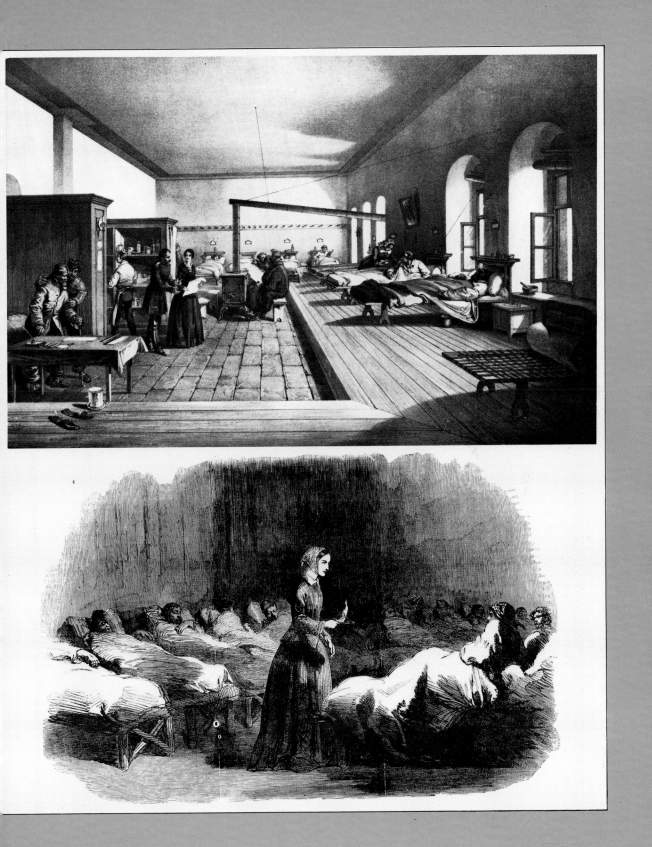

Miss Nightingale instead sat on the officials, and Strachey has a brilliant sketch of the irate lady ordering a government consignment to be forcibly opened while the responsible official stood by, 'wringing his hands in departmental agony'. What Miss Nightingale had witnessed was the destruction of a British Army not by enemy action but by male inefficiency and obscurantism. What she left in place of this tragedy was the beginning of a new nursing system based on the energy and imagination of dedicated women.

Statistics and centralization were to be the new orders of the day. In February 1855 she drove Lord Panmure, the new Secretary for War (appointed when the Aberdeen government fell in January) into setting up a Sanitary Commission to investigate military hospitals, with her supporter Dr John Sutherland from the Board of Health as chairman. Later Dr Sutherland was to describe himself to Florence as 'one of your wives'. The Commission 'saved the British army', she said. The death-rate at Scutari fell from 42 per 100 to 22 per 1000.

As the clean water, fresh air and nourishing food began to flow into the Barrack Hospital, the soldiers' love for their 'ministering Angel' knew no bounds: 'We felt we were in Heaven.' Certainly their love was not bounded by the Crimea. The effects of their adoration were felt at home. One popular song ran, 'She's the soldier's preserver, they call her their Queen.' She had suffered personally and physically with her 'children' the soldiers, who had been 'murdered' during those first frightful months of the war. She was writing, writing, writing reports, requisitions and demands in her cramped quarters for hours into each night, while unremitting visits to the wards drained her spiritual energy. Her slim black-clad figure with white collar, cuffs, cap and apron would glide with seemingly supernatural grace up to the table on which a man was to have his arm or leg sawn off without an anaesthetic. There she would sit with compressed lips until the operation was over, giving him courage and sharing as far as possible his pain. She allowed no man to die alone. If she could not talk to every one of the hundreds of patients every night, at least they could 'kiss her shadow' as it flitted softly by. At the same time she seemed the best man among them.

As soon as the tide of misery and mismanagement turned, jealousies again broke out. A proposed visit to hospitals at Balaclava on the Crimean mainland revealed to her a slip in her 'charter'. Her authority ran only in *Turkish* territory, and not on the Russian mainland. Dr John Hall, the hostile Inspector-General of Hospitals, made her life as difficult as possible. Then she caught the dreaded 'Crimean fever'. In her delirium she imagined she had an engine working inside her head. Her splendid constitution and Mrs Roberts's nursing dragged her back from death's door. After scarcely any convalescence she returned to Scutari, her locks shorn as close as Samson's but her strength unimpaired.

On the way to Scutari Dr Hall tried to kidnap her and send her home. He was foiled by her friends. The two Bracebridges, however, eventually did return to England, sated with sights of horror, and at once began criticizing the errant doctors. They thereby raised the kind of counter-storm in the Crimea that Florence had sedulously avoided.

There was also criticism among the women: ladies v. nurses, the 'Protestant Howl' v. the 'R. C. Storm', Mary Stanley and her new party of nurses v. Florence Nightingale and her original group. Mary was the sister of Queen Victoria's great friend Dean Stanley, and both were initially close friends of Florence. Mary Stanley was on the point of conversion to Catholicism and brought out a new batch of Catholic nuns to the Crimea. Miss Nightingale unkindly kept her waiting offshore, saying she was not wanted. It was not only their religion that Miss Nightingale objected to, although she had already had to quell objections to her own Catholic nuns, but the fact that she had not asked for extra nurses and had enough trouble controlling the original party. When Miss Stanley's nuns finally came ashore at Therapia they preferred to remain independent of Miss Nightingale's undenominational authority. Their leader, the Rev. Mother Bridgman, became to Florence 'Revd. Brickbat'. At times plain sex discrimination reared its Medusa head. 'Miss Nightingale was very wonderful, of course,' said Miss Wheare, one of Miss Stanley's ladies, 'but [I] could not get used to taking orders from a lady.' To obey Dr Hall seemed more *natural*.

At times Florence felt the officials would burn her if they could like Joan of Arc; Jesus Christ had been betrayed by only one person, Judas Iscariot, but she had been betrayed by almost everyone. Even her own nurses could not be relied on. Some got drunk, others got married. And her loyal supporter Lord Raglan died. People were always dying on Miss Nightingale.

There had been many things to be thankful for, none the less, before Sebastopol fell to the Allies and peace was signed on 29 April 1856. The Medical Staff Corps was established at her suggestion and a Nightingale Fund for training nurses was opened in 1855. She had a happy memory of a delicious ride over a hill near Sebastopol on a 'very pretty mare'. The troops, recognizing their even prettier benefactress, gave her three times three.

We now enter the last two years (1856–57) of her active and *mobile* life. Anything she did after 1857 – and she moved mountains – was done from a couch, bed, wheelchair or invalid carriage. But though she returned from the Crimea physically exhausted, her mind was still wound up to perform prodigies of mental labour. Naturally there was a colossal War Office cover-up, begotten of peace and a longing to forget. Dr Hall among others was made a KCB, what Florence called 'Knight of the Crimean Burial-grounds'. But despite the official white-washing she determined that her 'murdered children' in the Crimea should have an honour and a memorial more splendid and lasting than Dr Hall's: a Royal Commission which would forcibly shake the whole British Army into a new state of health. She was indeed a Niobe weeping for her children, but her tears were of anger.

Her first step was to visit Queen Victoria and Prince Albert at Balmoral in the autumn of 1856. She needed them on her side. The queen fell for the ladylike charm and masculine purpose – 'I wish we had her at the War Office' – as well as envying Florence's opportunity to do so much for the 'dear soldiers'. It is to Victoria's credit that she felt no jealousy of the lady who 'queened it' in the Crimea, describing her as 'one who has set so bright an example to our sex'.

Her two pillars of the proposed Royal Sanitary Commission on the health of the army were to be Sidney Herbert who was now out of office and Lord Panmure, the present Secretary for War. Lord Panmure was known as 'the Bison' because of his massive head, which he would move slowly from side to side in mingled menace and perplexity. Florence, however, had a 'powerful' head too (as the Queen wrote to Panmure) and while herself collecting, collating and even illustrating with charts all the figures necessary for the commission, she discovered that the Bison was 'bullyable'. Hounded down from his grouse-moors, Lord Panmure was bullied into bullying his own hostile officials, setting up the commission and appointing Herbert as chairman.

Sidney Herbert was one of those superlatively attractive characters who make the deserts of history, with their acres of commissions and blue books, almost romantic. Clever, handsome, a natural manager of men, idealistic and vulnerable, he shared with other aristocrats the honest conviction that only a sense of duty forced him into public life. How much happier he would be living peacefully at his beautiful home in Wilton or Ireland, fishing.

Florence Nightingale, however, had no time for male double-think. Herbert was again and again dragged back from his estates to undertake yet another essential piece of work for his implacable colleague. His evidently failing health she ignored or put down to 'fancy'. When Panmure excused a lapse in correspondence because of gout in his hands, Miss Nightingale joked sardonically, 'Gout is a very handy thing.'

By May 1857 the Royal Commisson had begun to sit with Herbert at its head. Before it reported, Florence was ready with a further scheme for four sub-commissions. As she noted, 'Reports are not self-executive.' Herbert was chairman of all four.

There were, however, still obstacles to her plans. Her family sought to possess her again, particularly now that she was such a credit to them, a national heroine. She asked herself how she could possibly read documents, interview witnesses, write her 1000-page *Notes affecting the Health, Efficiency, and Hospital Administration of the British Army*, or *Notes on Nursing*, or *Notes on Hospitals*, or all the other potential *Notes, Suggestions* and *Observations* which throbbed in her head like that Crimean engine, when her London base, the Burlington Hotel, was constantly invaded by her mother and sister? They got on her nerves to such an extent that after each visit she developed the symptoms of what was taken to be 'neurasthenia', breathlessness, nausea, fainting and palpitations.

Today 'neurasthenia' as a physical disease has been banished from the medical books, to have its place taken by a mental affliction with the same symptoms, 'psychoneurosis'. Instead of suffering from the after-effects of the Crimea and the continuing results of extreme overwork, as Florence was thought to be, she was a victim of anxiety and fear: anxiety about her mission to avenge her

**Florence Nightingale hated sitting for her portrait and gave
George Frederick Watts time only for this unfinished sketch.
Overleaf: 'Florence Nightingale at the entrance to Scutari' J. W. Barratt.**

murdered children and fear for her own sanity under the constant impact of these intrusive Nightingales.

In August 1857 she was sent to drink the waters at Malvern where the doctor gave a verdict that we may regard either as fortunate or misguided, according to our evaluation of the next half-century of her long life. She would risk total collapse and death, said her consultant, unless she submitted to complete rest for the remainder of her life, which would probably be a matter of months rather than years. Never get up again, he advised, and she virtually never did.

Why should she? She had achieved what her 'psyche' needed: freedom from anyone who agitated her (whenever Parthe, Mama or even Papa threatened to visit her, she threatened to collapse), a band of slave-companions including Aunt Mai and Aunt Mai's son-in-law the poet Arthur Hugh Clough, and a stream of the great and powerful from Whitehall. J. S. Mill summed up her position by saying 'I . . . share the admiration towards Miss Nightingale which is felt more universally . . . than towards any other living person.' Hardly a new Viceroy set off for India without calling on Florence Nightingale first, *by appointment*. (She saw no one, not even Clarkey from Paris, except by appointment.) Her business was 'to advise, to encourage and to warn' – the Royal Prerogative, no less. Indeed she was 'queening' it in London as she had queened it in the Crimea. But now with a poet to tie up her parcels.

Though Florence Nightingale was never actually 'on her deathbed' until she was ninety, she imagined herself to be in that ultimate state for something over a decade (1857–68) and acted accordingly. Time was short. She toiled heroically over stacks of paper-work; not only her own original schemes, but innumerable letters to co-workers, doubters, opponents. She could ignore the ill-health or unhappiness of friends caught in the toils of her 'little War Office' at the Burlington. Was she herself not defying death every day and night?

'So much to do, so much to do', she would sigh as one good cause inexorably led to another. The first ever training school for nurses was opened in 1860 at St Thomas's Hospital. It was followed the next year by a training school for midwives. In 1865 an Army Sanitary Standing Committee was set up, and in the same year she devised a cost-accounting system for the Army Medical Services that was still in use in 1947. The British Army's health depended on sanitation in barracks and nursing; nursing depended on training. The British Army at home led to the British Army in India, to the health of the people of India, to freedom from starvation, to irrigation. The India Office were just 'waddling' as usual. She would make them sprint. Barracks, with the sinister motto she had pinned on them – 'Soldiers enlist to death in the barracks' – led on to concern for deaths in workhouses, in maternity wards, in all large buildings where the unfortunate, including prostitutes, were crowded together in villainous conditions and where the mortality rate was always higher than in the poorest cottage or the worst slum. Florence Nightingale did not know about

Two prints showing life in the Crimea in 1854: the village of Kadikoi on the road to Balaclava *above* and nurses at Inkerman.

the processes of infection in, say, puerpural fever, but she could read the statistics.

It may be asked whether this woman of consummate genius could have accomplished as much in the way of research, drafting, proposing, getting her ideas accepted and carried out in the face of official inertia or opposition, if she had dispensed with her psychoneurosis and led a normal life. She would certainly have visited India, an enormous advantage which would have saved her from some ludicrous mistakes. She obstinately insisted, for instance, that all barrack windows should be open during the hot season. Lord Lawrence the Viceroy (and her committed admirer) for once had to put his foot down.

On the other hand, there is the fact that she worked best in silence and solitude, or with only the furry arm of a beloved cat round her neck. Again, her apparent vulnerability raised the tolerance level in those men and women whom she was bullying. If she had not been 'dying', surely Uncle Sam Smith would not have allowed his wife to break up her family life in order to live with and serve her 'Goddess-Niece'. Flo was to say of Aunt Mai, 'We were like two lovers'; and now she called Aunt Mai her 'Virgin mother'. When the 'Virgin mother' eventually decided it was her duty to return to her home and real children, the 'Goddess-Niece' refused to communicate again for twenty years. Arthur Hugh Clough, too, faded away, knotting string for the Goddess and waiting in vain for that 'westward' brightness over the land. Broken-hearted, Florence said she had been David to his Jonathan.

And Sidney Herbert? Could his wife have consented, as she did, to her husband being literally worked to death in the cause if she, Liz, had not also felt the searing, intoxicating breath on her cheek? Florence spoke of family life as a 'Moloch', the pagan god that immolated its worshippers. The Moloch of the Burlington also took its toll.

Lytton Strachey, in one of his periodic fits of good taste, decided to draw a veil over Miss Nightingale's destruction of Sidney Herbert. 'One fight more, the last and the best', she would urge him, quoting Robert Browning rather than poor Clough's, 'Say not the struggle naught availeth'. Perhaps she envied Browning's robust, masculine, undying service to Elizabeth Barrett. However, Florence's worst excesses may seem in the light of modern knowledge to be pitiable rather than cruel. In 1859 Herbert returned to the War Office. Without his directing hand, that most essential reform of all – reform of the War Office root and branch – would never be accomplished. But he was to let her down by dying. She refused to see him or write to him again between his resignation in June and his death in August 1861. On 8 June she had gone as far as to deny his illness, which was advanced kidney disease: 'I believe you have many years of usefulness before you.' This was the typical anger, as we may now guess, of bereavement: anger at desertion being one of the reactions that can flare up before changing into grief. When Herbert's colleagues criticized him after his death, Florence said, 'I too was hard on him' – a note of remorse for the death of one she was henceforth to call, 'My Master'. Herbert had died with Florence's name on his lips, 'Poor Florence . . . poor Florence, our joint work unfinished.'

**Florence Nightingale talking to Sir Harry Verney in the garden at
Claydon Hall, with her sister Parthenope.**

At last, in about 1868, the devouring flame died down. Her plans were no longer fiercely creative and original, nor had she the impulse to go on slogging at immense reports. Since 1861 she had lived in South Street off Park Lane, where she had five maids, a lady's maid and a man messenger.

Why did the change take place? Her powers may well have been exhausted, an exhaustion increased by the menopause. There was also no more quasi-sex stimulus from her co-workers, who had all died (except for Sutherland). Hilary Bonham Carter died of cancer in 1865, her artistic talent, said Florence, a sacrifice to the 'Fetich' of family life. Miss Nightingale would refer to her seclusion as a 'Robinson Crusoe' existence. Pickering thinks she may have become a morphine addict; she had found it beneficial physically, though not to her intellect, and addiction was relatively common in the nineteenth century. Most likely of all, perhaps, she realized at last that reform on a radical scale can never be 'finished', and so it was time for a change.

Mysticism, philosophy and theology more and more occupied her mind, as did a learned, intense and profoundly loving friendship with Benjamin Jowett, the redoubtable Master of Balliol College, Oxford. Having peremptorily ordered him not to work so hard after fifty, she may have taken her own good counsel. She helped him with a translation of Plato, and he helped her with deferential but privileged advice to subdue her 'wilfulness' and not overdo the ill-health. She once retorted by putting out her tongue at him. That he proposed marriage to her, however, is unproven. Her family said so; but there is nothing about it in Jowett's great collection of letters to her, now at Balliol.

She returned in some degree to family responsibilities, writing from Lea Hurst, 'I am becoming quite a tame beast.' Apart from bursts of resentment, she endured the fact that her mother was to live into her nineties, and Parthe, as an arthritic invalid, to seventy-one. Parthe indeed had brought new interests, including step-nieces and step-nephews, into Flo's life by becoming in 1858 the second wife of Sir Harry Verney of Claydon Hall in Buckinghamshire. (Of course he had proposed to Florence first but she had declined.) In her sixties there was an alteration even in Florence's face. It became large, round and agreeably catlike. Her health improved and she rose from her couch once or twice, to walk round Claydon lawn or to watch the widowed Queen Victoria open the new Law Courts and be congratulated by HM on looking so well.

Florence Nightingale outlived them all. Indeed the old Queen's heir King Edward VII, who gave her the OM, had been dead three months before Florence, a blind old lady lost in dreams once more, drew her last breath on 13 August 1910. She had refused to be buried in Westminster Abbey, insisting on a small stone cross in the Nightingale family graveyard: 'F. N. Born 1820. Died 1910.' Perhaps she still remembered her sinful dreams of 'reputation' and was determined not to be caught out before the Judgment Seat.

But if her memorial stone had instead contained even half the tally of her achievements, what a towering monument it would have had to be. The public image of soldiers transformed from 'scum' into human beings; nurses changed from Gamps into professionals. They could not have engraved the usual words about Florence being 'a devoted wife and mother', although she saw the soldiers and nurses as her own sons and daughters. Her potential as a wife can never be accurately gauged. She probably loved women more passionately than men; besides Marianne and Hilary her cousins, she was violently attached to Miss Pringle 'the Pearl' of St Thomas's as well as to Miss Williams her 'Goddess-Baby'; though even among goddesses the one she really worshipped was that clinical deity Hygeia.

On another level, she set 'a bright example to our sex' by transcending sex itself in her amazing combination of masculine and feminine genius. Women, provided they were brilliant enough, no longer needed to say they wished they had been born men. True, she opposed the women's movement. 'I am brutally indifferent to the rights and wrongs of my sex', she wrote to Miss Martineau in 1861. 'Vociferous ladies' always irritated her. Her own insistent pen did not seem to her so scratchy.

Certain aspects of her astonishing life are still almost inexplicable. For inst-ance, how did Miss Nightingale's extraordinary Indian influence come about? She laid down the law and earned the title of 'Governess of the Governors of India' without ever having set eyes on it. And how did she maintain her influence at home, at least until she went blind at eighty-one? No comparable case has ever existed: the case of a bedridden invalid – a woman at that – without official position who was none the less visited and consulted by a perpetual stream of bigwigs from the highest offices of state. The answer can only be in the magnetism of genius allied to the power of the 'legend-in-a-lifetime'.

JOSEPHINE BUTLER

1828–1906

Josephine Butler is the only Englishwoman among the 'Eminent Victorians' chosen here who enjoyed a long happy family life. Annie Besant and Ellen Terry were unhappily married for a short period or periods; Charlotte Brontë and George Eliot were happily married but only for a few months; Emily and Anne Brontë, Dr Barry and Florence Nightingale never married. At the same time no one worked harder for women than Josephine Butler, not even famous suffragists like Millicent Fawcett and Elizabeth Garrett Anderson. Yet where are Mrs Butler's honours? Mrs Fawcett was created a Dame; Dr Garrett Anderson has a hospital called after her, whereas Josephine Butler was until recently in danger of being forgotten. What happened?

The answer is simple. Josephine Butler did not champion the 'right women'. If she had had a hospital named after her it would have been one for the Voluntary Treatment of Venereal Diseases. She did indeed defend women's rights, but they were the rights of the destitute and prostitutes.

Josephine was the seventh child of John Grey and Hannah Annett, born at Milfield in Northumberland, four years before the first Reform Bill. Her kinsman Lord Grey of Howick was Prime Minister. Grey of Dilston, her father, organized support for Reform and for the abolition of slavery. He was also a firm believer in women's education and discussed all kinds of social problems with his daughters. Her cousin Charles Grey was Prince Albert's equerry. The Greys were a close clan. Of Josephine's three sons, one married her niece and another her great-niece.

Her mother Hannah was of Huguenot descent and was a firm evangelical, blessed as a child by John Wesley. From Hannah and her mother Margaret may have come Josephine's religious intensity. She was to write to her grandson about 'my grandmother's visions', which 'all came true'.

The Greys' childhood was free and happy. Josephine and her favourite sister Harriet, 'the belles of Northumberland', loved riding to hounds. They were once criticized by a gentleman for galloping too fast. When he heard who the reckless pair were he said, 'Then it's in the blood. They can't help it.' At eighteen Josephine almost died from a burst blood-vessel in her lungs. 'But I didn't – I belong to a family remarkable for *vitality*.'

The family was remarkable for other things besides vitality and physical courage. Her rebellious Aunt Margareta Grey of Milfield who married a Grey of Howick, wished to hear a debate in the House of Commons before there was a Ladies' Gallery. She got in dressed as a boy. Ladies' lives, she fumed, were bounded by visiting, note-writing, dressing for morning engagements, dressing for evening engagements, making calls, receiving calls. 'It is time to rise out of this, and for women of principle and natural parts to find themselves something to do.'

Josephine found that something in her first vision and 'call' to serve God, which involved a prostitute and occurred after a year of mental suffering when she was seventeen. She had passed through a 'dark night of the soul' during which she seemed to lose God. 'Who are you? Where are you?' she cried, wandering alone through the pine woods. At last He appeared to her, standing at the side of 'the woman who was a sinner in the city'.

In 1852 Josephine married George Butler and went to live in Oxford, where he was an examiner to the university. (The Butler family were and are distinguished in the academic field.) He also taught geography, gave lectures on fine art at the Taylorian Institute and became art critic for the *Morning Chronicle*. Josephine helped him with his work, which led to a commission to prepare a new edition of Chaucer. This gave her the entrée to the Bodleian Library, a hitherto male stronghold.

Apart from her family life Josephine was not happy at Oxford. A male celibate atmosphere prevailed. One evening a young don denounced Mrs Gaskell's *Ruth* for its portrayal of an unmarried mother, saying 'I would not let my mother read it.' Josephine later described the ensuing discussion: 'A moral lapse in a woman was spoken of as an immensely worse thing than in a man. . . . A pure woman, it was reiterated, should be absolutely ignorant of a certain class of evils, albeit those evils bore with murderous cruelty on other women.' Meanwhile the Butlers took in a girl from Newgate Prison who had murdered her bastard child. Josephine had a second mystical experience in which she heard the scream of 'a woman aspiring to heaven and dragged back to hell. ...'

The physical climate of Oxford did not suit Josephine either. When she was expecting her fourth child, her doctor ordered them to leave and George accepted an offer to become Vice-Principal of Cheltenham College in 1857. She quickly recovered. Cheltenham proved a more congenial home than Oxford, though there were strains when the Butlers supported the North in the American war, while their friends sympathized with the slave-owning South, considering *Uncle Tom's Cabin* 'unfair'.

But in 1864 there was a ghastly tragedy. The Butlers' one daughter, 'little Eva', was six years old. No less unlucky than the 'little Eva' of *Uncle Tom's Cabin*, this beloved girl rushed out to greet her parents one evening on their return home, leant too far over the banisters and plunged to her death on the stone floor of the hall.

Never can I lose that memory, [wrote Mrs Butler] – the fall, the sudden cry, and then the silence! It was pitiful to see her, helpless in her father's arms, her little drooping head resting on his shoulder, and her beautiful golden hair, all stained with blood, falling over his arm! Would to God that I had died that death for her!

Josephine was never really physically well after Eva's death, wrote her grandson. She joined the ranks of 'delicate' Victorian women, breathless at night and needing much fresh air. Four years later she had consulted nine doctors about her heart. 'They all said rest and quiet were the only things. They all said I would *never* be strong.' She added: 'But for Miss Garrett [the first British woman doctor], I must say of her that I gained more from her than from any other doctor....' Miss Garrett entered more into her 'mental state',

Harriet Grey's caricature of her sister's move from Oxford to Cheltenham.

111

Josephine explained, because she was able 'to *tell* her so much more than I ever could or would tell to any *man*'. Josephine was right to distrust the nine male doctors who prescribed 'rest and quiet', for she soon found that she felt well only during strenuous work – never in repose.

The tragic death of Eva in fact had a profound effect on Josephine Butler's whole development.

I became possessed [she wrote] with an irresistible desire to go forth and find some keener pain than my own – to meet with people more unhappy than myself . . . I had no clear idea beyond that, no plan for helping others; my sole wish was to plunge into the heart of some human misery, and to say to afflicted people, 'I understand. I, too, have suffered.'

It does not take a Freudian to make the connection between little Eva's fall, Josephine's 'plunge' into rescue work and the 'fall' of, say, little Marion, a Liverpool prostitute whom Josephine was soon nursing. For Liverpool was to be the Butlers' home from 1866 onwards, until Josephine was fifty-four, George having been appointed Principal of Liverpool College.

'It was not difficult to find misery in Liverpool', wrote Mrs Butler. It was the archetype of nineteenth-century sea-ports where vast inflowing wealth left a debris of hideous squalor. In its dockland abandoned orphans, as it might be young Heathcliff, could be picked up every day, while hundreds of half-starved Irish who had fled from the famine were left to rot like their own potatoes. Josephine found her way to the portentous Brownlow Hill Workhouse.

Here were noisome cellars crowded with down-and-out women and children, many of them prostitutes. Liverpool's street-walking population was 9,000 strong, 1,500 of them under fifteen and 500 under thirteen. The age of consent was twelve. Upon this scene of misery burst the astonishing vision of a beautiful lady, elegantly dressed but with an expression of deep sorrow in her blue eyes. She prayed with them and picked oakum with them sitting on the stone floor (their means of earning a few 'untainted' pence) and comforted the sick in their dark dens. She soon had enough influence to calm a riot where the authorities had failed. 'Fetch Mrs Butler', they would say in desperation.

She began taking the saddest cases into her own home, George courteously giving the visitor his arm upstairs. Marion was a young farmer's daughter, seduced by a hard-bitten debauché and thrown out of a brothel – her only home – when she became consumptive. She died under Mrs Butler's roof.

The Butlers' house became too small for the numbers of destitute and Josephine acquired a Home of Rest for them. She appealed to 'fashionable young men' to help pay the rent but found that only the 'good' subscribed. When two doctors gave their services free, she knew that her call had indeed come from God. Not so the fashionable women, who suspected devil's work. 'I hear Mrs Butler takes in *these creatures*', said a pained matron to Josephine's lady's maid, who boldly replied, 'Yes, Madam, I am proud to say she does.'

'Found' by Dante Gabriel Rossetti, who was a friend of the Butlers. It illustrates the horror of a countryman who finds his former love as a London prostitute.

George Butler, too, was criticized for not controlling his wife. Such un-Victorian male self-sacrifice did not assist his career. In those days there was only one career in a family and virtually only one fully developed human being. Indeed a pithy saying arose among suffragists: 'Husband and wife are one, and that one is the husband.' In the Butler household there were two, two equals.

Mrs Butler's fame spread as she began to seek employment for the girls she had rescued. 'Economics lie at the very root of practical morality', she was to say, anticipating Bernard Shaw's Preface to *Mrs Warren's Profession* in 1893: 'that prostitution is caused not by female depravity or male licentiousness, but simply by underpaying, undervaluing and overworking women so shamefully that the poorest of them are forced to resort to prostitution to keep body and soul together.' The anger that flickers through Shaw's Preface was already burning hotly in Josephine Butler during the 1860s. She identified her anger with Christ's 'humanness' rather than His divinity, causing Him to feel 'fierce human pity' towards the sinning woman and anger at man's injustice. Her message of love sent to a prostitute about to give birth to a bastard child shows how closely she identified her religion with the feminist cause:

You remember how sweet and lovely Jesus always was to *women*, and how He helped their *woman* diseases, and how respectful He was to them, and loved them and forgave the sins of the most sinful. And He was born of a woman – a woman *only*. No man had any hand in *that*! It was such an honour to women.

Mrs Butler's search for women's employment in Liverpool cemented her alliance with the women's movement in general. She pitied all frustrated women, not only prostitutes. True, prostitutes literally sold themselves to live. But upper class women 'sold' themselves for rank and pin-money. As Florence Nightingale had written in her *Cassandra*, 'The woman who has sold herself for an establishment, in what is she superior to those we may not name?' To Josephine Butler every woman had four 'rights', each leading on to the next: the right to earn, to be educated in order to do so, to decide the conditions of her life by exercising the vote, to own the money she earned. Yet the law regarded her as a 'feme covert' (*femme couverte*) a woman protected or 'covered' by a man.

The Crown Princess of Prussia (Queen Victoria's daughter Vicky) wrote enthusiastically to Mrs Butler, favouring women's training in the arts and regretting that the profession of actress was not yet 'proper'. Miss Emily Davies, co-founder of Girton College, won Josephine's admiration by persuading Cambridge University in 1865 to admit girls to their Local Examinations. Miss Annie Clough, later to be first Principal of Newnham, visited Liverpool the following year and appointed Josephine secretary and later President of the North of England Council for the Higher Education of Women. Another year passed and a petition for women's suffrage was presented to Parliament by J. S. Mill, signed by Josephine Butler among 1,498 others. By 1868 Mrs Butler was

A cynical caricature from *Le Rire* captioned with the words 'I know Monsieur Le Baron doesn't want to buy a pig in a poke!'

well-known enough to edit for Macmillans a book on *Women's Work and Women's Culture.*

Her prominence inevitably produced clashes with reactionary males. Frederick Harrison, a propagandist for Comte's new non-Christian creed which worshipped a calendar of Great Men, crossed swords with Mrs Butler on the subject of woman's 'place'. Not only should it remain strictly 'in the home', he believed, but outside the home there were to be '*no* occupations' for women; 'they ought *never* to work nor have the means of working'. Josephine retorted to this '*horrible*' letter with a biting question: What was to happen to the two and a half million 'surplus' women? Starvation or prostitution.

Prostitution, indeed, had surreptitiously entered a disastrous new phase that was again to change the direction of Mrs Butler's life. Up till 1864 there had been no legalized prostitution in England, apart from certain brothels in Southwark which functioned during the Middle Ages.

For some time past, however, there had been quiet moves by the medical profession and government to counter the spread of venereal diseases among the armed forces by introducing the Continental system of regulated prostitution. This system had been Napoleon's gift to France in 1802. As his conquering troops spread throughout Europe they brought with them the *maisons tolérées* – state brothels protected by special police.

The Liberal *Daily News* commissioned Harriet Martineau, a typical 'strong-minded' woman, to attack state brothels: they did *not* reduce venereal diseases, which could be better controlled by other methods. But the government was determined. A first instalment of Regulation entered the Statute Book in 1864 known as the Contagious Diseases Act. It was cunningly introduced under cover of a Contagious Diseases (Animals) Act of the year before. The public hardly noticed that slight change in wording.

Every licensed prostitute was attached to one of the eleven garrison towns or naval ports which had been experimentally endowed with a state brothel. She was compulsorily examined at regular intervals by none too delicate nurses and surgeons equipped with the dreaded 'instruments'. This ordeal, however, did not prevent a licensed prostitute from catching syphilis from a client between examinations.

Far worse than the surgeons were the new special police. This corps was instructed to arrest *any* woman or girl in the listed towns who was suspected of being a prostitute. 'Homeless' girls were particularly recommended to their attention. The suspect was carried off to the hospital for compulsory examination. If she refused, she could be imprisoned with hard labour. For though prostitution itself was not a crime, the new Act had created a crime in the refusal to comply with its dictates. There were no courts, no magistrates, no legal defences. However strongly a victim declared her innocence, she had no appeal against the decisions of an all-powerful and often corrupt police. And once the girl had been entered on the police register, there was little chance for her of a different life. As she grew older she might hope to become a procuress herself or a prostitute's maid.

Horrible mistakes were made. A widow committed suicide rather than face the bullying of an Inspector and the indignities of the examination. She and her daughter had been arrested on no other evidence than that they had been seen walking with two soldiers. After the inquest, which was used to whitewash the police, Josephine took the daughter into her home. Another girl was found to be a virgin, but not before she had been forced into the straitjacket, her legs held apart with metal clamps and she had finally rolled off the couch bleeding from a ruptured hymen. She was sent home with a few shillings of hush-money which fortunately did not 'hush' her.

The 1864 Act lapsed but was renewed in 1866 and extended in 1869. Government propaganda favoured applying the 'CD Acts', as they were now called, to more and more garrison towns and ports, if not to the whole female civilian population. In their despair, a group of opponents including Dr Elizabeth Blackwell, the first (American) woman on the British Medical Register, appealed to Josephine Butler to lead a campaign for repeal.

Josephine's blood boiled; though even more at the evil principle of the Act than at its practical results, however degrading. It constituted sex discrimination of a particularly ugly kind. It took two to make a prostitute. Nevertheless the age-old ideas of the double standard in sex for women and men – what was a 'vice' in one was a 'necessity' to the other – were trotted out again. Not only that, but *habeas corpus* was infringed every time a woman was seized and examined against her will. Josephine published an indictment of this aspect of the CD Acts entitled *The Constitution Violated*. The word 'violated' was shrewdly chosen, since the public would not at first think of physical 'violation' in connection with harlots. 'If women had possessed the franchise', wrote Josephine, 'the Contagious Diseases Acts could not have been passed.'

Nevertheless Josephine's first 'call' to this terrible task almost broke her down. She spoke of 'the anguish of that first plunge'. Today it is almost impossible to realize the horror in which the subject was held. After a Women's Liberal Federation meeting as late as 1892 on prostitution in India, Esther Bright wrote: 'The facts were so awful I could hardly restrain myself; I trembled all over, and most of the women wept. The speaker could not

Registration ticket issued to a prostitute in India four years after the repeal of the East India CD Act.

go on at one time, but almost broke down ... It is such a dirty, vile, unclean subject that we are afraid to touch it, and yet other women bear it.' Some further idea of educated feeling may be given by the fact that it was not till the Royal Commission in 1913 that 'Contagious Diseases' became 'Venereal Diseases' – CD into VD. Josephine was to be accused not only of indecency but of concealed personal sympathies with vice, much as anti-pornographers are today suspected of secret indulgence.

And how would her 'plunge' affect George? She wrote out her thoughts and carried them to his study. 'I hesitated and laid my cheek against his door, and as I leaned I prayed.' Then she went in and gave him the paper. It was several days before he could discuss it. At last – 'Go! and God be with you.' He gave her complete freedom for her work and never complained when it kept her from him. She had told him, 'I feel as if I must go out into the streets and CRY ALOUD, or my heart will break.'

She wisely kept the detailed news of her new crusade from George's family. Their motto was, *Intuta quae indecora* – 'Improper things are unsafe.'

In the early months of her campaign Mrs Butler made two discoveries. Working-men were the most reliable male supporters but women must in the end rely on themselves. The Second Reform Act of 1867 had given the vote to male householders in the towns; these were the fathers whose daughters were most at risk under the CD Acts. The men were to show Josephine their realization of the fact by enthusiastically welcoming her at her inaugural meeting, an unexpectedly crowded gathering of railwaymen in the Mechanics Institute at Crewe. It was Professor James Stuart of Cambridge, a lifelong disciple and adviser, who first told her to watch the enfranchised workers.

Women, however, were her spearhead. A Ladies' Association for the Repeal of the CD Acts was founded in the autumn of 1869, and Josephine became president. Reluctantly she resigned from the presidency of her Council for Women's Higher Education, for she could not lead both. Many of her educated friends deplored her choice. Did not the Rev. Frederick Denison Maurice, first Principal of Queen's College for Girls, approve of the CD Acts? Not to mention John Morley, editor of *The Fortnightly Review*, who saw the opposition as sacrificing the unborn to the 'rights' of harlots. Even Dr Elizabeth Garrett supported the government.

On the last day of December 1869 Josephine published the Association's manifesto. Its eight clauses contained her social philosophy on the subject, from which she never swerved. And she never swerved because *God* had spoken. The spiritual inspiration of Josephine Butler can never be over-emphasized. At the top of each column of statistics, at the bottom of each clause, in the centre of each Parliamentary debate she saw Christ's face.

The signatories of the manifesto none the less represented many different philosophies. There was Miss Harriet Martineau who did not believe in Christianity, Miss Mary Carpenter the reformer of reformatories, almost every prominent Quaker lady, and Florence Nightingale from her West End bed. Florence had asked Dr Jowett what to do about Mrs Butler's Manifesto. Leave it

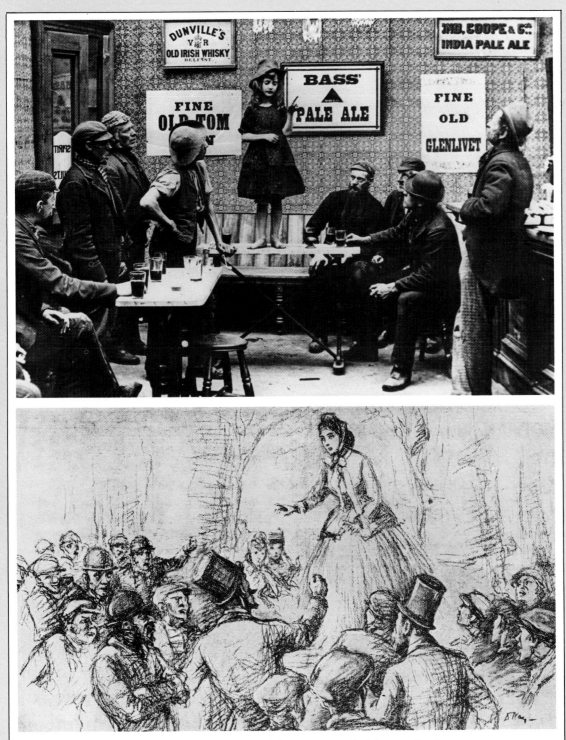

Top: a young girl entertaining patrons of a Liverpool pub.
Above: Josephine Butler campaigning for the repeal of the CD Acts.

alone, said the Master of Balliol in so many words. 'Mrs Butler takes an interest in a class of sinners whom she had better left to themselves.' Mrs Butler was a fanatic, though she had 'a touch of genius'. Florence signed. She thought the Acts 'disgusting'. And as an administrator she saw they could never work. But Jowett stuck to his guns and was in due course, as Vice-Chancellor of Oxford, turning down a proposal for Josephine to address the dons.

The gist of the manifesto was practical. On the Continent, for instance, especially in Paris where women had long been 'outraged' by this system, public health was worse than in England. With 'wiser teaching', the causes of moral evil could be better controlled. To her arguments Josephine in time added many stirring aphorisms, for instance: 'Women are called to be a great power in the future. . . .'

In 1870 she founded her first propaganda organ *The Shield*. Her aim was to rub home the injustices of the law. Women were invariably regarded as temptresses, men as victims of a natural urge. On a wet evening *The Shield's* sub-editor disproved this myth. A man's head suddenly appeared under her umbrella.

'May I have the pleasure of escorting you home?'

'I will escort you to a policeman.'

He fled.

In the same year that Josephine Butler started her first periodical, William Acton published a revised edition of his book entitled *Prostitution*, urging that the powers of the CD Acts should be extended to the civil population. Prostitution was well organized, he argued, with its different types of brothels such as 'dress houses, introducing houses, accommodation houses'. Preventive measures against syphilis should be organized equally well.

By June Josephine had covered over 3,000 miles, spoken at nearly 100 meetings, and published the first of her 38 pamphlets and 36 books. But her first physical battlefield was the Colchester by-election of the same year. The Liberal government, eager to quash this women's nonsense, put up a General as their candidate. He had helped Florence Nightingale in her Crimean crusade but he was an ardent exponent of the CD Acts which he wanted extended to cover soldiers' and sailors' wives. His name was Sir Henry Storks, known to Josephine as 'the bird'.

Colchester was a safe Liberal seat, and mobs were easily recruited on the General's behalf. After one rough meeting, Mrs Butler had just gone to bed when the manager asked her to leave his hotel: hooligans were threatening to burn it down. She escaped by a window and lodged with a working-class family. From another meeting she had to flee with a shawl over her head into an empty warehouse, whence she was conducted by a prostitute to a local grocer's; there she awaited the all-clear behind a rampart of soap and candles. Her supporters were continually pelted with mud and stones. The Press refused to report her speeches, as being 'unfit for print'. Storks's argument, such as it was, turned on one point: continence being impossible for servicemen, the women they required were better off in every way under state regulation.

But when the result was declared, 'the bird' had been more than winged. He was defeated by the Conservatives with a majority of 400 votes. A telegram of three words was sent to the Butlers: 'Bird Shot Dead'.

The excitement was unprecedented and two years later the militant ladies almost did it again at the Pontefract by-election, the Liberal candidate retaining his seat with a much reduced majority. The riff-raff, however, were even more violent than they had been at Colchester, for they were organized by the brothel-keepers. It was difficult to hire halls for meetings and Josephine had one horrific experience in a stable loft. Access to it was by a single ladder, the floor had been sprinkled with cayenne pepper and smoke was soon drifting up from burning hay below. For a time it seemed that Josephine and her supporters might be asphyxiated, thrown from a window or raped by a gang who blocked the trap-door exit. She felt that only 'some unseen power' was holding these creatures back. Eventually she broke through and leapt to safety.

Meanwhile 'this revolt of the women', as one rueful MP called it, had forced Parliament to adopt at least a substitute for action – a Royal Commission. Twenty-five men, only one favourable to repeal, were appointed towards the end of 1870 to enquire into the working of the CD Acts. On 18 March 1871 Mrs Butler was summoned to give evidence. She arrived alone at the House of Lords, the only woman in a roomful of hostile men, the only woman to be interrogated. She made her most controversial points with perfect lucidity: that girls were bought and sold by men, that the lower classes were tyrannized over by the upper classes, that the age of consent must be raised. Mrs Butler wanted to let in 'a floodlight on your doings'. What did she mean by '*your* doings'? asked a member of the Commission; did she mean them personally? 'No, I mean the immorality which exists among gentlemen of the upper classes. I will give an illustration if you like. . . .' Hastily the Chairman took the next question.

Mrs Butler's peroration was as uncompromising as her answers: 'All of us, who are seeking the repeal of these Acts,' she declared, 'are wholly indifferent to the decision of this Commission. . . . We have the word of God in our hands, the law of God in our consciences.'

Next month a great petition for repeal was presented to Parliament amid raucous laughter. Josephine was unperturbed. When a member of the Commission came up and asked if she had not been nervous when giving evidence she replied: 'Not at all. But my soul was deeply troubled at the sight of so many men with so base a moral standard as you seem to have and such utter scepticism about God and human nature.' The poor man looked at his boots. 'I fear it is true.' Nevertheless he and his colleagues published a report in which the obnoxious double-standard was restated:

There is no comparison to be made between prostitutes and the men who consort with them. With the one sex the offence is committed as a matter of gain, with the other it is an irregular indulgence of a natural impulse.

That cynical phrase, 'an irregular indulgence of a natural impulse' was to sicken Josephine for years.

The report, however, was not without redeeming features. It did refer to the traffic in girls and recommended an end to the examination of suspects together with a raising of the age of consent to fourteen. Nothing was actually done. But two members were converted, the Rev. F. D. Maurice and Charles Buxton MP. Indeed all were impressed by the courage and conviction of Josephine Butler in this, her finest hour.

A new battle developed over 'Bruce's Bill' in 1872. Bruce, the Liberal Home Secretary, hoped to split the women's ranks by proposing some practical ameliorations while extending instead of repealing the Acts. Josephine had met Bruce on a deputation the year before. She had been advised to 'lard' her speech to him with 'Right Honourable Sir's – but still she failed to move that 'proud stomach' behind the tightly buttoned coat. Now she stood fast against the advice of her own moderates. When they argued, 'Half a loaf is better than no bread', she replied, 'Not if it is poisoned.' She demanded repeal, wholesale repeal and nothing but repeal. 'My motto is no legislation at all on prostitution, for all such legislation will press on women only. And even if it did not, I have no faith in it.' Her positive programme, which included *voluntary* medical treatment and rescue work – 'this deep, difficult, holy work' – could be done only by dedicated people independently of the state.

Though Bruce's Bill was withdrawn, Josephine's movement seemed weakened. Two years later a worse blow fell. The Conservatives won the General Election of 1874 and hailed their victory as the country's endorsement of Regulation. But good came out of evil. The Right Honourable James Stansfeld, a Liberal leader, was now free to push the cause inside Parliament. As W. T. Stead, her journalist friend, remarked with his usual acerbity, 'all Right Honourables' had hitherto shrunk from the 'odious' duty to vote for repeal. With her new powerful ally at home, Josephine decided on a daring advance. She would carry her personal crusade into the enemy strongholds abroad.

On the whole she always preferred spontaneous thrusts to organized campaigns. 'You know I have not a good head for organization', she told a colleague; 'My one gift, if I have one, is to breathe a little fire and courage into *individual* workers. . . .' And so in the bitter winter of 1874, accompanied by her son Stanley, she threw her jet of flame into Paris. With introductions from Lord Derby the Foreign Secretary and Cardinal Manning, she entered intrepidly into the luxurious lions' den – the plush and gilt palatial offices of M. Lecour, the chief of moral police. The sky was grey outside but she could see a speck of blue. 'I held on to that speck.'

Refusing a chair and looking him straight in the face, she asked in fluent French if the vice figures were falling under the 'moral' regulations. 'Oh, no . . . they go on always increasing, always increasing' – due to the Commune . . . to women's growing 'coquetry'. Never due to poverty? Never.

'Madame, remember this: that women constantly injure *good* men, but no man ever injures a good woman.'

'No seductions of innocent girls?'

'Oh, that's the region of romance where police can do nothing.'

'Has not the system failed?'

'Who hopes for perfect results?'

'Those too I suppose belong to the region of romance?'

M. Lecour, courteous in his invulnerability, gave this formidable lady permission to visit St Lazare, the prison-cum-hospital for vagabond women. She knocked on the door but no one answered. Then she remembered some haunting words that had come to her before leaving home: 'Behold I have set before thee an open door, and no man can shut it.' She picked up a stone and banged hard. A nun answered and showed her round. Afterwards Josephine described the silent, half-dazed girls staring at her in the exercise yard. She never spoke or wrote of what went on inside; it was too horrible. 'My heart was ready to faint within me.'

Her friend Yves Guyot, however, made a detailed report on which Glen Petrie in 1971 based his book *A Singular Iniquity*: the filthy young bodies, never allowed to be completely undressed for fear of encouraging vice; the infected syringes; the stench; the wooden sleeping-cages for children, to prevent lesbian practices; the apprenticeship to state brothels for such as were eventually released but were homeless.

And this was what poor England in her folly was preparing for her children also. Sick at heart and in body, Josephine visited her sister Harriet in Italy, after George had taken her for a family holiday in southern France. Hostile English doctors bustled about Roman conference chambers with bundles of *The Lancet* under their arms. The battle, she told Harriet, 'was like running one's own breasts upon knife points'. But there must be no retreat. Things were moving. Controversy was actually breaking out in the Italian press – *against* licensed brothels as well as for. Josephine wrote, 'The fire is lighted it seems.'

Back in Liverpool she decided to found an International Federation for Abolition. 'Abolition' was now the name of their cause, based on memories of slave-trade abolition. Her son George became her press secretary, Stansfeld became president with Stuart and herself as joint secretaries; 'her name is a banner', they all said. Her call went forth:

Injustice is immoral, oppression is immoral, the sacrifice of the weaker to the stronger is immoral, and all these immoralities are embodied in all the systems of legalized prostitution, in whatever part of the world or under whatever title they exist.

The streets of Geneva – their future headquarters – were said to be entirely free from bad women – 'how beautiful!' scoffed Josephine. 'They are carefully *locked up*.' Yet corruption was increasing. 'There may be evils *even worse* than our wretched London streets': the evils of state-sanctioned, state-offered, state-taxed prostitution in which the state invested and on which *tenanciers* grew fat. The abolitionists were to face riots, wrecked meetings and arrests in Geneva; for the vested interest in vice persuaded people that Josephine was a rich Madame herself, bent on ruining the Swiss trade in favour of the English.

Josephine was soon able to bring impressive new strength to the cause. Supported by two Quakers, Alfred Dyer and George Gillett, she unearthed a villainous white slave traffic at Liège in Belgium, where wagon-loads of children were brought from all over Europe like cattle. The Belgian age of consent was, creditably, sixteen. But this made girls from England, with one of the lowest 'ages' in Europe, particularly desirable. Children of eleven and twelve were bought or abducted and cruelly beaten if they refused to perform or tried to escape. A corrupt police co-operated. Josephine's allegations were indignantly challenged and she was threatened with extradition. After thoroughly substantiating her accusation on oath, she was able to enunciate a most telling truth: wherever there were licensed brothels there was an active market for prostitutes and the traffic flourished; where there was no state regulation there was no white slave traffic.

She had not long to wait before another political swing in the pendulum swept forward the women's cause. The Liberals won the General Election of 1880; by now many of their successful candidates were abolitionists. The working-men's vote was extended from the towns to the counties, providing new strength. The government was forced to re-examine the CD Acts and Josephine Butler was again interrogated on 5 May 1882. How different was her experience from the last time. Six of the fifteen-strong committee were now abolitionists. She was able to relate her recent Continental discoveries to her home crusade, and also to describe in detail a whole night she had spent in visiting the licensed brothels for servicemen at Chatham in April 1870.

Chairman: I believe you are of opinion that these Acts have an effect upon the soldiers, as stimulating them to immorality, and you have some experience of that?
Mrs Butler: Yes . . . My heart was moved to speak to them, and there, in that brothel, I gathered them round me, or rather they gathered themselves round me, and I spoke to them as a mother to sons. I did not speak to them altogether in a directly religious manner; I spoke to them lovingly. . . .

'Why do you come here?' she asked their informal spokesman.

'Oh, the soldiers all come here, and these are the Government women.'

A soldier was pushed forward. 'Here is a lad, very young: he has just joined; couldn't you get him out of this? He doesn't understand what it means. . . . It is a shame that they don't give us some proper amusement. . . . They expect us to be bad, and of course we are.'

Josephine saw at once they would have been delighted with 'anything like a lecture or a penny reading with singing and music'.

There were about 200 women in the saloon, all 'solemn as hell itself, with no look of pleasure in any face; a businesslike exhibition of superintended vice'. The girls had their tickets fastened to their dresses and the soldiers with tickets pinned them on their hats, 'passing them to one another with remarks as to the date of the last examination'.

Chairman: You talked with a view to reclaiming the women?
Mrs Butler: And with a view to reclaiming men quite as much.

Her reply was sharp.

George had always been censured for permitting and indeed assisting his

W. T. Stead

Canon George Butler

Josephine nursed her husband in his last illness, but never stopped her work for women.

Finsbury-pavement, which has an experience of thirty-one years, has kept for twenty-five years a record of the ages at which those whom they have rescued lost their character. The following are the numbers of the rescued who were seduced at the ages of twelve and thirteen for 1862 to 1875, when the close time was raised to thirteen—33, 55, 65, 107, 102, 103, 77, 60, 78, 62, 40, 43, 30 : total, 855, or 66 per annum between the ages of twelve and thirteen. From 1875 to 1883 the figures are as follows : 22, 24, 19, 20, 16, 14, 15, 10, 7 ; total, 147 ; average, 16 per annum. Allowance must be made for the fact that the total number rescued in 1883 was only half that rescued in 1867, but even then the number of children seduced at twelve and thirteen would have been reduced by one-half owing to the raising of the age. All those who have the best means of knowing how the law would work, gaol chaplains and the rest, are strongly in favour of extending the close time. The preventive operation of the law is much more effective than I anticipated, for it is almost the sole barrier against a constantly increasing appetite for the immature of both sexes. That this infernal taste prevails is unfortunately beyond all gainsaying, and for proof we need go no further than the reports of the numerous refuges and homes for children which have been opened of late years in the neighbourhood of London. But in the ordinary market the supply is limited to girls who are over thirteen.

THE RUIN OF THE VERY YOUNG.

There is fortunately no need to dwell upon this revolting phase of criminality, for it is recognized by the law, and the criminals when caught are soundly punished. My object throughout has been to indicate crimes virtually encouraged by the law ; but it is necessary to refer to cases where even penal servitude has not deterred men from the perpetration of this most ruthless of outrages, in order to show the need for strengthening the barrier which alone stands between infants and the brutal lust of dissolute men. Here, for example, is a portrait of a tiny little mite in the care of a rescue officer of our excellent Society for the Protection of Children. Her name is Annie Bryant, and she is now just five years old. Yet that baby girl has been the victim of rape. She was enticed together with a companion into a house in the New Cut on May 28, and forcibly outraged, first by a young man named William Hemmings, and then by a fellow-lodger. The offence was completed, and the poor little child received internal injuries from which it is doubtful whether she will ever entirely recover. The scoundrel is now doing two years' penal servitude, but his accomplice escaped. A penny cake was the lure which enticed the baby to her ruin. As I nursed her on my knee, and made her quite happy with a sixpence, the matron of the refuge where the little waif was sheltered told how every night before the baby girl went to sleep she would shudder and cry, and whisper in her ear. And not until the poor child was solemnly assured and reassured that the door was fast, and that no "bad man" could possibly get in, would she dare to go to sleep. Every night it was the same, and when I saw her it was nearly three weeks since her evil fate had befallen her ! This instance of a child of such tender years being subjected to outrage is not an isolated one. A girl of eighteen who is now walking Regent-street had her little sister of five violated by a "gentleman" whom she had brought home. She had left the room for a few minutes, and he took advantage of her absence to ruin the poor child, who was sleeping peacefully in another corner of the room. The man in this case escaped unpunished. As a rule the children who are sent to homes as "fallen" at the age of ten, eleven, and twelve, are children of prostitutes, bred to the business, and broken in prematurely to their dreadful calling. There are children of five in homes now who, although they have not technically fallen, are little better than animals possessed by an unclean spirit, for the law of heredity is as terribly true in the brothel as elsewhere. One child in St. Cyprian's was turned out on to the streets by her mother to earn a living when ten. At St. Mary's Home they do not receive any children over sixteen. Sister Emma has at present more than fifty children in her home in Hants. She receives none under twelve. In only four cases was the man punished. The proportion of victims among the protected is, however, comparatively small to those who have passed the fatal age of thirteen. If Mr. Hastings, who would fix the age of consent at ten, or Mr. Warton, who was in favour of even a lower age than ten, was allowed to have his way, we should probably have to start homes to accommodate infants

ONE OF THE VICTIMS.

of four, five, and six who had been ruined "by their own consent." What blasphemy !

THE CHILD PROSTITUTE.

It has been computed, says the report of a Hampshire Home, that there are no less than 10,000 little girls living in sin in Christian England. I do not know how far that is correct, but there is no doubt as to the existence of a vast and increasing mass of juvenile prostitution. The Report of the Lords' Committee in 1882 says :—

> The evidence before the Committee proves beyond doubt that juvenile prostitution from an almost incredibly early age is increasing to an appalling extent in England, and especially in London. They are unable adequately to express their sense of the magnitude, both in a moral and physical point of view, of the evil thus brought to light, and of the necessity for taking vigorous measures to cope with it.

Unfortunately the evil, instead of being coped with, is in the opinion of the chaplains of our gaols rather on the increase than otherwise. The victims are for the most part thirteen, fourteen, and fifteen years old.

At West-end houses of the better sort, that is to say, houses where nothing can be done without a preliminary expenditure of a sovereign in a bottle of champagne, and where the ordinary fee, without allowing for tips and wine, is £5, they are very timid in purveying very young girls. I should have had much less difficulty in establishing the fact but for the awe that has fallen upon the unholy sisterhood since the chief among them all was compelled to plead guilty in order to save her clients from exposure. Houses French, Spanish, and English in fashionable localities where, according to current report, you might either meet a Cabinet Minister or be supplied with any number of little children, are now indignant at any application by a stranger for the accommodation which they only extend to their old clients. But at one villa in the north of London I found through the assistance of a friend a lovely child between fourteen and fifteen, tall for her age, but singularly attractive in her childish innocence. At first the keeper strenuously denied that they had any such article in the house, but on mentioning who had directed us to her place, the fact was admitted and an appointment was arranged. There was another girl in the house— a brazen-faced harlot, whose flaunting vice served as a foil to set off the childlike, spirituelle beauty of the other's baby face. It was cruel to see the poor wee features, not much larger than those of a doll, of the delicately nurtured girl, as she came into the room with her fur mantle wrapped closely round her, and timidly asked me if I would take some wine. Poor child, she had been out driving to the Inventories that morning, and was somewhat tired and still. It seemed a profanation to touch her, she was so young and so baby-like. There she was, turned over to the first comer that would pay, but still to all appearance so modest, the maiden bloom not altogether having faded off her childish cheeks, and her pathetic eyes, where still lingered the timid glance of a frightened fawn. I felt like one of the damned. "She saw old gentlemen," she said, "almost exclusively. Sometimes it was rather bad, but she liked the life," she said, timidly trying to face the grim inexorable, "and the wine, she was so fond of that," although her glass stood untasted before her. Poor thing ! When I left the house as a guilty thing, shrinking away abashed from before the presence of the child with her baby eyes, I said to the keeper who let me out, "She is too good for her trade, poor thing." "Wait a bit," said the woman, with a leer. "She is very young —only turned fourteen, and has just come out, you know. Come again in a couple of months, and you will see a great change." A great change, indeed. Would to God she died before that ! And she was but one.

HOW CRIMINALS ARE SHIELDED BY THE LAW.

This frightful development of fantastic vice is directly encouraged by the law, which marks off all girls over thirteen as fair game for men. It is only in the spring of this year that a man was sentenced to a term of imprisonment for indecent assault upon a child. It was shown in evidence that he had violated more than a dozen children just over thirteen, whom he had enticed into backyards by promises of sweet-meats, but though they did not know what he was doing until they felt the pain, they were over age, and so he escaped scot free, until one day he was fortunately caught with a child under thirteen, and was promptly punished. The Rev. J. Horsley, the chaplain at Clerkenwell, stated last year :—"There is a monster now walking about who acts as clerk in a highly respectable establishment. He is fifty years of age. For years it has been his villainous amusement to decoy and ruin children. A very short time ago sixteen cases were proved against him before a magistrate on the Surrey side of the river. The children were all fearfully injured, possibly for life. Fourteen of the girls were thirteen years old, and were therefore beyond the protected age, and it could not be proved that they were not consenting parties. The wife of the scoundrel told the officer who had the case in charge that it was her opinion that her husband ought to be burned. Yet by the English law we cannot touch this monster of depravity, or so much as inflict a small fine on him."

A CLOSE TIME FOR GIRLS.

Before the 14th of August it is a crime to shoot a grouse, lest an immature cheeper should not yet have a fair chance to fly. The sportsman who wishes to follow the partridge through the stubbles must wait till September 1, and the close time for pheasants is even later. Admitting wife's activities. By 1882 he felt he had to resign from Liverpool College. To enable him to do so the Butlers' friends, headed by Robert Martineau, Henry Wilson and Stansfeld, collected a fund to provide an annuity of £200 a year. Then, in the autumn, George was appointed a canon of Winchester Cathedral, 'the answer', he wrote to Josephine, 'to prayers offered up by you, as I know, for so long'.

At the opening of Parliament on 28 February 1883 a first attempt to introduce abolition into the Debate on the Address was talked out. While the men talked the women prayed and wept in a hotel nearby, 'outcasts' kneeling beside society ladies. One American woman rose from her knees: 'Tears are good, prayers are better, and women need a vote in the ballot box behind every tear.'

Intense excitement grew throughout April. Prayer meetings multiplied up and down the country. Some of them were for Mr Gladstone, that he might realize his responsibilities as Prime Minister. Josephine had noticed his evasiveness as a politician but always admired his purity as a man. She never knew how great were his temptations in his own work for prostitutes, and that he had to maintain his purity with self-flagellation.

On 20 April the end came. The Rt Hon. James Stansfeld moved against compulsory examination. A feeling of victory was in the air. There was a long cheer when the figures were read out – 182 to 110. Josephine ran down from the Ladies' Gallery into the starlit court below. It was 1.30 a.m. 'Say unto Jerusalem', she quoted, 'that her warfare is accomplished.' For the Acts were suspended forthwith.

Repeal followed inevitably, but not before there had been another spectacular piece of warfare for 'Jerusalem'. W. T. Stead formed a 'Secret Commission', of which Josephine and her son George were members, to investigate the London brothels and the white slave traffic. Glen Petrie quotes a letter dated 5 June 1885, in which Josephine wrote: 'O! What horrors we have seen.... My dear son has volunteered to go in disguise to one of the high class dens where there are *padded rooms*....' No wonder she later said, 'There is no need for anyone to press upon me the reality of Hell ... for I have been in Hell.' The Commission's horrible findings were published in a series of articles in Stead's influential review, the *Pall Mall Gazette*, under the title of 'The Maiden Tribute to Modern Babylon'. In one issue Stead demonstrated how easy it was to buy and sell an English child. At his request Josephine had put him in touch with a reclaimed prostitute named Rebecca Jarrett. The reluctant Rebecca was persuaded to procure a child named Eliza Armstrong from her unmarried mother for £5. Eliza was shipped to the Salvation Army in Paris (instead of to the usual state brothel). The effect of the article was prodigious. Unluckily, however, Eliza's natural father, a drunkard, complained to the police that his permission had not been asked. Stead was imprisoned for three months and poor Rebecca for a year. Bernard Shaw called the whole thing a put-up job. Nevertheless, the lesson of the

A page from the *Pall Mall Gazette* in which W. T. Stead exposed the outrageous traffic in girls from England to Continental brothels.

'Maiden Tribute' was effective. A striking correlation had been established for all to see between licensed brothels and the traffic to supply them.

The Repeal Bill was introduced by Stansfeld on 18 March 1886; he moved the Second Reading simply by raising his hat; the Royal Assent was given on 15 April. It took less than a month to undo the mistakes of years. For the figures showed that the cases of VD among the home forces were just over 260 per thousand in 1865, and after the Acts had been operating for eighteen years the figures were – 260 per thousand.

Josephine's home life was shattered by her husband's death in 1890. She had to leave Winchester and went to live with her eldest son in Wimbledon, where she wrote *Recollections of George Butler*, 'to show . . . that he was even more to me in later life than a wise and noble supporter and helper in the work which may be called especially my own. . . .' But there were still journeys to make, foreign centres to be encouraged, the Empire to be saved. It was found that State regulation of prostitution in India was being secretly practised, despite repeal at home and the denials of Lord Roberts, the Commander-in-Chief. An order from the Quartermaster-General, known as 'The Infamous Memorandum', came to light; in it he demanded more and better quality women for the troops. The whole scandal was exposed by two American doctors, Kate Bushnel and Elizabeth Andrews. 'Bobs' apologized and the Government paid £800 for their expenses. 'So we fought them with their own money!' rejoiced Josephine. But licensed brothels were not finally banished from Indian cantonments until 1918.

There were many defeats in Europe especially in Geneva, where the system existed into the 1920s. A long battle nevertheless might well be God's will. 'The longer and more earnest our struggle is', wrote Josephine, 'the more effectually it will loosen the chain of wickedness in other parts of the world.'

She died in 1906 at Wooler in her beloved Northumberland aged seventy-eight. As an old lady she had retained the beauty of fragility, speaking at meetings in her grey dress, cap of black velvet and violets, and silk cloak trimmed with 'good black lace'. (Every lady wears only *real* lace, said Miss Nightingale.) Leaning slightly forward from the rostrum, Josephine Butler looked like the Winged Victory.

'The seed which she has sown can never die', said James Stuart. But weeds sprang up and still do. There are professional female 'child-catchers' in the East today. The President of the International Abolitionist Federation recently told the slavery group that child prostitution exists in rich countries as well as poor. The present Josephine Butler Society quotes a man whose own 'infamous memorandum' recommends *four* as the age of consent for child-sex, 'provided only that they enjoy it'. The fight goes on, from India to Southampton, in fact across the world.

Josephine's name has been commemorated in the Noble Women windows of Liverpool Cathedral and in the Church of England Calendar of Saintly Worthies, under the date of her death 30 December: 'SOCIAL REFORMER, WIFE, MOTHER.'

In Josephine Butler's words – perhaps her own best memorial – 'God and one woman make a majority.'

~⚜~ ANNIE BESANT ~⚜~

1847–1933

O f all great Victorian women Annie Besant was the most extraordinary. Perhaps the comparison is not quite fair to the others, for the strangest part of her life took place in India during the twentieth century. She lived further into the next century than any other of our eleven women. Nevertheless, even without her later experiences, the Victorian years of Annie Besant seemed to be a microcosm of everyone else's problems. Marriage, sex, work, the law, science and religion, motherhood and birth-control, poverty and socialism were all there in acute form, all the problems of Victorian women, including a tendency to hear 'voices', when the voices of Darwin and Huxley should have silenced such supernatural phenomena for ever.

Though Annie Besant was born in London on 1 October 1847, her later memory-images went back to a race of Celtic kings. Apart from the royal strain, her descent was three-quarters Irish, she insisted, and her heart all Irish. Her paternal grandmother was Irish and so were both her maternal grandparents. Annie's Irishness came out early. The child was a gay, 'sunshine Annie', but also 'mystical and imaginative, religious to the finger-tips, and with a certain faculty for seeing visions and dreaming dreams'.

No less interesting was the English quarter of Annie's blood. Her father, William Burton Perrse Wood, was descended from that radical firebrand Matthew Wood, once Lord Mayor of London. The senior branch of the Wood family had since become eminently respectable, boasting Lord Chancellor Hatherley in its ranks and later Sir Evelyn Wood; though Kitty O'Shea, née Katherine Wood, was perhaps a blot on these cousins' escutcheon. As a clever member of the junior branch, William Wood went in for scepticism. He would read aloud Shelley's *Queen Mab* to his pious wife.

Annie was precocious. She could read at five, and remembered being unswathed from a curtain where she was deep in a book and sent out to play; or sitting on the tombstone locally known as 'Byron's grave' at Harrow-on-the-Hill where her widowed mother lived, reading Byron and *Paradise Lost*. Milton's Satan was her special 'companion', she said, and she would declaim his speeches from the Hill. Here were the first signs of the future orator and rebel.

Her brother's education was looked after, by Harrow School, but Annie's was not; until kindly Miss Marryat, sister of Captain Marryat the novelist, offered to educate her. Miss Marryat believed in a progressive education for girls, anchored to intensive religious training. The lives of the saints pre-occupied Annie and she longed to be a Christian martyr like St Agnes or St Cecilia. 'Why then and not now?' she asked herself. She wondered nervously if she was really saved. Since she was already a believer, she could not, alas, enjoy the glamorous flash of conversion. Annie was to make up for this youthful disappointment by adult conversions ad lib, not to mention martyrdoms.

In her seventeenth year she was returned to Harrow, having travelled abroad and grown dangerously pretty. Miss Marryat several times had to change hotels when young gentlemen tourists became too attentive. A black-eyed Annie with dark curls and a trim, tiny figure appeared at the Harrow balls and inspired several proposals of marriage. It was after staying with her maternal grand-parents at Stockwell near London and while on holiday at St Leonards-on-Sea that the acceptable offer was made.

Annie had had no girlish love-dreams. The reading of novels was absolutely forbidden; hence all her nascent passions had been focused on Jesus Christ her Saviour and Mrs Wood her mother. In assessing the place of motherhood in Annie's life, this early passion for her mother must not be overlooked. As for the Jesus Christ, Annie met a schoolmaster named Frank Besant who, as a deacon to the local church, also seemed to be dedicated to Christ's service. The two young people were thrown together. Frank thought he ought to propose and Annie felt obliged to accept. When she discovered during their engagement that her feelings for Frank were merely friendly, she tried to break it off; her mother, however, regarded such a thing as shameful. They were married at St

**Bernard Partridge's portrait of George Bernard Shaw, 'Ahenobarbus at Rehearsal'.
Shaw rejected Annie Besant's proposal of 'free marriage'.**

Leonards in December 1867, Annie being just twenty and never having experienced the slightest rebuff, correction or unkindness in all her short life. In her *Autobiography* Annie was to add that she had never been exposed to evil in the outside world either, but this was an exaggeration. Her mother had taken her to Manchester in the summer before her marriage, where they had witnessed mob violence before the execution of the young Fenians known as 'Manchester martyrs'. Again the 'martyr' theme had appeared. Annie burned with the flame of liberty for Ireland.

Whatever she may have learnt about political martyrdom it was nothing to the sudden revelation of martyrdom in marriage. Frank, seven years older than herself, shocked and terrified her on the wedding night. Son of a Portsmouth draper, he had won a scholarship to Cambridge and a first in mathematics. Under a cool exterior he had a hot temper, which was more than matched by the angry wilfulness of his undisciplined wife; she called herself 'as proud as Lucifer'. She was bored by the talk of babies and servants among the Cheltenham College wives, where Frank became assistant master. Unfortunately it was soon after the Butlers had left for Liverpool, otherwise Annie might have found a friend in Josephine. After Annie's own babies, Arthur Digby (known as Digby) and Mabel, were born in January 1869 and August 1870 respectively, she felt that she had had enough of pregnancy for the time, particularly as Mabel nearly died of bronchitis. As the young mother sat for days and nights on end inside the steam-tent with her choking infant, she dwelt resentfully on the sins of her two ogres, Frank and the Almighty.

Her husband had struck her while she was carrying Mabel for suggesting family limitation, causing a premature birth. On her doctor's advice she read about physiology and sex; during her famous trial in 1877 she was to tell the judge: 'When I was first married my own doctor gave me the work of Chavasse, on the ground that it was better for a woman to *read* the medical details than it was for her to have to apply to one of the opposite sex to settle matters which did not need to be dealt with by the doctor. . . .' Her horror of Frank was to grow. On various occasions he threw her over a stile, kneed her and pushed her out of bed so that she crashed on the floor and was badly bruised.

In order to mitigate the unhappiness of her domestic prison she began writing short stories. The *Family Herald* took one entitled 'Sunshine and Shade', paying her thirty shillings. Frank took away the money. As Annie remarked, he had high ideas of 'a husband's authority and a wife's submission'. Her story described the trial of a wife who adored riding (as did Annie) but was confined to a wheelchair for thirty years after a fall. She turned to helping others more unfortunate than herself. 'Sunshine and Shade' was prophetic. Annie's 'fall' into the loathsome pit of sex with Frank was in time to bring about her campaign on behalf of harassed mothers.

When it came to the Almighty, Annie could not believe that a loving Father

'Bradlaugh's Dream'. A song encouraging the electors of Northampton not to vote the atheist Bradlaugh into Parliament.

would allow 'an innocent babe' like little Mab to suffer the torments of bronchitis. What made it worse was that, through her kinship with Lord Hatherley, she had obtained for Frank the living of Sibsey, near Lincoln. She was now the wife of a vicar instead of a schoolmaster. Church-going became her duty. Yet she could no longer believe in God.

Annie's loss of faith could not but affect her already crumbling marriage. She refused to stay for Communion after morning service. Frank exploded. She must either take Communion or go. She went. But not before her life at Sibsey had revealed to her two important things about herself.

During a typhoid epidemic she visited the afflicted cottagers and discovered that she possessed a special gift for nursing. Just as her devotion had saved little Mabel, some interior power enabled her to drag the sick poor back from the threshold of death. 'I think Mother Nature meant me for a nurse', she wrote, 'for I take a sheer delight in nursing anyone, provided only that there is peril in the sickness ... the struggle between the human skill one wields and the supreme enemy, Death.' A sense of power and compassion were both strong in Annie Besant, as they were in Florence Nightingale. But it was a female strength. Annie had replaced 'God the Father' with 'Mother Nature'.

She also owed to Sibsey her first awareness of her oratorical skill. One day after practising the organ in Sibsey church, she decided on impulse to see what it felt like to preach. She mounted the pulpit and suddenly she was pouring out a torrent of eloquence. Her golden voice, thrown back from the stone walls and pillars, was a revelation to her. For the first and last time in her life she spoke to empty seats. She felt a 'rush of language that moves and sways', makes passion and emotion gush forth from a thousand hearers, as from a rock. Speaking, she knew, was to be one of the deepest delights of her life.

Meanwhile life was hideous. What was she to do? A formal deed of separation had been drawn up in October 1873, by which the Rev. Frank Besant allowed his wife £110 a year – enough for 'respectable starvation'. On this she had to keep herself and Mabel, while Digby lived with his father and was largely paid for by his generous uncle, the writer (Sir) Walter Besant. Frank buried himself in research on church registers for the rest of his life. There were to be exchanges of the children during the summer holidays. Annie's brother Henry (later Sir Henry Wood) was willing to have her with him at Brompton, provided she would 'keep quiet'. Keeping quiet was not one of Annie's gifts and she refused. She tried living at Folkestone with some kindly aunts, then as the inevitable governess. Because of her heretical ideas, she failed like Harriet Martineau in her attempts to start an educational establishment of her own. But just before her beloved mother died she took Communion with her, thanks to the broad-mindedness of her friend Dean Stanley of Westminster. In almost her last words to Annie, by now an avowed unbeliever, Mrs Wood said: 'You have always been too religious'; and then rubbed in the paradox, 'Yes, it has been darling Annie's only fault; she has always been too religious.'

Through Annie's deep interest in religion and its opposite, she ultimately managed to keep herself and Mabel, albeit with hardship and ill-health. The

Annie Wood with her mother.

year before her separation she had visited Langham Place to hear a sermon by the Rev. Charles Voysey, a Dissenter who had quit the Church of England. His preaching stirred her. She realized that others had searing problems and were not beaten by them. At the Voyseys' home in Upper Norwood – a salon for high-minded heretics – she met Thomas Scott, editor of the *National Reformer*, a journal for freethinkers, as well as Charles Bray and Sara Hennell, George Eliot's friends. Annie wrote a sceptical article on the divinity of Jesus for Scott, defiantly signed 'By the wife of a beneficed clergyman.' Walter Besant spotted the culprit. Her normal pen name on the *Reformer* was Ajax, the hero who had implored the gods for light. But she began the new year of 1875 by writing proudly as Annie Besant. One concession was made to Frank, whose name it was. Whereas Frank and Walter were Besant to rhyme with cant, Annie pronounced it Besant to rhyme with pleasant.

It was only a matter of time before Annie came under the influence of Charles Bradlaugh, the leading secularist of the day. He was to be the first great influence on Mrs Besant's career. Bradlaugh had heard her defending free thought at the South Place Institute, Finsbury, in August 1874 and marked her speech as the best he had ever heard by a woman. And what a woman! Beautiful and slender with brilliant eyes that could express anger as well as anxiety. Her speeches began in an agony of nerves and rose to an ecstasy of power.

Bradlaugh himself was as powerful a man as he was an orator. Tall and immensely strong, he used his eyes with hypnotic effect, sometimes freezing his audience, but more often fanning their passions. Born in 1833 of a working-class family, at fifteen he was hurrying to Bonners Fields, the Hyde Park of East London, for Chartist rallies. Under the inspiration of George Jacob Holyoake young Bradlaugh became a radical and atheist, or secularist as he and his friends called themselves. Like Annie he was turned out of his home. Two years in the army, when he assisted at the eviction of a peasant family from their cabin in Ireland, made Bradlaugh as strong a supporter of Irish Home Rule as Annie herself. At twenty-five he replaced Holyoake as leader of the secularists and within the next ten years had founded the National Secular Society with their Hall of Science in Old Street, Finsbury. By the time Annie's marriage was on the rocks in 1870, Bradlaugh's had been wrecked by his wife's alcoholism. He had always been a teetotaller and abhorred free love as much as he worshipped free thought. In 1873 and again at a by-election in 1874 he stood for the constituency of Northampton, enduring the same rebuffs as Mrs Besant at her lectures.

For Annie now added to her role of battered wife that of a speaker dodging the kicks of savage opponents, ducking the glass from shattered windows and making her escape in fast cabs. In this she shared the experience of violence in the 1870s with Josephine Butler. And indeed Mrs Butler's fight for down-trodden women, particularly prostitutes, was enthusiastically acclaimed by both Mrs Besant and Bradlaugh.

It was in 1875 that Annie really launched herself into public life as a leading advocate of secularism. She freely took on all the odium attached to atheism, but she could not have gone through it without Bradlaugh's support, as she herself admitted. 'My quick, impulsive nature found in him the restful strength it needed, and learned from him the self-control it lacked.' Bradlaugh's old-fashioned courtesy to women assuaged the personal bitterness that Annie had developed after life with Frank. One thing, however, Bradlaugh did not teach her, and that was to moderate the viciousness of her attacks on the Bible. In later life she was to confess that she had been unjust towards Christianity, ignoring its services to mankind and concentrating solely on its 'crimes'. Annie's youthful stridency none the less was an essential part of her victory over her husband. The God of her heated imagination was simply another version of the Rev. Frank Besant, and in denying His existence she was purging herself of *him*.

Her fanaticism built up unnecessary hostility against her, as well as excessive adulation. No doubt the main body of secularists hailed her as a lady of refinement and genius; she was so witty, sparkling, sarcastic and intelligent, their new 'Star of Freedom'. But there were enemies who called her shrewish, a vixen, an animal, bestial, foul. Even some sympathizers had to qualify their praise. Bradlaugh's two devoted daughters Alice and Hypatia found her 'absolutely insensitive to the feelings of others'. One young man, enchanted by the youthful vivacity of her manner and impressed by her cogency and 'indignation', yet noted sadly that 'the relieving touches of wit and humour seldom found a place in her discourses'.

At one of her meetings she was accused of having written a book advocating free love. It was in fact Dr G. R. Drysdale's *Physical, Sexual and Natural Religion*. The hubbub reached the ears of Frank Besant and he made his first attempt to take Mabel away from her atheistical mother. He failed this time, for Mabel could still recite the Lord's Prayer and was occasionally taken to church.

The accusation of free love, mainly directed against Annie's relations with Charles Bradlaugh, was totally unjustified. Nevertheless the pair were deeply in love and would have married if each had been free. Charles did become free in May 1877 when his wife died. But Annie was to find to her dismay that her legal separation from Frank Besant was held to mean that she had condoned his cruelty – cruelty being the ground on which she might otherwise have obtained a divorce. In vain Annie raged sarcastically against 'the beauty of the English law' which made a wife a chattel not a person. Mr Frank Besant's 'chattel' was effectively prevented from ever transferring itself to a new owner.

One must ask, however, whether Annie would have been happy in the married state, even with Charles Bradlaugh. 'I ought never to have married', she wrote in her *Autobiography*, 'for under the soft, loving, pliable girl there lay hidden ... a woman of strong dominant will, strength that panted for expression and rebelled against restraint, fiery and passionate emotions that were seething under compression – a most undesirable partner to sit in a lady's arm-chair on the domestic rug before the fire.' Bradlaugh had a hearth too, and though Annie loved him, it is doubtful if she would have loved his fireside.

Though Annie could not marry Charles, even when he was free in 1877, that year marked a close and dramatic partnership with him that was never to be equalled. Indeed their joint struggle with a bench of inquisitorial males was to produce her finest hour.

The story of Besant's and Bradlaugh's trial in the Court of Queen's Bench opens, according to Annie's memoirs, with the marketing by a 'disreputable' Bristol bookseller of a well known medical pamphlet, to which had been added 'improper pictures'. The booklet in question had been published in America over forty years before, and was the careful work of a Dr Charles Knowlton on birth-control as a check on population growth. Knowlton had been prosecuted and imprisoned but the booklet went on selling steadily. In England there had been no prosecution until the new illustrated edition, when the bookseller and publisher were both charged with obscenity.

Now it happened that the publisher was Charles Watts, a member of the Secular Society and also publisher of their journal the *National Reformer*. Urged by his wife Kate, an amateur actress, Watts pleaded guilty and was discharged. But utter consternation reigned in the Secular Society, for the population problem was taken most seriously by Mrs Besant and Bradlaugh. Britain's population had nearly doubled during the first half of the nineteenth century, growing from 11 million in 1801 to 21 million in 1851.

Dr Knowlton, holding that late marriage was as dangerous as over-population, causing male resort to prostitutes, self-abuse and seduction, advocated early marriage and physical checks on the birth of children. He described in medical language female organs such as the uterus and fallopian tubes, through which the checks should be exerted. His preferred method of control was a syringe filled with a sterilising solution to be used 'after connection'.

So what was the duty of secularists? Besant and Bradlaugh, after studying the 'plain yet chaste' language of Dr Knowlton, resolved to give the British public, especially the poor, a chance to read it for themselves. Their decision split the Secular Society, Charles Watts and George Jacob Holyoake resigning. Pretty Mrs Watts in any case was jealous of pretty Mrs Besant, while Holyoake found the booklet's language 'coarse' rather than chaste.

The title at any rate of Dr Knowlton's book was far from salacious: *The Fruits of Philosophy*, with the sub-title *The Private Companion of Young Married People*. The word 'Philosophy' in the title, however, required interpreting. To its defenders it simply meant social science, to people like Holyoake it meant pornography.

Pursuing their mission, Besant and Bradlaugh republished *The Fruits* on 24 March 1877 with a preface of their own. In this they first stated the public's 'fullest right' to free discussion of all great social questions including population, followed by their own belief in 'scientific checks'. They wrote: 'We think it more moral to prevent the conception of children than, after they are born, to murder them by want of food, air, and clothing' – or by abortion, which to Annie was 'so horrible, so revolting'. The police had been notified of the publication date of this high-minded bombshell, since Besant and Bradlaugh intended their trial, if any, to be a test case for freedom of discussion. Calling themselves the Freethought Publishing Company, they hired a tiny office in Stonecutter Street, Shoe Lane. Five hundred copies at sixpence each were sold in the first half-hour. A detective was among the purchasers. The knowledge that the publishers might be arrested sent up Dr Knowlton's hitherto sluggish sales to 133,000 copies by 6 April, when the arrests were duly made.

Here it seemed was the ultimate in martyrdom, enough to satisfy even Annie. Things had been getting worse for her during the year before the trial. Anonymous hate-letters, cayenne pepper at her meetings as at Mrs Butler's and congestion of her right lung added to the strain of constant writing, speaking and travel. When she first consulted her doctor about her weak lungs he said work would either kill her or cure. As with most Victorian ladies, work cured.

The oldest anti-atheist chestnut was falsely attributed to her: the story of a speaker who lays his watch down on the table crying, 'If there be a God, I give him five minutes to strike me dead.' When the five minutes is up the speaker triumphantly declares, 'There is no God!' Annie's alleged challenge to the Almighty was denounced as 'ginger-beer blasphemy and the ravings of a half-drunken woman'.

All this and prison too. Such was Annie's sense of melodrama that she had ordered Bradlaugh's daughters to help her hide copies of *The Fruits* all over his garden in St John's Wood and under the floor-boards, lest the police should seize them prematurely. Bradlaugh told the ladies not to be silly. He had given Annie a St Bernard dog (very like himself) to look after her in her spacious new house, also in St John's Wood. But now she needed every ounce of Bradlaugh's personal support. He was risking his whole political career and the chance to win Northampton. But she – she was risking worse: 'scandal the most terrible a woman can face', the end of her 'pure reputation'. (Frank had her watched by detectives but never discovered a sexual sin.) Yet she could not retreat. Indeed with her St Bernard by her side she decided to do without professional counsel and defend herself in court. It would be considered unwomanly, she knew; but that prejudice should be balanced by the honour given to courage.

The trial opened before the Lord Chief Justice, Sir Alexander Coburn, who secretly sympathized with the Besant-Bradlaugh attitude. Sir Hardinge Giffard, the Solicitor-General, accused the pair of issuing a lewd, filthy, bawdy and 'obscene libel' (*libellum* being the Latin for book) advocating indecent, obscene, unnatural and immoral practices and thus corrupting the morals of youth. (Since 1857 the law had defined obscenity as writing intended to corrupt and deprave.) Dismissing the 'colourable' claim that *The Fruits* was aimed at married people, Giffard insisted that its true object was to promote sex outside marriage; as witness its open sale on the streets for sixpence, a sum which boys and girls could afford.

Annie's defence was unerring. She swept aside all idea of self and began at once by raising the whole issue to the highest plane:

... It is not as defendant that I plead to you today, not simply as defending myself do I stand here but I speak as counsel for hundreds of the poor, and it is they for whom I defend this case. My clients are scattered up and down the length and breadth of the land ... among the fathers, who see their wage ever reducing ... amongst the mothers worn out through over-frequent child-bearing. .... I find my clients among the little children.

She told the twelve gentlemen of the jury about the appalling conditions she had seen in slums, all of them dominated by ignorance of the facts of life which led to that dreadful trio, pauperism, crime and higher poor rates. That last 'horror' would surely touch the gentlemen of the jury. It was they and their class who would have to pay for the surplus population.

Refusing to descend from her plateau, Annie indignantly repudiated Giffard's references to 'promiscuous intercourse' and his suggestion that *The Fruits* would encourage it. She would not have mentioned anything so 'foul' had not the Solicitor-General used the word first. As her flow of oratory gained in power, she ventured to interrupt herself with a mild joke. Her sympathies, she confessed, were with the learned counsel. 'I do feel the position is especially painful for him, because if he does not get a verdict against a *woman*, it does make the position of learned counsel very painful. [A laugh.]'

For the most part, however, Annie was deadly serious. She pointed out that sex was taught to boys and girls at the South Kensington science classes sponsored by the government. Was Lord Salisbury the Prime Minister to be prosecuted? The text of the Contagious Diseases Act could be bought by anyone for a shilling. Her own daughter (then eight years old) would in due course be enlightened. 'I say to you deliberately as the mother of a daughter whom I love, that I believe it will tend to her happiness in her future, as well as to her health, that she shall not have made to her that kind of mystery about sexual functions that every man and woman must know sooner or later. . . .' Why should the poor be the only ones not to know how to limit their families to the number of children they could afford?

She then dealt with the so-called 'natural checks' on population growth, which in her view were too barbaric to contemplate: war, famine, disease. For a moment she plunged bravely into a discussion of Darwinism. The great man had written to her and Bradlaugh arguing for *some* struggle for survival or the race would 'sink into indolence'. The population must not get too small for healthy competition. Moreover, if better types used 'checks' while the lower types continued to breed recklessly, the former would be supplanted in society. Annie wisely refrained from answering Darwin's last argument. She stuck to *less* breeding, not *selective* breeding, making the point that Darwin's 'natural checks' were being eliminated by science.

Her confidence was greatest when she was describing her experiences in the slums. Excessive child-bearing caused its own diseases, she said, foremost among them being 'falling of the womb' (prolapse). Here she was on strong ground, and it is significant that as late as 1915 the Women's Co-operative Guild, founded in 1883, created a sensation by publishing *Maternity*, a collection of poignant letters by working-class mothers, most of whom suffered from prolapses. One mother wrote that since the war (1915) preventives were largely used. 'Race suicide if you will, is the policy of the mothers of the future. Who shall blame us?'

Who should blame Annie, when she reached her emotional peroration?

Unless you are prepared, gentlemen, to brand me with malicious meaning, I ask you as an English woman, for that justice which it is not impossible to expect at the hands of English men – I ask you to give me a verdict of 'Not guilty', and to send me home unstained. [Applause – promptly suppressed.]

The verdict was a compromise, owing to the foreman of the jury, Arthur Walter, son of the proprietor of *The Times*. Walter worked hard for a verdict of 'Guilty' despite a summing-up favourable to the defendants. He finally announced, as foreman, that while *The Fruits* was calculated to deprave, the defendants had no corrupt motives in publishing it. The baffled Lord Chief Justice had to say this meant a verdict of 'Guilty' – though it was later quashed on the grounds of a technical error. Meanwhile, Mrs Besant had concluded on a note of defiance reminiscent of Mrs Butler's.

If you commit this wrong [said Mrs Besant] then, from your verdict of guilty, we appeal to the verdict of a wider court, a grander jury. . . . We appeal from yours to the verdict of history . . . that weighing us in the far off to-morrow, shall say that this man and this woman . . . did good service in their day and in their generation – that history shall say to us, 'Well done', whatever your verdict may be.

Unfortunately the Rev. Frank Besant did not take the same view as history, though he did have Annie's idea of appealing to another court. Mabel in fact was made a ward of Chancery, on the double ground of her mother's atheism and propaganda for contraception. In her memoirs, Annie describes graphically the scene when the screaming child was torn from her. She did not take advantage of her limited access to her children, for the sake of their own stability, relying on their return to her when they came of age. This they duly did, both of them later helping their mother in her work.

Annie's legal battle for her children was not in vain. By once again pleading her own case in person she encouraged other women to study the law, despite the bench's opposition. 'Appear in person?' the scandalized judge had exclaimed, when Annie was pleading for custody of Mabel. 'A lady appear in person? Never heard of such a thing!' The legal profession were to hear more and more of such things; but less and less of the Shelley-Besant syndrome, by which a parent was deprived of his or her children because of irreligion. A blow was also struck by Annie Besant for the rights of wives. 'If you are legally your husband's wife', she wrote, 'you can have no legal claim to your children; if legally you are your husband's mistress your rights as mother are secure' – because the *wife*, unlike the mistress, was the man's property.

Meanwhile in 1878, after a severe breakdown and delirium when Bradlaugh visited her daily and nursed her 'like a tender mother', Annie decided to compensate for the loss of her daughter by being 'a mother to all helpless children'. And to fit herself for this work, she resolved on a course of higher education. She attended the science classes at South Kensington, studying first for the London Matriculation and then for a science degree. Hypatia Bradlaugh joined her.

Annie's academic career, though brilliant, was constantly impeded and perhaps ultimately thwarted by the violent prejudices against her. After matriculating with a first class in botany (the only woman in her year) and other firsts and seconds, she was not allowed to further her research in the Royal Botanical Gardens, Regents Park, lest she should corrupt the Curator's daughters who worked there; but the great Sir James Hooker got her into Kew. She failed, however, three times in her chemistry practical finals, owing, she felt sure, to the examiner's prejudice. She therefore never obtained a degree. Yet her studies were amply rewarded, not only by her teaching qualifications but also by the arrival of a new man in her life.

Her science teacher was that dazzling but wildly irresponsible *petit maître*, Dr Edward Aveling of London University. Annie merely called him 'the very ablest teacher she ever met, with an ardent love of science'. She did not draw attention to his even more ardent love of women and money. His eyes, said Shaw, were those of a basilisk and he might well have been exhibited in the zoo as a specimen of reptile. Aveling would make his girl students pay in advance and then cut the courses. The lucky ones got a letter of apology. 'The others were seduced and had their microscopes appropriated.' A married man separated from his wife, he was an inveterate sponger on other people's emotions and bank accounts, including those of his mistress Eleanor 'Tussy' Marx, youngest daughter of Karl Marx. With tentacles stretching through the world of the theatre, Aveling invited Ellen Terry to make him a loan but Shaw warned

Charles Bradlaugh MP being thrown out of the House of Commons.

her off the deal. In 1897 his wife died and he secretly married an actress. When Eleanor Aveling (as she called herself) found out, she swallowed prussic acid.

Before Shaw himself stepped in to be Annie Besant's third man, it is almost certain that Edward Aveling had asked her to live with him but that she did not do so; perhaps because Eleanor Marx cut her out. Nevertheless Annie was in love with Edward, as she demonstrated by a piece she wrote for the Secular Society Almanac of 1880, in which 'a new teacher' in her life was likened to one of two streams that 'flow into each other'. Her loss of Aveling was to be another silent martyrdom for Annie.

Shaw followed Aveling as inevitably as socialism followed science and secularism in Annie's cycle of conversions. Not that either of them ousted Bradlaugh. Indeed 1880 was Bradlaugh's great year. At the General Election he at last won the battle for Northampton. The jubilant Secular Society presented him with that sign manual of gentility, a silver salver. Immediately afterwards began his six-year battle to take his seat as an atheist. The House of Commons refused to let him either swear on the Bible or 'affirm' his loyalty (as in the courts of law) and Bradlaugh refused to leave the Chamber. Cavendish Bentink MP urged members to 'debag' him. Instead he was removed to 'prison' in the Clock Tower of Parliament, where sympathizers heaped his table with visiting-cards – no doubt on his silver salver. His expulsion was rescinded and he took his seat after 'affirming'. The following year the process was reversed, Bradlaugh was expelled, his seat declared vacant – and Northampton re-elected him. And so the farce was to repeat itself until a Tory government allowed him to 'affirm'.

Annie had worked furiously but not always wisely for him during the recurring fracas of 1881. She became vice-president of a new League for the Defence of Constitutional Rights and suggested that reprisals against the government should take the form of a run on the savings banks and pledges against taxable drink and tobacco. This showed, alas, that whatever else she had learned from Dr Aveling, it was not economics. Finally she held the mob at bay while Bradlaugh tried in vain to stop himself being thrown out of the House by ten hefty officials. He arrived in Palace Yard to the sound of splintering wood and breaking glass, where Annie received him.

It was in May 1884, the year of Aveling's elopement with Tussy Marx, that Annie first saw Shaw. Characteristically he was defending socialism in a series of ironical sallies while Bradlaugh, the confirmed individualist, solemnly attacked it. Shaw thoroughly foxed Annie by describing himself as a socialist 'loafer'. She gave him a governessy 'snarl' (her word) in the *Reformer* for admitting to 'so shameful a life'. Then she climbed down after discovering that by 'loafer' Shaw meant 'he did not carry a hod'. Unknown to her secularist friends the snarl was rapidly melting into a smile.

Shaw always said that Annie Besant joined each new movement 'at a bound'. Her bound into socialism took place in January 1885, when Fabians and secularists met again in hot debate. Everyone expected her to demolish Shaw. Instead she left the job to a subordinate – and then demolished the demolisher. After the meeting she invited Shaw to put her up for membership of the Fabian Society and to come to dinner. Socialism attracted her for two reasons: its defence of the underdog and its ideal of universal brotherhood. From now on Shaw and Annie developed what he called an intimate personal relationship that never went beyond friendship. There was a moment, however, when it might have developed into a 'vulgar intrigue'.

The affair foundered on Annie's heavy-handed intensity. She responded to his invitation to cohabit by producing a list of her terms for his signature. G.B.S. exploded in laughter: 'Good God! This is worse than all the vows of all the churches on earth. I had rather be legally married to you ten times over.'

Mrs Besant knew that legal marriage was unattainable. Her contract with Shaw was intended to tie down the incorrigible philanderer in accordance with the new socialist philosophy: a 'free marriage' or marriage à la Marx (Eleanor Marx and Edward Aveling). Annie burst into tears at Shaw's laughter, sent back his letters and demanded hers in return. He was to treat her less scurvily in his play, *Arms and the Man* (1894) where she appeared as Raina of 'the noble attitude and the thrilling voice'.

If Annie did not teach G.B.S. 'the higher love', G.B.S. did teach her the higher socialism. She objected to the rancour and violence of the Social Democratic Federation and preferred the Fabians for their intellectuality and moderation. The SDF reciprocated by attacking her for being a 'born enthusiast' – but not born near enough to working men and women. Annie retorted that in 1873 and 1874 she had known real poverty. Then the SDF specifically picked out her crusade for population-control as irrelevant. 'We simply laugh to scorn the ridiculous idea', they wrote, 'that the reconstitution of Society depends upon the poenis [*sic*].'

The Fabians were more her cup of tea with ladylike Mrs Beatrice 'Bo' Webb despising Tussy Marx for her slovenliness. Mrs Besant, though now become 'Annie Militant' on the way to being 'Annie Triumphant', was still every inch the lady. Her waistline had increased; she was stocky, stout and grey-haired. But her beauty could not be dimmed as long as her fire blazed so brightly.

During Annie's socialist militancy she fought the Fabians' battles under their higher command. Some of her old friends now became enemies. They called her 'a female St Athanasius in petticoats' (Athanasius being the saint who was against the world), or the lady with 'the mind of a milkjug', for ever pouring in and out. Three aspects of her campaign for socialism stand out: Bloody Sunday, the Bryant & May match-girls' strike and the Tower Hamlets School Board. Each of these three was floated on a sea of writing, editing and speaking. Her new paper, *Our Corner*, gave Shaw opportunities to write; he needed a corner somewhere, being very poor. She travelled to the Edinburgh slums, where a chance meeting with an old woman dying of cancer showed Annie's gift for illuminating her experiences with a striking phrase: 'And so, year after year, the misery grows, and every city has on its womb a cancer, sapping its vitality...'

Bloody Sunday on 13 November 1887 had been boiling up for many months. Poverty and unemployment had taken a disastrous new plunge in the 1880s, and marches and meetings were the workers' traditional means of making their voices heard. Anger and despair were producing their usual toll of minor brawls and arrests. But when it was learned that Trafalgar Square, London's traditional platform and sounding-board, was to be shut by the police that Sunday, a great surge of determination to assert their right of assembly swept thousands of people towards the square.

Annie and Shaw were in one of the processions, marching behind their banners. When things got tough Shaw advised her to go home. But she mounted a wagonette and tried to get the driver to block the advancing police. Instead he fled with her to the Embankment, where she jumped down and hurried back to the scene of battle. Suddenly there was a rattle of cavalry and the Guards trotted in. 'Go home, go home', shouted the organizers. They were too

'Bloody Sunday' 13 November 1887: special constables being instructed in their duties before the march *top* and one of the many fights that broke out between marchers and the police *above*.

late. As the square emptied, a mass of injured people was revealed, all 'respectable workmen'.

The aftermath of Bloody Sunday meant a new spell of frantic activity for Annie. She and W. T. Stead organized a Defence Fund for the victims, Annie popping up in police-courts and prisons, bailing out the accused and caring for the discharged. She bought hats for the men from Millbank Prison before giving them their fares home. Yet another paper appeared, *The Link*, in which she exposed cases of sweated labour ('A finisher of boots paid two shillings and sixpence per dozen pairs, and find your own polish and thread.') Bad landlords, insanitary workshops, cases of cruelty to children were all reported to Annie by her 'Vigilance Circles' and published in *The Link*. But who would invigilate the vigilantes? Some people thought that another set of vigilantes was necessary to curb Annie's self-assumed powers.

The climax came with the strike of Bryant & May's match-girls next year. Here there was not only sweated labour – 'twopence farthing per gross of boxes and buy your own string and paste' – but also industrial diseases, especially 'phossy jaw' caused by working with phosporous-headed matches. *The Link* published 'White Slavery in London' (W. T. Stead was co-editor with Annie) and the firm sacked Edith Simcox the girls' leader. Fourteen hundred of them came out on strike, Annie organizing strike pay, meetings, questions in Parliament. By July a settlement was reached with improved wages and conditions and a Matchmakers' Union. In November Annie and Edith Simcox were the Matchmakers' delegates to the International Trades Union Congress in London.

Her third achievement was to be elected to the School Board for Tower Hamlets, where she was at last able to work directly for the 'helpless children', to whom she had dedicated herself after losing custody of Mabel. It was thought that she had topped the poll because she was a woman. She fought among other things for better wages and more schooling for child-actors (*pace* Ellen Terry) and school meals. 'For these child martyrs of the slums', wrote Mrs Besant, 'Society has only formulas, not food.'

Why is it, that with her proud achievements in so many causes dear to the women's movement, her name does not figure more prominently in their records? Ray Strachey's *The Cause* and Mitchell and Oakley's *The Rights and Wrongs of Women* give her no mention whatever, while in both Sheila Rowbotham's *Women, Resistance and Revolution* and Roger Fulford's *Votes for Women* she is mentioned only once; Fulford quotes her bold statement, 'If the Bible and Religion stand in the way of women's rights then the Bible and Religion must go.'

The answer lies in that very religion which Annie had said 'must go'. Most of the 'strong-minded' ladies of the era could face the absence of religion with fortitude, even if some of them, like Beatrice Webb, regretted it. But when Annie herself brought back religion – and religion in a highly esoteric form – her friends of the Victorian progressive movements felt she had never really been one of them. Her name was quietly dropped, as though she were a black sheep who had committed some unmentionable offence.

**Annie Besant (centre top row) with the Strike Committee of the Matchmakers'
Union, whose action achieved better pay and conditions.**

Tramping around Bethnal Green in the late eighties on behalf of her half-
starved families, Annie would ask herself, 'Where is the cure for sorrow, what
the way of rescue from the world?' She was never quite at home with the
Fabians. Shaw believed they were too sophisticated for her, expressing their
consciences through wit and irony. She needed intensities dragged up from the
very bottom of the heart. Shaw could sometimes make her laugh at him, never
at herself.

The mysticism of her youth began returning in waves of nostalgia. She
sought 'some hidden thing, some hidden power'. One evening at dusk she
heard a 'Voice' saying, 'Take courage for the light is near.' A fortnight later
W. T. Stead sent her Mme Blavatsky's book on Theosophy called *The Secret
Doctrine* to review for the *Pall Mall Gazette*. In those two fat volumes Annie
found 'the light'.

As usual she plunged headlong. Obtaining an introduction from Stead to the
author of *The Secret Doctrine*, Annie took her socialist friend Herbert Burrows
with her to pay a call on the priestess of Lansdowne Road. It was a 'soft spring
evening' but Mme Blavatsky's voice was 'vibrant, compelling', rather than soft,
her handshake firm, her hair almost fuzzy and her cast of countenance masculine
and rugged. The magnetic eyes that Annie looked for in her idols and had seen
in Bradlaugh, were Mme Blavatsky's outstanding feature. She incessantly
rolled the cigarettes with which she would sometimes produce psychic
phenomena, making them disappear and turn up in unexpected places. Un–

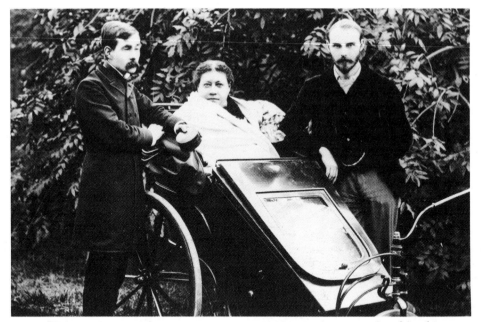

Helena Petrovna Blavatsky (or H. P. B. as she was known to her friends), the founder of modern Theosophy.

gainly in bulk and weighing sixteen stone, she sat in a huge wheelchair which travelled with her on her journeys to and from India. On this first occasion she talked only about commonplace subjects. Annie bade her a 'commonplace' goodbye, due to what she afterwards called 'a flash of the old unbending pride and an inward jeer' at this new folly.

Her pride was not to last, for she needed the 'hidden thing' possessed by this strange woman too much. At Mme Blavatsky's behest, Annie read the *Report* by the Psychical Research Society in which her theosophical and occult activities in India had been exposed as fraudulent. There were references to trap-doors and sliding panels, foreign accomplices and fake letters from gurus.

On 10 May 1889 Mme Blavatsky summoned Annie to pass judgment on the *Report*. For answer Annie knelt down, seized Mme Blavatsky's hands and begged to become her disciple 'in the face of the world'. It was Annie's final and most satisfying bid for martyrdom.

'You are a noble woman', said the new teacher, placing her hands on Annie's grey curls. 'May Master bless you.'

'Master' or 'Mahatma' – Master Morya to be precise – was Annie's future guru. The existence of these Masters lay at the heart of Theosophy, as expounded by Mme Blavatsky. They were human beings, albeit 'supermen', living in Tibet. Their supreme gift was World Unity, that Brotherhood of Man which Annie had tried and failed to find in socialism.

Once she lost her faith in doubt, Annie was prepared to extend her beliefs almost indefinitely. She jumped from the denial of one afterlife to the assertion

**A meeting of the Theosophists at Oman Camp _c_. 1924. Krishnamurti is
seated in the centre, with Annie Besant on his right.**

of many afterlives: the repeated reincarnations of the soul until its attainment of
perfection released it from the wheel of Karma. Annie's Master was to reveal
that she had been the pagan martyr Hypatia in an earlier incarnation.

Within six months of the first meeting Annie had become Helena Petrovna
Blavatsky's right-hand man – or rather right-hand woman, for the male role
was conspicuously played by this remarkable Russian, a kind of benign Rasputin in her power over human beings. Annie Besant's biographer, A. H. Nethercot, says that 'The Lesbian overtones of the situation in 1889–91 cannot be
overlooked.' Mme Blavatsky would write to Annie as 'My darling Penelope',
signing herself, 'Your ... female Ulysses'. Colonel Olcott, co-founder of
modern Theosophy in 1875, believed her to be no female but 'a wonderful
man', and a Hindu man at that.

Mme Blavatsky and her temple of Theosophy were moved from Lansdowne
Road to Annie Besant's home in Avenue Road, St John's Wood. Annie was put
in charge of the Inner Group or 'Esoteric Section' of the Society, whose 'occult
room' had secret access to Mme Blavatsky's own apartment. Annie became
editor of the Theosophist magazine _Lucifer_. She had thus moved from 'Ajax'
crying for light to 'Lucifer' bringing it. _Our Corner_ and _The Link_ both folded. At
meetings H. P. B. would leave Annie to answer all the disciples' questions –
'Annie! _you_ explain' – while she smoked and smoked and let her magnetic eyes
rove round the company. When she died in 1891 (the same year as Bradlaugh)
Annie took on the leadership in Blavatsky Lodge.

She had long severed all connection with the secularists. Her conversion convinced Bradlaugh that her judgment was no longer to be trusted. Shaw took it more lightly. 'Why go to Thibet for a Mahatma?' he laughed. 'Here and now is your Mahatma. I am your Mahatma.' The offer was too late. With a flash of wit Annie explained that her mind might have been weakened by her becoming a vegetarian – like him!

The rest of Annie Besant's story is equally extraordinary but in a twentieth-century context which does not belong here; except in so far as it underlines her escape from every Victorian myth, and most counter-myths. She moved from clericalism and materialism, male chauvinism and extreme feminism into what seemed to her to be the truth. The only 'ism' from which she never wholly retreated was socialism.

It was in India that Annie achieved the final synthesis of her political and mystical ideals. She founded a Hindu college at Benares which Pandit Nehru was to attend, and for which £3,000 was contributed by Mrs Jacob Bright, sister-in-law of John Bright the great radical. Esther, Mrs Bright's daughter, was an adoring disciple of Annie. 'You might call me "mata", mother,' said Annie, 'if that name suits you.' After the college was secure Annie hoped to raise the girls of India. 'See what an ambitious, restless creature I am.' But the war came and she threw herself into the Indian nationalist movement. In the spring of 1917 the government interned her – surely the highest tribute to an old lady of seventy – only to find her elected that August, in a whirlwind of popular enthusiasm, as first woman President of the Indian National Congress. She was released the next month.

The mistakes she made were over people: getting tied up with the Rev. C. W. Leadbeater who looked like Bernard Shaw but had had trouble over choir boys; fighting a law-case for the guardianship of two young Brahmin brothers and hailing the elder, Krishnamurti, as the Theosophists' messiah – until Krishna resigned from the Society. Nevertheless, when he was an independent spiritual teacher, he visited her at Adyar, the Theosophists' headquarters near Madras, where she lay dying. The golden voice had become thin and her memory had failed. But she managed to whisper, 'I brought you up, didn't I?'

She loved to be called the 'Mother of India', and as President of the Theosophists she sponsored a new divine personality, the World Mother, possibly a reincarnation of the Virgin Mary and embodied by a Mrs Arundale. For despite Mrs Besant's famous trial and her work for population control, it was motherhood that filled and overflowed her Victorian soul. Deprived for so many years, she needed a continent as rich in humanity as India to satisfy her.

She celebrated her jubilee at the Queen's Hall, London, in 1924. White-haired, white-robed, she received tributes from the Prime Minister, the Indian Viceroy, many Indian leaders and Sir Robert Baden-Powell the Chief Scout. He honoured her for having founded the Indian Boy Scout movement and presented her with the Order of the Silver Wolf.

It was surely a she-wolf; the same that had brought up Romulus and Remus, Krishna and his brother Nandya, and had failed to bring up Digby and Mabel. At her centenary Digby Besant was to sum her up in one word, 'Mother'.

⤙⤚ ELLEN TERRY ⤙⤚
1847–1928

There was always one profession in which women were free to earn as much as the market would pay. I do not mean prostitution, but acting, though no doubt Victorian prudes saw no difference between them. The stage was to be the favoured profession of Ellen Terry: a lady who became extremely well paid, independent, envied, admired, loved by geniuses, and the recipient of birthday telegrams from Queen Alexandra. Yet in spite of this success there were tensions between the private and public woman. For the Victorian ideal of motherhood was not so easily shaken out of the system, even when it stood in the way of £200 a week.

Ellen Terry was born with a 'property' spoon in her mouth; or so said Bernard Shaw. For she was born to the theatre, of the theatre and in theatrical lodgings. The stage claimed both her parents; with her siblings Kate and Fred she was to establish a brilliant theatrical dynasty. Gielguds, Nielson-Terrys and Craigs all descended from humble Mr and Mrs Ben Terry who in 1847 were still no more than strolling players.

151

Ellen, their fourth child, was born in Market Street, Coventry, on 27 February 1847. She always thought the date was 1848 but the Coventry register says otherwise. Afterwards she took her birthplace as a good omen. The great tragic actress Sarah Kemble had married William Siddons there; and Coventry was in Warwickshire, Shakespeare's county.

Ellen's first memory was of a solid oak bureau on which she would stand to watch the Coventry factory chimneys burst into flame as the fiery sunsets faded. She said she had not then seen a stage. But the bureau was surely the first platform on which she became part of a dramatic vision.

Her father Ben was of Irish extraction. From him may have come her sensitivity, wit and occasional inconsequence. On the same side of the family was the American painter John Singleton Copley and whether or not because of him Ellen had a highly developed pictorial sense. Her mother Sarah Ballard had a Wesleyan Methodist lay preacher for a father. But despite her religious upbringing, the lovely Sarah was playing 'the fourth singing witch' in *Macbeth* soon after her daughter Ellen's birth. Like Josephine Butler, Ellen Terry may have inherited the ability to speak in public from her Methodist ancestors; though the thought of their gift being exploited on the stage, of all places, would have horrified them.

The stage was not anathema to Methodists alone. When Ellen was born the profession was still in the process of climbing towards respectability, having travelled from the Restoration 'low', up through the age of the Kembles and Mrs Jordan, when royalty seemed less afraid of being contaminated than humbler folk, and onward with the Keans and Macready. It was not till late in the second half of the Victorian age that an actor was knighted (Sir Henry Irving) and the first player-pair (Sir Squire and Lady Bancroft) entertained at Balmoral by Queen Victoria herself. When William Terriss was stabbed to death at the stage door in 1897, everyone knew his assailant would get off, since Terriss was 'only an actor'. 'Poor dear Terriss', said Ellen, 'I do hope he lived long enough to realize that he was murdered. How he would have enjoyed it!' In 1929 Shaw wrote that actors and actresses were at last 'ladies and gentlemen of the professional class' and no longer 'players'.

Meanwhile Ellen had far to go both physically, up and down England with her family caravanserai of players, and in knowledge of life and love. She was her father's favourite child. Though she inherited her mother's tall graceful figure, hair of pale gold and luminous blue-grey eyes, she was totally without Sarah's tight sense of discipline. Indeed, travelling around with Ben brought out in Ellen a lasting enthusiasm for untrammelled nature and the 'open road'. Her biographer Roger Manvell believes that this companionship steered her away from Victorian prejudices at the most impressionable period of her youth.

The Terrys lived through a romantic theatrical era, as distinct from the classical heroics of the earlier Kembles. Ellen's chief instructress, Mrs Charles Kean, had married into the second generation of Edmund Kean's great stage family, and it seemed that his innovatory romantic style of blood and thunder, horror and rapture had come to stay.

Kate and Ellen Terry in a drawing-room comedy.

In 1853 Ben Terry brought his family to London and was fortunate enough to join Charles Kean's company at the Princess's Theatre. The clever little Terrys, Kate and Nellie, were soon on the boards with Ben, racing about backstage – Nellie once bumped into the great Macready and took the opportunity to admire his 'beautiful wavy mouth' as he accepted her apology – or falling asleep in the wings. Mrs Kean would sit in the gallery checking up on Ellen's elocution. 'A E I O U, my dear, are five distinct vowels.' She must not mix them all up, making a 'pudding' of them. (It was a pity Mrs Kean did not teach Henry Irving too, for he made such a strange pudding of his vowels that carping critics complained of feeling sick.) At seven, as at seventy, Ellen had the most perfect enunciation. Her charm, beauty and cleverness were her own, but she owed her technical skill to Mrs Kean. 'I have always loved women with a somewhat hard manner', wrote Ellen, remembering Mrs Kean's beaky nose and shrill insistence that concealed a generous heart.

Ellen's first success came when she was nine. Her acting of young Mamillius in *The Winter's Tale* won applause both from *The Times* reviewer and the Rev. Charles Dodgson (Lewis Carroll). Between them they praised her 'vivacious precocity' and the 'remarkable ease and spirit' of 'a beautiful little creature'. The little creature herself always remembered the crises more clearly than the compliments, though she could not forget the audience's sobs and shouts for

'Arthur! Arthur!' when she played the blinded prince in *King John*. On the very first night as Mamillius (she played it for 102 times in 1856) she tripped and fell flat in front of Queen Victoria and Prince Albert. As Puck in *A Midsummer Night's Dream* she once broke her toe at the end in a trap-door on the stage. Kate and Mrs Kean rushed to her rescue, the latter promising untold wealth if only she would be brave and carry on. 'Finish the play, dear, and I'll double your salary.' So Nellie stuck it out, interspersing Puck's last lines with appropriate cries of anguish – 'If we shadows have offended/Think but this, and all is mended (Oh, my toe!)' – and bringing her family thirty shillings a week instead of fifteen. For the rest of their stay in London the Terrys were able to afford a house of their own.

By 1860 the Keans were in the United States and the Terrys again fending for themselves. They made an 'odd little troupe', wrote Ellen. At the end of two years Nellie was back in London with her father at the Royalty. Now a long-legged fourteen-year-old, she would tuck her shamefully big hands under her arms. 'Take down your hands!' Mme Albina the director would scream at her. '*Mon Dieu! It is like an ugly young poulet going to roost!*'

It was at the Royalty that the poor little chicken had her first shock of stage fright. Cold shivers ran down her spine. Icy centipedes crawled through her hair, her knees wobbled, her eyes bulged, her mouth opened—but no sound came out.

Her talented sister Kate was rounding off her theatrical education with a first-rate stock company (repertory) at the Theatre Royal, Bristol. Nellie and the rest of the family joined her there in 1862, when the two girls captivated a 'wonderful family' of devoted Bristolian theatre-goers named Godwin.

Mrs Godwin was beautiful, Mr Godwin aesthetic and brilliant. Still in his twenties, he was an architect of repute and full of ideas about everything including the stage. At first Nellie was chiefly conscious of him as the creator of her costume for Titania, which he showed her how to damp and wring dry before she wore it, 'all crinkled and clinging', for the performance. This was the very first of her many lovely dresses.

The Godwins' house in elegant Portland Square seemed to her a veritable Palace of Art. Beauty had hitherto passed her by, apart from nature and her own handsome family, but the Portland Square house was full of beautiful things. When Nellie returned to work in London at the Haymarket, she discovered that glamour had left the stage. She thought that the trouble lay in the way the actors teased her and talked cheap scandal. But the truth was that for the last year in Bristol she had fed on honeydew. Nothing else would satisfy her now.

By a curious chance a new draught of honeydew was already being prepared for Ellen by one of the Terrys' family friends, Tom Taylor the critic. She was to sip it in Little Holland House, a pleasure-dome even more fascinating than 21 Portland Square.

Taylor introduced the Terry girls to the artist George Frederick Watts, who was soon painting 'The Sisters' in his large studio with the red baize door at Little Holland House, Kensington. In the portrait both girls look ethereally lovely; but it is the younger, Nell, who fills the foreground of the picture with her languorous yet vital pre-Raphaelite beauty. Her face is in profile and she is looking slightly upward with parted lips; looking for something or someone. Watts thought it might be for him. In reality Nell was drinking in the spirit of this marvellous house and looking for beauty's essence.

Little Holland House was rented from Lord Holland by Mr and Mrs Thoby Prinsep. Watts had arrived, a genius tortured with dyspepsia, in the 1850s, to be looked after by Mrs Prinsep. 'He came to stay for three days; he stayed for thirty years', Sarah Prinsep wrote with excusable exaggeration, for he did stay over twenty years. Sarah came fourth in a famous septet of sisters, the Pattles, sometimes known as the 'Pattledom'. The best looking was Virginia, who married Earl Somers although Watts had been in love with her. Sarah Prinsep made the deepest impression, while Julia Margaret Cameron, the plainest, was also the most brilliant, being the greatest artist among many Victorian pioneer photographers. The trio were called Beauty, Dash and Talent. Dash had invested her house with the cool blue-green atmosphere beloved of contemporary artistic taste. The ceiling in the drawing-room was painted a deep blue and covered with golden stars; but hardly more thickly than the carpets beneath. For Sarah Prinsep loved to act as hostess to the stars of art, poetry and

One of Lewis Carroll's studies of the Terry family, 1865. Ellen (fourth from left) wrote of this time: 'I hated my life . . ., and everything in the world'.

politics. This was where Ellen Terry first met them: 'old Madox Brown' who loved her, Leighton whose paintings she detested, Rossetti whose death was later to seem like the loss of the last member of her family, the smartly dressed Browning appearing even more incomprehensible as a man than a poet, Gladstone the possessor of volcanic fires beneath a grey crust, Disraeli with straggling black curls that shook as he walked. Disraeli seems to have intrigued Ellen more than anyone else. Observing him in Piccadilly one day, she crossed the road and bumped into him on purpose. 'Excuse me', he said, not recognizing her, and passed on; but at least she had tried to look into those veiled eyes.

Her starry-eyed delight and wonder at the place naturally spilled over in affection for the eccentric 'old' artist – forty-six to her sixteen – who was painting her. In youth Watts had looked romantically Byronic, with skin as pale, hair as dark and eyes as brown as Godwin's. But at thirty, according to his most recent biographer Wilfrid Blunt, Watts was disillusioned and often physically ill. He was also emotionally unstable, sexually frustrated and probably sexually ignorant. Nevertheless he felt that he ought to get married. An apparently docile and certainly loving young actress might rejuvenate him.

He told his confidante Lady Constance Leslie that he intended to remove the younger Miss Terry from the 'temptations' of the stage, educate her, and if she still loved him, marry her. He admitted that it would require much time and the support of friends to make 'the poor child' into what he wished, and into what Sarah Prinsep ardently wished for him. A dialogue has survived, however, between Watts and a friend showing that at least one of his circle was sceptical:

Watts: 'I am thinking of adopting Ellen Terry. . . .'
Friend: 'I think she is too old.'
Watts (later): 'I am thinking of marrying Ellen Terry. . . .'
Friend: 'I think she is too young.'

Did Watts feel the unwonted sap rising as he kissed his younger model in the studio one day? That first kiss was merely 'all tenderness and kindness', Ellen told Shaw many years later. But the second kiss was different enough to make her think Watts had given her a baby as well. Her frank account to Shaw was too hot even for post-Victorian days and was excluded from *Ellen Terry and Bernard Shaw; a Correspondence*, edited by Christopher St John in 1931. Here it is:

Then I got ill and had to stay at Little Holland House – and then – he kissed me – *differently* – not much differently but a little, and I told no one for a fortnight, but when I was alone with Mother she looked so pretty and sad and kind, I told her – What do you think I told the poor darling? I told her I *must* be married to him *now* because I was going to have a baby !!!! and she believed me!! Oh, I tell you I thought I knew everything then, but I was nearly 16 [*sic*] years old then – I was *sure,* THAT kiss meant giving me a baby.

'Choosing' by George Frederick Watts. Ellen Terry is seen choosing scentless camellias in preference to the humble but sweetly scented violets.
Overleaf left: Ellen Terry as Hiordis. Shaw often tried to persuade her to act in Ibsen's plays but her choice of *The Vikings* was disastrous.
Overleaf right above: Ellen Terry's costumes for Portia and Lady Macbeth.
Overleaf right below: her simple bedroom at Smallhythe Place.

Hiördis.

When Ellen herself had a young daughter with problems, she was to apostrophize Shaw in one of her first letters to him (1892), 'What fools we are in bringing up our children!'

Again to Shaw, Ellen said later that her parents 'hated' the marriage, though in her own *Memoirs* they were 'delighted'. She may have been confusing her mother's original horror with her later relief at learning that Nell was not to be a pregnant bride after all. The wedding took place at St Barnabas' Church, Kensington, on 20 February 1864. Ellen remembered her wedding dress, as she remembered all her clothes. 'On that day I wore a brown silk gown which had been designed by Holman Hunt, and a quilted white bonnet with a sprig of orange-blossom, and I was wrapped in a beautiful Indian shawl.' Holman Hunt had painted the popular 'Light of the World' and Nellie Terry felt herself to be just that. After the wedding Nell wept copiously. 'Don't cry', said Watts. 'It makes your nose swell.' He had bought beauty not sentiment.

His own lack of personal attraction seemed all too obvious to Lady Constance Leslie, who described the 'atrabilious' groom moving slowly up the aisle with his 'radiant child bride dancing up it on winged feet.'

Ellen was to be seventeen in seven days' time, her 'Signor' forty-seven in three days. (The youngest Pattle had christened George Frederick Watts 'Signor', as it seemed more appropriate than the commonplace George or Fred.)

Little Nellie Watts was soon in the throes of life with a reverend Signor, a Poet Laureate, and a changing selection of the Pattledom; the one constant presence was Sarah Prinsep in whose house Ellen lived as with a resident mother-in-law and a dragon at that. The Prinseps with Signor and Ellen in tow went in the spring to stay in the country; first with the Camerons at Freshwater, Isle of Wight, where the Tennysons also lived. Ellen had no difficulty in charming the Laureate on their evening walks, he with flowing cape and beard, she in a round brown mushroom straw hat with a red feather around it and a ribbon to tie it under her chin, for she still wore her hair loose. She responded enthusiastically to his information on wild flowers, bark of trees and flight of birds. 'Always I was quite at ease with him.' So ravishing was she that Julia Margaret Cameron got her into the Tennysons' bathroom and photographed her in her nightdress. Perhaps the loveliest of all Mrs Cameron's portraits, it shows Ellen in one of her melting moods. At other times her spirits bubbled over and she preferred the company of boisterous youth: 'playing Indians and Knights of the Round Table with Tennyson's sons, Hallam and Lionel, and the young Camerons. . . .' It bored her to sit indoors 'noticing what the poet did or said' – or for that matter, what the painter did or said. Watts she considered old for his age and 'always teetering about in goloshes'.

Ellen was to mutiny during the second country visit, when she lunched with the Spencer Stanhopes at Cobham in Surrey. Lilla Spencer Stanhope recalled

'The Sisters' by George Frederick Watts. While he was painting this portrait of Kate and Ellen Terry the artist was ensnared by Ellen's beauty.

Ellen as 'quite a schoolgirl and a decided tom-boy', who staged a scene between Sarah Prinsep and herself soon after luncheon:

Suddenly the latter, with an air of supreme boredom, leant back over the arm of the chair in which she was seated, and shaking her head to and fro loosened the pins from her hair which tumbled about her shoulders like a cloak of shining gold. . . . Mrs Prinsep was horrified. 'Ellen! Ellen!' she cried, 'put your hair up instantly.' And Ellen, flashing a wrathful glance at her tormentor, grasped the waving mass of gold, coiled it carelessly upon her head, and stabbing it with pins, sat there looking lovelier than ever, a petulant, scolded child.

Ellen was to go one better when she 'bounded' into dinner at Little Holland House dressed as Cupid – perhaps the famous 'Cupid' dress that she had worn in Bristol. This scene, described by Ellen's daughter, was blown up during the Naughty Nineties into the story of a naked Cupid dancing on the Prinseps' table before an astonished audience of bishops. Thus Nell Terry graduated into a mixture of Nell Gwynne, Emma Hamilton and Cora Pearl in an episode that may have given rise to a recent misunderstanding at the Watts Gallery near Guildford. A visitor informed the curator, who was as astonished as the mythical bishops, that Watts had married Nell Gwynne and painted her as 'Hope' on top not of a table but of the world.

In retrospect, Nell's marriage seemed to her none the less happy, particularly when she was sitting as a model to her famous husband. Her 'thirst for beauty' – beauty both in herself and in her surroundings – was well satisfied. She would sit or stand for Watts hour after hour, almost in a dream. One day, dressed in heavy armour for 'The Watchman', she fainted across his arm, causing him to stab his canvas with a spot of pink paint. The spot is still there.

Nothing exact is known of how the marriage broke up. Long afterwards both Ellen and Watts dropped hints; Ellen accusing Watts of being 'so impatient' with his child bride, and herself 'so ignorant and young', as if the trouble were between a disappointed master and his naughty pupil. This indeed was just how Sarah Prinsep saw Ellen – except that she regarded Watts's bride as her own rebellious pupil. Watts cited 'incompatibility of temper' in the legal separation. In the subsequent divorce (1877) he mentioned, along with adultery, her 'very artistic and peculiar nature', which he had somehow failed to control, and also the 'demands' she made on him which he could not satisfy. Were these 'demands' sexual? And was the marriage consummated?

There is still no agreement on these questions for the evidence remains inconclusive. David Loshak is chief advocate for the view that the marriage was consummated. Writing in the *Burlington Magazine* (1963), he based his conclusion on a picture of 'Paolo and Francesca'. Watts painted three versions, but in only one is Ellen the model for Francesca. In that painting Ellen/Francesca is nude and generating with Watts/Paolo a strong sensuous and erotic feeling. Loshak takes this to mean that they were lovers. It may be so. On the other hand, Watts was quite capable of conveying erotic feeling long before Ellen Terry appeared on the scene. His 'Satan and Sin', a picture of a naked couple dated about 1850, could hardly be more suggestive of mixed-up sex.

The majority of Watts's biographers deny that the marriage was consummated (Ronald Chapman) or doubt it (Wilfrid Blunt), or, if they lived in the nineteenth century, ignore the whole question. In the *Annals* of Watts's life by his second wife Mary Fraser-Tytler, Ellen Terry is not even mentioned by name.

I confess myself to be a 'doubtful'. Most of the gossip and rumours do point to an unconsummated marriage, though there is no evidence whatever that Watts was impotent. The story of Ellen in tears outside the bedroom door on the wedding night sounds more like a Victorian genre picture ('Rejected') than reality. The Rev. Charles Dodgson, a family friend of the Terrys, suggested that it was no marriage at all. Ellen was justified in saying of Watts, wrote Dodgson, 'He never loved me and I do not believe, in God's sight, we are man and wife.'

Whether or not Ellen was still a virgin, she and Signor were quarrelling so badly by September that she had to leave the 'wonderland' that was the studio and spend Christmas 1864 at home. She blamed not Signor but Sarah: 'God forgive her, for I *can not*....' She was to meet Watts once more in a Brighton street: 'He told me that I had grown!' And years later Watts was to see her through a hedge between two gardens. The sight wrung from him a written apology for spoiling her life, which she accepted, together with a beautiful portrait of herself. She did not know that the angry old man destroyed many other pictures of her and intended to do away with 'Choosing' also. Fortunately 'Choosing' had already been sold, and its new owner rushed to claim it before it reached Watts's bonfire.

Ellen was back in the theatre by 1865, in no very cheerful frame of mind. Indeed she had been 'thunderstruck' to hear she was to be legally separated from her husband. The deed was drawn up on 26 January 1865, allowing her £300 a year 'so long as she should lead a chaste life', and not return to the stage, when her allowance would drop to £200. She, however, had no choice but to act, though she had never been remotely 'stage-struck'; indeed she had cut short a successful run in *The American Cousin* without a pang, to marry Watts. Since then she had tasted honeydew and seen the real countryside rather than stage scenery. To that she returned as soon as possible.

Her chance came through Edward Godwin, the fascinating architect she had first met in Bristol and whom she may have met again at Little Holland House. There was an unsubstantiated rumour that Ellen had once gone to nurse Godwin and innocently stayed the night, thus giving Watts his chance to get rid of her. It may have been Godwin's wife who was ill, for she died in 1865. The following year Ellen spoke of a visit to Paris with 'a friend', possibly the bereaved Godwin. One brief, tragic incident stuck in her memory; she saw a betrayed French peasant girl clinging to the outside of her seducer's carriage and being literally dragged along at his chariot wheels. Much as Ellen detested her life at home and on the stage – doing the mending while Kate strummed the Moonlight Sonata or playing Helen Heartwell in *The Hunchback*, then 'not a very desirable person to *be*! *I* think! *although no harm in her*' – Ellen would be saved from the fate of the French girl by her earning power in the theatre.

Left: **G. F. Watts at the time of his marriage to Ellen Terry.**
Right: **Edward Godwin, the father of Ellen Terry's children Ted and Edy Craig.**

Her depression deepened, however, when Kate left the stage to marry Arthur Lewis, a wealthy businessman who lived on Campden Hill, close to the Holland Park paradise from which Ellen had been ejected.

Suddenly without a word of warning she eloped. Her last move had been to return 'permanently' to the theatre on 8 June 1867. Rather less than a year later she had vanished. The next six years are sometimes called 'the lost years of Ellen Terry'. No one knew her whereabouts. It was only when a drowned girl was picked out of the river and identified by some of the Terrys as Ellen that the runaway revealed herself. She was living with Godwin in Hertfordshire. The Terry family were relieved to know she was alive. But as she was living in sin, relations with her family remained severed.

Though near enough to London for Godwin to pursue his architectural career, Ellen was in fact buried in Hertfordshire, at Fallows Green, Harpenden, where they finally settled in a house built by Godwin. Ellen's taste for adventure in the country (she used to leap down a whole flight of cottage stairs outside Bristol and over gates and out of trees at Freshwater) was now fully indulged. On a pitch-black night a drunk boarded her pony-trap saying 'My God, it's a gal!' and had to be clubbed out with her whip-handle. She was once marooned all night alone in a wood, surrounded by a vast assemblage of speckled yellow frogs. Godwin encouraged her to commune with the moon by sleeping out-doors. She said she drew lasting benefit from this practice. And despite frogs, she was lyrically happy. She would never consider, she wrote, 'all the sweet human things of life' well lost for art; 'absolute devotion to another human being means the greatest *happiness.*' For a time she had it.

Her daughter Edith was born in 1870, a pretty dark-haired child with decided views. Two years later Edward arrived, plump and fair. The children learned to refer to themselves before the servants as 'Miss Edy' and 'Master Teddy'. Social standards must be maintained despite the ambiguous situation.

After the children's birth the parents began to grow apart. Ellen was increasingly uneasy about their financial position. Shakespeare criticism and all sorts of unprofitable subjects distracted Godwin from building houses. Fallows Green was invaded by the bailiffs. Then occurred one of those extraordinary coincidences, stranger than fiction, which change people's lives.

Mrs Godwin, as Ellen called herself, was driving along a lane near her home one winter's day when a wheel came off her pony-trap. As she stood contemplating the disaster a middle-aged bearded figure in hunting pink suddenly jumped his horse over the hedge into the lane. Seeing a lady in distress, he approached her.

'Good God, it's Nellie. Where have you been all these years?' The huntsman was Charles Reade, popular novelist, playwright and actor-manager. He had taken a great interest in Kate and Nell as young actresses. Nell replied almost wholly truthfully.

'I've been having a very happy time.'

'Well, you've had it long enough. Come back to the stage!' She hesitated. Then remembered the prospect of more bailiffs.

'Perhaps . . . if someone would give me £40 a week!'

'Done!' He promised her that and more if she would act the part of the heroine in his own play *The Wandering Heir* at the Queen's Theatre. And so the 'wandering heir' to all the glory of the English stage returned to it permanently at last on 28 February 1874.

She had played truant for nearly six years, behaviour which Shaw was severely to condemn as trifling with her career. Her son Teddy, on the other hand, saw his mother's dilemma in terms of a genuine tug-of-love, as poignant as Charles Reade's *Cloister and the Hearth* except that it was between the theatre and the hearth. In his memoir *Ellen Terry and Her Secret Self* (1931) her son wrote that there were two Ellens, the 'little mother' or 'little Nelly' and the great Ellen Terry the actress. In a sense Ellen Terry subscribed to this duality herself, sometimes signing letters to Shaw with the invented name 'Nellen', to remind him that she was also Nell. Shaw however would have none of 'Nell', eloquently writing that 'Ellen Terry is the most beautiful name in the world; it rings like a chime through the last quarter of the nineteenth century.'

That was just what Teddy objected to. He adored his natural father, Godwin, dedicating the memoir to him. Teddy never accepted that his 'little mother' needed to leave Fallows Green in order to earn the money that Godwin failed to provide. Teddy considered the 'bailiffs' to be a figment of Great Ellen's imagination; Little Nelly could perfectly well have remained in her peaceful private

Above right: Edward Gordon Craig's woodcut of Henry Irving.
Above left: Ellen Terry's annotated copy of *Macbeth*.
Below: caricature of the Americans' reception of Henry and Ellen.

Souvenir of

Madame Sans-Gêne

Presented at the Lyceum Theatre
By HENRY IRVING

Price One Shilling

Above left: Edward Gordon Craig's woodcut of Ellen Terry.
Above right: souvenir programme of one of the magnificent Lyceum productions.
Below: Henry and Ellen with William Terriss in *Charles I*.

home with her babies – as every mother should. But Teddy's sister Edy took exactly the opposite view, not only fighting strenuously for women's work and careers but ultimately choosing a woman, Chris St John, for her lover rather than a man. (This dénouement was to be brought about partly by Ellen herself, who opposed two possible marriages for her daughter as unsuitable.)

Ellen herself managed to avoid being pulled apart between her son and daughter by agreeing first with one, then the other. Yet there remained some dualism in her to the end, as there did in most independent Victorian women; and it was part of her genius that she never let it seriously disrupt her private or public happiness. Indeed her great charm on the stage came from presenting herself as a happy integrated personality.

Teddy was right over one thing, however. The 'damned *magnet*' of the stage itself, not only the £40 to be earned there, had affected his mother's decision to return. Yet Ellen Terry did not even mention it. Torn between the two worlds of actress and mother, she covered up the fact that she had freely chosen the former by arguing nothing but economic necessity.

The Godwins returned to London in 1874, living uncomfortably in Blooms-bury. He was forty, Ellen twenty-seven with two illegitimate children. Her relations with Godwin deteriorated fast when he took into his office a young girl trainee – he believed in professional women architects – who was almost certainly Beatrice Phillips, his future wife. In 1877 Watts divorced Ellen for adultery with Godwin by whom, ironically, she had been abandoned two years before, in November 1875. It was a wonder, as her son wrote later, that his broken-hearted mother had not killed herself, for Godwin he maintained was the one great love of her life.

In her desperate sorrow Ellen was saved and defended by the stage and two of its leading figures, Squire Bancroft and Charles Reade. Mrs Squire Bancroft had found her in 1875 sitting disconsolately in the Bloomsbury house, surrounded by empty spaces from which the furniture had been removed, and dressed in a yellow and brown speckled tabard. It must have made her look like one of the frogs in the Hertfordshire wood, particularly as she was painfully thin. She was swept off by Marie Bancroft to the Prince of Wales Theatre, where she beguiled her audience as never before playing Portia in *The Merchant of Venice*.

Charles Reade did not let her down either. Her acting was simply '*wonderful*' in his *Wandering Heir*, wrote Lewis Carroll. Her success was due largely to Reade's robust direction. Ellen, who called him 'Papa', was to remember him fondly as 'Dear, kind, unjust, generous, cautious, impulsive, gentle Charles Reade'. Never must she decline into limpness, he urged; no loose lines, limp business or limp exits. Exits must always be 'ardent'. Invigorated and sustained over these three difficult years, Ellen made an 'ardent exit' from the world of Reade and Bancroft in 1878. As Roger Manvell writes, there was now established 'the greatest partnership in the history of the English Theatre' – that between Ellen Terry and Henry Irving.

And the year 1878 was in other ways an *annus mirabile* for Ellen. While playing the heroine in *Olivia,* an adaptation of Goldsmith's *Vicar of Wakefield* by

W. G. Wills, she met an actor named Charles ('Kelly') Wardell, who had fought in the Crimea. She fell in love with the big burly fellow or, rather, with the owner of an available name. A 'legitimate' surname for her children and herself seemed worth any marriage, even with a man who drank and whose heavy footsteps on the stair Teddy greatly disliked. After the marriage the Terry family rallied round her once more. She was respectable. The little Godwins became Wardells and suddenly abounded in aunts, uncles and grandparents. 'Mrs' Godwin had had many would-be lovers, including young Johnston Forbes-Robertson, but no status: Mrs Wardell was every inch a leading lady.

Ellen Terry was by no means unknown to Henry Irving. They had acted together once on Boxing Day a few months before her elopement with Godwin. The play, *Katherine and Petruchio*, was Garrick's version of *The Taming of the Shrew*. Ellen had characteristically made Katherine as unshrewish as possible, to balance Irving's violent Petruchio. But it was when Irving saw her as Olivia ten years later that he decided she should be his leading lady at the Lyceum. Like Ellen, Irving had a past. His past, indeed, more or less synchronized with hers, though he was the elder by nine years. In 1869, while she was in Hertfordshire, he had married Florence O'Callaghan, who gave him two sons but no encouragement whatever in his career. When she mocked even his sensational success in *The Bells*, he stopped their carriage, sprang out and never saw her again. She refused to have a divorce or to die so that Irving was never able to choose a new wife. It might otherwise have been Ellen herself. She was soon freed again, for Wardell died in 1885, having agreed to a separation four years earlier. Ellen told Shaw she would have died herself if she had lived with Charlie one more month. 'I gave him three-quarters of all the money I made weekly, and prayed him to go.' This was the period – the eighties – of Ellen's greatest admiration for Henry Irving, both as man and actor.

Henry Irving, born Brodribb in Cornwall, had an overwhelming sense of style. He quickly changed his surname to something more impressive and created a heroic world of his own at the Lyceum Theatre, a world of scenic opulence, grand acting and powerful emotions. His first tremendous success had been as a Polish Jew in *The Bells*, when his intense feeling seemed to tear him to pieces. Indeed, violent emotions were always dangerously to slow up his acting, and so to slow up Ellen's too. But so loyal was she to her master that she played her own parts in the manner that would best contribute to his. When she played Portia opposite his Shylock, for instance, she had to make up for Irving's unorthodox, mournful presentation of the Jew by injecting extra liveliness into her own relations with Bassanio. 'She touched him!' whispered the more prudish members of the audience in horror.

Ellen sometimes wondered if Henry ever quite realized how physically beautiful he was. (Only an exceptionally sweet character like Ellen could have had any doubts.) Tall, with a thick curtain of hair, highbridged nose and noble bearing, he could make his rather small brown eyes 'shine like an immense bowl of dark liquid with light shining through'. As for his mouth, it was 'firm, firm, firm' – since firmness was necessary in the greatest actor-manager of the age. If he had faults in Ellen's eyes, she was eager to forgive them, even his egotism. For she was 'our lady of the Lyceum' (Oscar Wilde's phrase) and Henry was its supreme lord. Everyone had to revolve around him, but at an appropriate distance.

Bram Stoker, author of *Dracula*, was proud to be Irving's manager, and in his company was the young playwright Arthur Wing Pinero. Famous painters such as Sir Laurence Alma-Tadema and Sir Edward Burne-Jones were ready to design Irving's sets. It was Alma-Tadema who produced what Ellen considered her most beautiful dress, for Imogen in *Cymbeline*. Henry's green and gold costume for Othello was so splendid that Ellen salvaged it after it was finished with and had it made up to wear as the Nurse in *Romeo and Juliet*. The finest of all Ellen's marvellous dresses and the most famous theatrical costume ever made was Alice Comyns-Carr's design for Lady Macbeth. It is now exhibited at the Ellen Terry Museum. Her friend the painter W. Graham Robertson has described it:

Long plaits of deep red hair fell from under a purple veil over a robe of green upon which iridescent wings of beetles glittered like emeralds, and a great wine-coloured cloak, gold embroidered, swept from her shoulders. The effect was barbaric. . . .

Oscar Wilde said that Lady Macbeth, while patronizing local industries for her husband's clothes, took care to buy her own in Byzantium.

When Irving and Ellen went on tour, even to America, he travelled as a prince of the theatre, taking an enormous retinue and all his scenery and costumes. Ellen approved. It brought them enormous prestige. Up to 1881 the Lyceum at maximum capacity had only been able to take £230 a night. Irving enlarged it, so that the takings became £350. The expenses were fabulous, but so were the profits. Ellen was his partner, his leading lady, but her salary was forty per cent to his sixty per cent. In fact it was a 'partnership' such as the suffragettes might have ridiculed. 'Henry and Ellen were one, and that one was Henry.'

Nevertheless the Lyceum made Ellen Terry, and the public went wild over her increasing skill and beauty. True, Lewis Carroll longed in vain for 'the gush of animal spirits' that she had once shown. But her public were more than satisfied with the vivacious charm, geniality and responsiveness of a supreme comedy actress. In her gift for remaining herself while playing somebody else (the essence of a comedian) she was sometimes compared to that royal mistress Mrs Jordan, of whom Hazlitt wrote: 'It was not as an actress, but as herself, that she charmed every one.'

Ellen's beauty seemed miraculously to keep pace with each change in fashion. As a girl she had been the ideal of every Pre-Raphaelite artist, with her dreamy look and 'harvest-coloured' hair. She herself still revered the teachings of that period, learning from a disciple of Ruskin to spin real yarn for a production of *Faust*. In womanhood she enthralled the new 'aesthetic' age. Her Ophelia seemed to Henry James, the American novelist, aesthetic: 'not only her garments but her features themselves bear a stamp of the new enthusiasm.' Oscar Wilde described her Ophelia in a sonnet as, 'Like some wan lily overdrenched

'Henry Irving at Bournemouth' by Edward Gordon Craig.

with rain'. It sounded a little soggy but Ellen expressed delight. That was just how she meant to play the part. In fact Irving's abnormally slow Hamlet had necessitated a drooping Ophelia. Bram Stoker commented on 'the large, graceful, goddess-like way' in which Ophelia walked.

Though Graham Robertson could not deny that she had 'Pale eyes, rather small and narrow, a broad nose slightly tilted at the tip, large chin, pale hair not decidedly golden yet not brown...' he quickly switched to the truth: 'Yet out of these was evolved Ellen Terry, the most beautiful woman of her time.'

No doubt Ellen, like Irving, had faults of character and technique. Irving took himself too seriously, Ellen too light-heartedly, often breaking out in giggles on the stage when something seemed to her funny or absurd. To do her justice, the audience loved it. Irving was as obsessively punctual as the Prince of Wales, Ellen as maddeningly unpunctual as Princess Alexandra. Ellen was usually still slapping on her make-up when the call-boy sang out for the third time, 'Miss Terry. . . .'

She was seldom word-perfect, preferring to chatter with a group of adoring girls rather than learn her part. As time went on her memory became as bad as her concentration, and she had to plaster the stage furniture with pieces of paper on which she had written out her lines.

She was prone to cry on stage, being in fact England's greatest 'sob-stuffer' according to her son. Of course Teddy blamed the English public, who in the eighties always had their handkerchiefs at the ready. The real Ellen kept a small demon of wit and irony somewhere deep down inside her, but faced with her public she dared not let it out. So she and they wept happily together.

She was a fidget. Unlike the great Sarah Siddons who earned the praise of King George III for her repose, Ellen Terry could not keep still. It was partly the same hyperactivity that had assailed her in Freshwater (in a skit on *Faust* called 'Faust-and-Loose', the actress caricaturing Ellen made her stage entry by leaping over a stile) and partly the exhilarating effect of being in front of an audience: 'Though I may *seem* like myself to others', Ellen wrote to Shaw, 'I never *feel* like myself when I am acting, but someone else, so nice, and so young and so happy, and always in-the-air, light, and bodyless.' She felt literally carried out of herself. In order to hold her down, a mass of precious stones were sewn on to her dress for Queen Katherine in *Henry VIII*, until poor Ellen was so heavily weighted that she could not stand up and had to order half the ballast to be cut off and thrown overboard. The ageing Irving found her a considerable weight, however, as the dead Cordelia who had to be carried bodily on to the stage. Ellen would lie down on a table-top, Irving would whisper, 'Now then – ready?' spit on his hands, and off they went.

Shortly before their first American tour in 1883, the Irving-Terry partnership put on *Romeo and Juliet* at the Lyceum. Henry James was sarcastic about 'the large, the long, the mature Miss Terry' – aged thirty-six when Juliet was fourteen. But Ellen's reception in America matched her send-off from Liverpool by Oscar Wilde and Lillie Langtry, herself the mother of a natural daughter and an actress whose beauty might have made her a rival had she possessed even half of Ellen's talent. Ellen was to spend a total of five years of her life in America, and she came to feel 'half American'.

It was the American women with whom she had her real love-affair.

They share in her fame . . . [wrote Joseph Hatton in the *New York Tribune*] There is a sort of trades unionism among the women of America in this respect. They hold together in a ring against the so-called lords of creation, and the men are content to accept . . . a happy form of petticoat government.

During the eighties Ellen's daughter and son were christened, given god-parents, several new first names and their third new surname. While travelling in Scotland Ellen had seen the great rock Ailsa Craig. 'What a good stage name! A pity you can't have it Ted. I shall give it to Edy.' So Edy became Ailsa Craig when she first went on the stage and remained Edith Craig when she took to costume design; while Ted became Edward Gordon Craig, the distinguished designer of stage architecture. Their mother had magicked both Godwin and Wardell away.

Perhaps one reason was Ellen's absorbing devotion to Irving. As over her relations with Watts, there is an insoluble controversy. Those who believe they were not lovers argue the unacceptable risks of Henry's leading lady suddenly being cast from her pedestal by the arrival of an illegitimate child. There is also an argument from temperament, Henry being too much the complete egotist and Ellen cherishing an artist's inner citadel against all mankind. Shaw called her an *'aluminium*-hearted wretch'. The argument in favour of their being lovers seems stronger. Blanche Patch, Shaw's future secretary, used to hear Ellen and Henry talking in their next-door garden at Winchelsea, and see Ellen dancing on the grass in a transparent nightdress. They certainly 'cohabited' in a literal sense. They arrived at and left the theatre together, driving about London in a carriage 'like two great babies in a giant perambulator', scoffed Shaw. Ellen mothered Henry by warming his numbed feet on her stomach under her dress. Or was it mothering? George Meredith in his poem *Modern Love* (1897) was to write, 'My feet were nourished on her breasts all night.' Was Ellen's maternal love 'modern love' after all? When actually asked by Marguerite Steen, a companion in her later years, whether she had been Irving's mistress, Ellen replied, 'Of course I was. We were terribly in love for a while.' However, this may have been nothing more than the hyperbole of theatrical language.

Whether or not Ellen and Henry became technically lovers they certainly exchanged letters in the language of love. 'With all my love my dearest dearest', Henry wrote in 1885. In 1887, 'You were very lovely my darling – You yourself – alone – and there is nothing in the world beside you. . . .' In 1891, 'My own dear wife, as long as I live.' In a letter dated 23 October to Henry, Ellen wrote, 'Dear – I'm better now and hope to come back to work to-morrow – I was dreadfully ill. . . . Thank you for *missing* me! and for your loving letter. Your Nell.'

Halfway through the nineties, their partnership was beginning to crumble. Ellen's diary often referred to quarrels, and Henry was dispirited at the appearance of rivals to the Lyceum and Shakespeare: modern English drawing-room comedies by Pinero, Jones and Wilde, and Norwegian problem-plays by a fellow named Ibsen. It was not till 1902 that the Lyceum closed its doors, but the ties between Ellen Terry and Henry Irving had already fallen apart. He had a new love in Mrs Eliza Aria, a Jewish journalist who had fallen for his sympathetic rendering of Shylock. One day to Ellen's amazement Irving failed to find a role for her. 'Oh, well for the present, at all events,' he said, 'there's no chance of acting at the Lyceum. For the present, you can, of course, er, *do as you like*!'

The loyal Ellen blamed Shakespeare rather than Irving for not giving old ladies enough good parts. As Dame Peggy Ashcroft was later to remark, Juliet's Nurse was unique. Why did Shakespeare write so few parts for *mothers*? asked Ellen, showing her mixture of 'Little Nelly' and the feminist Ellen Terry.

Meanwhile in 1892 the greatest correspondence of Ellen Terry's life began and at the same time the great love of Bernard Shaw's. There is no doubt Shaw loved Ellen with all his heart and imagination, though they did not really meet for fourteen years; an astounding story. A mere photograph of her glimpsed in the street would shake him with desire. Nevertheless theirs was to remain 'a paper courtship'. Because of Shaw's sexual problems, Ellen became his 'Mother-Sweetheart', the woman who would 'found a divine race' with him – but only in dreams. No doubt there were moments when he longed to scrap his own phrase and live with her – for Shaw had experienced sex with two women, one of them the feminist actress Florence Farr.

No doubt Ellen also had lonely moments, particularly during her disenchantment with Irving and before Shaw married Charlotte Payne-Townshend in 1898. Then perhaps Ellen would have liked their love to be recorded on something less flimsy than paper; perhaps even on the deeply peaceful double bed so much acclaimed by the great star Mrs Pat Campbell in comparison with the 'hurly-burly of the *chaise longue*'. Nevertheless the wonderful series of Terry-Shaw letters would have been sadly curtailed if they had 'kept house' together, and we must be thankful that neither of their citadels fell.

Shaw's ostensible purpose in maintaining for so many years his tremendous paper barrage of adoration, praise, criticism, wit and banter was to wean his glorious Ellen ('Ellen, Ellen, Ellen, Ellen, Ellen, Ellen, Ellen, Ellen, Ellen, Eleanor, Ellenest') away from that agreeable fool Irving ('intoxicated by the humming of his words in his nose . . . no brains') and to turn her either towards Ibsen, or better still towards Shakespeare's only rival, the 'greatest', the only, the inimitable G.B.S. He lambasted the Terry-Irving partnership for not fulfilling its highest destiny. 'Irving's thirty years at the Lyceum', wrote Shaw, 'though a most imposing episode in the history of the English theatre, were an exasperating waste of the talent of the two artists who had seemed to me peculiarly fitted to lift the theatre out of its old ruts and head it towards unexplored regions of drama.' At the Lyceum he found 'the woman who OUGHT to have played [Ibsen's] The Lady from the Sea – the woman with all the nameless charm, all the skill, all the force, in a word, all the genius – playing – guess what? why, a charade. . . .' The 'charade' was Reade's *Nance Oldfield*, a popular favourite though certainly unworthy of Ellen's talent.

But Shaw's 'unexplored regions of drama', particularly when they led to the Northern darkness of Ibsen, could never be Ellen's forte. Mrs Siddons, the great tragedy queen and 'an appalling creature on the stage', could have given Hedda Gabler plenty of ferocity, whereas Ellen Terry was all happiness and human sympathy.

There were touches of Ellen in Shaw's *Candida* (the 'Virgin-Mother') and in his *Man of Destiny* (the tall 'Strange Lady' with her 'vigorous hands and feet' and 'radiant charm'). But Shaw could never make a 'New Woman' of Ellen, as he had of the Ibsenite actress Janet Achurch; and after his marriage to Charlotte he virtually gave up trying. The nearest he got was when, after many false starts, he eventually persuaded Ellen to act in his own *Captain Brassbound's Conversion* in 1906, playing the part of Lady Cecily Waynflete; a part specially written for Ellen some ten years before and based on a mixture of her character and Mary Kingsley's.

Ellen and G.B.S. had to meet at last for rehearsals, thus breaking that strangest of touch-me-not spells. And Ellen did not feel she ever played Lady Cecily exactly as G.B.S. wanted. It was not her fault. Shaw was making a point about Ellen, through Lady Cecily, that was only half valid. In Lady Cecily he had drawn the newest New Woman, a 'renunciator' of sex who converts and reforms other people because she never gets involved herself. The nub of Shaw's message came in the play's last line, when Captain Brassbound has almost mesmerized Lady Cecily into loving him. At the very peak of their sex-duel, news suddenly reaches him which sends him hurrying back to sea. Lady Cecily recovers herself, bringing down the curtain on the words, 'And what an escape!'

That Ellen could never escape her double role of sexy Little Nelly and untouchable Great Terry was aptly proved by an event during the first rehearsal. A well-built young American with black hair and high Indian cheekbones named James Carew had been hired to play Captain Kearney. 'Who's that?' asked Ellen. She crossed over to him with her famous long rhythmic stride and 'lilywhite' hands outstretched. There was no 'escape'. They toured together and were married in 1907 in Pittsburgh. But though a 'good actor and a good fellow', poor Jim could not stay the course. As William Siddons said of his Sarah, 'She's too big for me.' They separated amicably, leaving behind only kind feelings which incidentally gave rise to the best anecdote of Nell's old age. Carew came to visit her at Smallhythe. Her memory had almost gone and her sight had failed.

'Tell me, Jim,' she suddenly said, '. . . did I kick you out or did you kick me out?'

'Well, dear, I think we arranged it between us, didn't we?' A pause. Then Ellen again,

'Yes, so we did. Dam' fools weren't we.'

Apart from Shaw's comedy, Ellen Terry made one other attempt to get away from the old Lyceum repertoire. After the parting from Irving she decided to become an 'actress-manageress' (Shaw's expression) and put on Ibsen. The result was disastrous. She chose Ibsen's *Vikings*, whose stormy heroine Hiordis was beyond even Ellen's empathy. Ted Craig her son contributed to the fiasco by designing a set so magnificent that it bankrupted his mother. She lost all her savings. For Ellen was no Sarah Bernhardt, an actor-manager of genius and the best man among them.

When Ellen could no longer act she took the same way out as Mrs Siddons, giving seductive lectures and readings, which she regarded as her contribution to the women's movement. Ellen's speciality was Shakespeare's women, whom she professed to find generally 'strong' characters. At the back of her mind may have been several considerations: a bold attempt to contradict Shaw by showing that Portia and Beatrice were every bit as 'strong-minded' as his Mrs Clandon and Gloria, the New Women in *You Never Can Tell* – and much more charming; a demonstration that if Shakespeare's women were 'strong', Ellen who impersonated them could not be 'weak', as some critics averred. Her alleged weakness had shown chiefly perhaps in Lady Macbeth. She 'humanized' her as she had 'humanized' Katherine the shrew and Helen Heartwell, by seeing the good in them. 'She was a woman', wrote Ellen of the character she called familiarly 'Lady Mac', just as she called the fatal banquet in *Macbeth* a 'royal tea-party'. Henry Labouchere the journalist, theatrical owner and MP, criticized Ellen's Lady Macbeth for being 'an aesthetic Burne-Jonesy, Grosvenor Gallery version'. Perhaps Ellen did indeed find it easier to impersonate Bunthorne's bride than Macbeth's.

Lastly there was Ellen's need to keep working. As she once said to her son, 'One's work is the best of us all – don't you think so? With most folks I've met, I've loved their work better than them.' Her high, humble idea was to be a 'useful' member of the great theatrical profession.

After moving about in London, from comfortable 10 Barkston Gardens to charming 215 Kings Road, to a dark flat in St Martin's Lane, she settled in her timbered Tudor cottage at Smallhythe in Kent. There she would ride 'a lovely tricycle' – 'it made me feel better' – and drive a pony-trap. Her bedroom was a model of simplicity and her silver-backed hand mirror so small that she could not have seen half her face in it. She wrote at Teddy's old school desk. On her bedside table were a small crucifix and a Shakespeare.

Her rural peace was probably less deep than it might have been because of the animosities between Ted and Edy. Ted said the female threesome living next door in the Priest's house bossed Ellen unmercifully. They were Edy, Christabel Marshall ('Christopher St John' the writer) and the painter Clare ('Tony') Atwood. Edy said that Ted neglected Ellen. Certainly Ellen could never see enough of her son and his children. She did not meet the most romantic of all her many grandchildren, legitimate and illegitimate, for Deirdre, the love-child of Ted and the great dancer Isadora Duncan, was tragically drowned in the Seine with her half-brother Patrick.

Ellen's theatrical honours had been lavish. At her Golden Jubilee matinee on 12 June 1906, Enrico Caruso, Eleanora Duse, Herbert Beerbohm Tree, Johnston Forbes-Robertson and a great 'Pride of Terrys' performed. Over two hundred theatre people autographed a huge sheet of paper for her. George Bernard Shaw wrote for her:

> Oh, Ellen, was it kind of Fate
> To make your youth so thrifty
> That you are young at fifty-eight
> Whilst we are old at fifty.

Henry Irving was old at sixty-seven and had died the year before.

Ellen Terry in old age.

Ellen Terry died on 18 July 1928, the centenary year of Ibsen's birth. In 1925 she had been created a Dame Grand Cross; Irving had been knighted in 1895. She was buried in the actors' church of St Paul's, Covent Garden; he in Westminster Abbey. Why the difference? Her admirers were outraged that their petition for the Abbey was turned down. Quite simply she was a woman. Of course she had been divorced whereas Irving had merely deserted his wife. But the double-standard went deeper than the divorce. Its root had been brilliantly stated on behalf of all her sisters by Sarah Siddons in conversation with the poet Samuel Rogers. Sarah was comparing the retirement honours of her brother John Kemble with her own. 'Ah, Mr Rogers,' she sighed, 'perhaps in the next world women will be more valued than they are in this.'

HARRIET BEECHER STOWE

1811–1896

'Dear Reader', as Mrs Stowe would say when introducing a controversial idea into her story, 'dear reader', you may well ask why the author of the most famous of all American novels, *Uncle Tom's Cabin*, is suddenly discovered in a gallery of Victorian women. I must admit that Mrs Stowe's presence here might seem a case of sleight of hand. Her admission can be defended none the less without guile. She was what we mean by 'Victorian' in many of her feelings; her dates correspond; she made three trips to Victorian England and fitted in as neatly as a billiard ball dropping into its pocket; her influence on the Victorians was enormous, her friendships – especially with Lady Byron and George Eliot – were both baleful and benign and her popularity was as prodigious in Britain as in America and lasted longer. She was indeed an honorary Victorian.

Harriet Beecher Stowe, to be hailed by Professor Denis W. Brogan as 'one of the most important women of modern times', was born on 13 June 1811 at Litchfield in the state of Connecticut, New England, the seventh of nine children. Her father, Lyman Beecher, was a renowned Congregationalist minister. In the preface to the novel *The Minister's Wooing* (1859), Harriet recommended her work 'to the kindly thoughts of that British fireside from which the fathers and mothers of America first went out to give English ideas and institutions a new growth in a new world'. The New England woman, she wrote, possessed 'a sort of trim well-kept air of ladyhood that sat jauntily upon her'. Among the men, those old English ideas had produced a 'tone of life' in New England that was 'habitually earnest and solemn'. However, Lyman Beecher was more original and eccentric than solemn. All the Beechers in fact were known for eccentricity among their conventional neighbours.

Tales were told of this formidable man's extravagant acts in the home, such as ducking his beloved eldest daughter Catherine in the wash-tub and dangling her out of the window to see how long she could endure without crying. (She endured as long as he kept her there.) And in his library he kept the poetry of Byron. Like Byron himself, Dr Lyman Beecher was deeply moved by Milton's Satan. He felt he might have understood and converted both the fallen angels, given the chance. Harriet was allowed by her father to read Byron and Scott as a girl, even though romantic literature, novels and plays were taboo among Calvinists. The twin strands of rebellion and intense piety were thus interwoven in Harriet's mind from childhood.

Her mother Roxana Foote, a charming lady of good Episcopalian family, was much admired in her day. Unfortunately she died when Harriet was five; Harriet not only lost a mother, but also found a mythical saint. It was generally accepted among Roxana's bereaved children that she watched over them from above. As a result the adult Harriet tended to translate her fictional females to heaven halfway through her novels, which made for weak plots. Lady Byron was to be in a sense the 'Saint Roxana' of Harriet's real life.

When Lyman remarried in 1817 (he was twice widowed and had a total of eleven children) little Harriet said sharply to her beautiful young step-mother, Harriet Porter of Boston, 'because you have come and married my pa, when I am big enough I mean to go and marry your pa.' The six-year-old child already had a strong sense of justice.

In the home of grandmother Foote, with whom she lived for some time after her mother's death, she found much kindness. Nevertheless at eight Harriet was considered an 'odd' little girl who pulled faces and liked being laughed at. The reason for her faces may have been hidden in her intense shyness. She probably suffered from the kind of 'tic' that many bright children display and felt too shy to explain that she didn't grimace on purpose; in any case she was pleased to win attention. Two years later she was shyer and odder than ever, having become a bookworm. She began with the *Arabian Nights*, found in her father's attic. The eyes fixed on the pages of romance were the Beecher blue-grey. The hair, which fell forward, was brown and thick, the parted lips sensual. She was physically as tiny as Charlotte Brontë; indeed when Charlotte enquired about her height during her first fame, it pleased her to find that the great Harriet Beecher Stowe was only five feet tall.

She was fortunate in her siblings. One of her three brothers, Henry Ward Beecher, had from the beginning been as dear to her as Isaac Evans was to his sister Mary Ann (George Eliot). Henry was to describe the Litchfield of his and Harriet's past as 'blessed for childhood'. Her sister Catherine was a powerful influence in Harriet's early life. Thanks to Catherine's own genius for teaching, Harriet escaped the Brontë-type horror of boarding-school for motherless girls and afterwards the servitude of a governess. Catherine Beecher had been engaged to a Professor Fisher who was drowned off the Irish coast. He left Catherine 2,000 dollars, with which she started a girls' school of her own at Hartford, Maine. Catherine's tragedy was Harriet's opportunity. She entered her sister's Hartford Female Seminary at thirteen, as a student, then became an assistant to Catherine and finally, at eighteen, a teacher.

As a deeply religious girl brought up a Calvinist, Harriet could hardly expect to escape a crisis of moral self-doubt. The year she went to Hartford she had been 'converted'; that is, she had become supernaturally aware of belonging to the small body of 'elect' whom God had pre-ordained for heaven. Harriet's faith in her election, however, was not strong enough to bring her through her teens without religious trials. 'I do nothing right. . .', she wrote at fourteen to her eldest brother the Rev. Edward Beecher; 'I am beset behind and before and my sins take away all my happiness.' Next year Edward was listening to a fresh wail: 'I wish I wish I could die young . . . rather than live, a trouble to everyone.' She was not really a 'trouble' to anyone but herself. Though her father struck up a close relationship with his odd daughter when he moved to Boston in 1817, her devoted brother Henry still saw her as 'owling about', blind to all but her books. She had no gift for communication, except on paper. A pathetic record of a youthful attempt to break down her shyness has survived:

I am trying to cultivate a general spirit of kindliness toward everybody. Instead of shrinking into a corner to notice how other people behave, I am holding out my hand to the right and to the left, and forming casual or incidental acquaintances with all who will be acquainted with me. In this way I find society full of interest and pleasure. . . .

In fact, Harriet's pleasure in other people was that of a potential novelist: watching Aunt Esther Beecher for the future Miss Ophelia of *Uncle Tom's Cabin* and memorizing anecdotes of the past for *Oldtown Folks* or *Poganuc People*. Henry James, many years later, was to describe her as 'vaguely observant, slightly wool-gathering, letting her eyes wander all over the place. . . .'

Though there were occasional recurrences of depression, Harriet had the dual key to her happiness in her possession by the time she was sixteen. Dual, because it opened the way to serving God and to serving her God-given talents at the same time. 'I do not mean to live in vain', she wrote. 'He has given me talents, and I will lay them at His feet. . . .' Teaching she did not feel was one of those talents. While Catherine wanted to stretch her wings and organize girls' education on a grand scale, Harriet wished to write – schoolbooks if necessary. Great changes were to come in all their lives when Lyman Beecher was invited to be president of Lane Theological Seminary, Cincinnati. The Beecher family moved west in November 1832.

View of Cincinnati across the Ohio *c.* **1835. Apart from one visit to a plantation,
Harriet's view of the slave state of Kentucky was all she saw of slavery.**

Domestic life for Harriet during the Cincinnati years was not the true rain that watered her developing genius. Nevertheless it comes first in the story. She was still living at home as a teacher and listening dutifully to her father's 'Beecheriana'. He would pray, 'O Lord, grant that we may not despise our rulers – and grant that they may not act *so we can't help it.*' His daughter wrote 'A New England Sketch' as a sideline, won a prize in a literary magazine and published a best-selling school geography. Whenever she needed a pen name she became a man, 'Franklin'.

Meanwhile a newly-wed girl named Eliza was brought to Cincinnati by her young husband Calvin Ellis Stowe, the learned biblical scholar appointed to Lane Seminary under Dr Beecher. Harriet took one look at the ethereal bride and 'I fell in love with her directly'. Alas, Eliza died young. Harriet does not seem to have fallen in love with the bereaved Mr Stowe 'directly' or even passionately, but she consented to marry him on 6 January 1836. She had nursed the dying Eliza. Now it was her duty to 'mother' the widower. He like her father was what the family called a 'hypo'. In Mrs Stowe's opinion all good wives became mothers to their husbands whether the husbands were hypochondriacs or not.

She and Calvin did not make a handsome pair. He was stocky and inclined to fat, being excessively greedy. His huge head was already balding though he was only thirty-three; his eyebrows were too bushy and his humour too folksy. Harriet at twenty-four had a little too much of everything except legs, which tadpoled off to almost nothing. She also had too much character, energy and genius for Calvin Ellis Stowe, and wore the trousers while 'mothering' him. Mothering meant teasing, criticizing, warning, nursing, loving and gratefully accepting his love.

The Stowes also shared certain powers and character defects. With his neurosis about his health Calvin had a propensity to see visions. Harriet was also to have her visions at a later date, but Calvin from childhood had been a natural medium, conducting psychic arguments with Goethe and the Devil, the latter of whom he drove off 'barking'.

In the 1840s he had religious doubts which Harriet was able to clear up for him in the 'thrilling paragraphs' of her bracing letters, such encouragement being a 'woman's part' in the home. He seems to have doubted even his power to resist wine and women but again had his morale boosted by his wife.

What terrible temptations lie in the way of your steps [she wrote to him in 1844] – till now I never realized it – for though I did love you with an almost *insane* love before I married you I never knew yet or felt the pulsation which showed me that I could be tempted in that way – there never was a moment when I felt anything by which you could have drawn me astray – for I loved you as I now love God – and I can conceive of no higher love – and as I have no passion – I have no jealousy, – the most beautiful woman in the world could not make me jealous so long as she only *dazzled the senses* – but still, my dear, you must not wonder if I want to warn you not to look or *think* too freely on womankind. If your sex would guard the outworks of *thought*, you would never fall. . . .

What did Harriet mean by writing of her almost *insane* love for Calvin before marriage? She cannot have meant physical passion, for this she specifically ruled out. 'Obsessive' may be near to her meaning; if so it suggests that her sexual feelings, never strong, were atrophied by life with Calvin, which incidentally included excessive and painful child-bearing. A substitute for erotic feeling was later to be found in other tumultuous emotions, such as righteous indignation, compassion and the 'pulsation' of the creative urge.

Harriet herself was something of a 'hypo'; with more excuse. The poverty of her life during the 1840s was perpetually wearing if not grinding. From 1838 onwards she had been writing to augment the family income. The births of six of her seven children took place in Cincinnati, and one of them left her a wretched invalid for months. By 1845 she was writing with her pen dipped in the kitchen sink:

My dear Husband, – It is a dark, sloppy, rainy, muddy, disagreeable day, and I have been working hard (for me) all day in the kitchen, washing dishes, looking into closets, and seeing a great deal of that dark side of domestic life. . . . I am sick of the smell of sour milk, and sour meat, and sour everything . . . and everything smells moldy; and altogether I feel as if I never wanted to eat again.

Rather surprisingly considering their straitened circumstances, Harriet was able to take the 'water-cure' in Brattleboro, being away from May 1846 to the next March. She conceived her sixth child immediately on her return, and the old hard cycle started up again. Calvin followed her to Brattleboro and while he was absent in 1849 Harriet went through the worst experience of her life. Cholera was recurrent in Cincinnati, but 1849 brought a scourge of horrific proportions. On 4 July over 1,000 victims were buried in a town whose population had been only 6,000 a decade before. Harriet herself fell ill and her new baby Charley sickened and died. She never completely lost the humility which these unhappy years brought her. That they were indeed unhappy is shown by many throw-away sentences in her letters.

'I must have a room to myself, which shall be *my* room', she demanded of Calvin, desperately trying to write something more paying than letters to an unsympathetic husband. To Georgy May, her old school friend, she plaintively described how 'dolefully uninteresting' she had become, but hoped to 'grow young again one of these days'.

Calvin could be as critical of her as she of him. He lists some of his 'grievances' in a letter to her of 1845:

I must clean the stable, wash the carriage, grease the wheels, black my boots, etc. etc. but you scorn to sweep the carriage, you must always call your servant to do it, and not stoop yourself to so menial an art. This makes me mad, for you are not too good to do in your line what I am everyday obliged to do in mine ... affectionately C.E.S.

Yet however ironical that word 'affectionately' may sound, Calvin was as dependent on Harriet as she was loyal to him. 'If you were not already my dearly loved husband', she once wrote during this dismal period, 'I should certainly fall in love with you.'

If Harriet's domestic life in Cincinnati was to bring her moral strength through her own misery, her strength as a writer was virtually created by the misery of others. For Cincinnati was within striking distance of human misery on a vast and poignant scale.

The Ohio river marked the boundary between the 'free' state named after it and the Southern 'slave' state of Kentucky. From a vantage point in Ohio Harriet could look across the water and see Kentucky's nearest slave settlements. Now and then a slave would escape from a plantation, flee over the water and hope to be helped on his way to the free North, perhaps as far as Canada. Some of the Ohioans would wish to help him, others to hunt him. The Beechers and Stowes once found themselves among the helpers. Harriet and Calvin were employing a black girl who said she was free. It turned out that she was a hunted slave and Calvin, aided by Henry Beecher, helped her to escape North by the famous 'underground railroad'.

This girl was not the first escaped slave to come to Harriet's notice. There were always public advertisements for runaways.

A 100 DOLLARS REWARD

A. W. Gains of Boone County, Kentucky, would pay the above reward for the recapture of 'Humphrey', a slave, who is about 17 years of age. . . .

In this case there was nothing about a reward for capturing the fugitive 'alive *or dead*'. But that was soon to come. The Beechers had arrived in Ohio at the very time when American history was taking a twist into regions of hideous danger, violence and ultimately of heroism.

American slavery and the causes of the Civil War of 1861–65 are still under discussion. Sufficient for Harriet's story that the new technology on the plantations, coupled with the acquisition of new American territories, brought about a great increase in the economic value of slaves. As the progressive slave-owner Mr Clayton says in Mrs Stowe's *Dred* (1856): 'From the day that they began to open new territories to slavery, the value of this kind of property mounted up so as to make emancipation a moral impossibility.' More slaves could pick more cotton and clean it more efficiently than ever before.

True, the African slave *trade* had been abolished three years before Harriet was born. But slavery was self-perpetuating unless drastically dealt with, for slaves bred slaves – or rather slaves were bred from slaves for the market, as in battery farming. There was in fact an internal slave trade still.

But the Northern states had liberated all their slaves by 1776, the year of

This poster, printed one year before the American Civil War, is typical of its kind. Under the Fugitive Slave Law of 1850 all American citizens were obliged to hunt down runaway slaves, but many people shared the Beechers' defiance of the law.

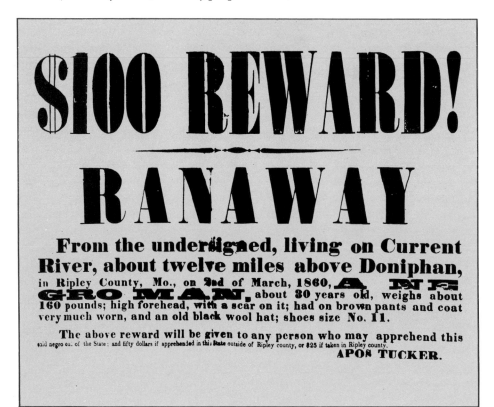

American Independence from Britain. It was not till nearly sixty years later, in 1833, that Britain followed suit, declaring the emancipation of slaves in West Indian plantations.

The year 1833 had also been a landmark for Harriet Beecher. She had paid her first and only visit to a slave plantation, when she was twenty-two. A quiet retiring girl, her friends noticed she was particularly quiet on this occasion. Could she be bored? Far from it. Harriet Beecher was at her favourite game; this time deeply engrossed in observing the black boys and girls, black 'uncles' and 'aunts', who in twenty years' time were to be described clustering round their weak but well-intentioned Kentucky 'mas'r', Mr Shelby, in *Uncle Tom's Cabin*.

Perhaps as the Beecher party returned to Ohio on the ferry they discussed the horrors of slave uprisings. Only two years earlier, an educated slave and preacher in Virginia named Nat Turner had thrown off his chains. Was he hero or hell-hound? Fifty-five whites had been murdered. The year 1831 also saw the publication of William Lloyd Garrison's *Liberator* in Boston, with his anti-slavery trumpet call, '*I will be heard*'. And then, only two years after Harriet's visit to Kentucky, there was white violence in Cincinnati itself and disruption in Lane Seminary over the anti-slavery issue.

Tempers were rising as the economic implications of slavery made the South more tenacious and the North more censorious. One of Dr Beecher's students who had entered Lane in 1833 was Theodore Dwight Weld. In him Harriet saw her first 'abolitionist' who was to become famous. The abolitionists distinguished themselves sharply from moderate opponents of slavery like Harriet's father Dr Beecher. Within two years Weld had hived off from Lane, taking with him the best of Beecher's students. (He was later to marry one of the two famous Grimké sisters, champions of both Negro emancipation and women's rights.) At the same time racial tensions in general were boiling up. A clergyman in Alabama was hanged by a white mob for distributing anti-slavery literature, and another abolitionist who had been tortured by a Mississippi mob hanged himself. The following year race riots broke out in Cincinnati, whipped up by young whites of 'the better class'. A Negro quarter was destroyed and the offices of *The Philanthropist*, an abolitionist journal published by a Quaker, were sacked. On the second day of violence Harriet found her brother Henry pouring lead. 'What on earth are you doing?' she asked him. 'Making bullets, to kill men with.' However, the show of force by Henry and other volunteers brought the riots to an end.

This was only fringe activity, the small bubbles round the edge of a seething cauldron. Harriet heard about things at the heart of the struggle in the Deep South from her brother Charles, a clerk in New Orleans where the notorious slave-markets were held. Strangely, Harriet never visited New Orleans herself, though she was to write of Uncle Tom being sold there. Perhaps for this reason her picture of the beautiful and cruel city lacks atmosphere. Little Eva's house in New Orleans has the grandeur of a film set. Where are the fascinating balconies of Spanish ironwork or the exquisite secluded patios?

If Charles Beecher could not give his sister atmosphere he did give her a formidable model for her fiction. Simon Legree, the odious tyrant and slave-owner in *Uncle Tom's Cabin*, was based on a white overseer whom Charles had met on a Mississippi steamboat. The overseer showed Charles his huge fist, hard, swollen and knotty as an oak burl. He made Charles feel it and told him: 'I got that from knockin' down niggers.'

The year 1849 turned out to be Harriet's last year of misery and her last in Cincinnati. Calvin Stowe was offered a professorship at Bowdoin College, Brunswick, in Maine, and Harriet was glad to be trekking North once more. Her baby was left behind in his grave with all the other cholera victims. But Harriet was now carrying within her *Uncle Tom*.

The Stowes arrived in the North in 1850, the same year as the government took another big stride along the road to war. It was a legislative act known as the 'Compromise of 1850'. The Southern states had felt aggrieved because the new territory of California had been declared 'free', and to pacify them the government offered a *quid pro quo* in the form of a strengthening of the law against escaped slaves. The new Fugitive Slave Law of 1850 made it obligatory for all American citizens, of North or South, to hunt down and recapture slaves rather than aid their escape. Freedom in California was thus traded for tighter national shackles.

The North erupted with fury. 'Hattie, if I could use a pen as you can,' wrote the Rev. Edward Beecher's wife to her sister-in-law, 'I would write something that would make this whole nation feel what an accursed thing slavery is.' After reading this aloud to her young children and getting their enthusiastic reaction, Hattie declared, 'I *will* write something. I will if I live.' Her favourite brother Henry backed her up: 'Do it, Hattie.' He would see that whatever she wrote was circulated. But Uncle Tom could cut his own way through the growing tangle of argument.

Harriet and Henry were secret abolitionists; secret, because their revered father was always a 'meliorist' who believed in making things better gradually, without the abolitionists' explosions and corrosions. Many good people thought at this period that but for the abolitionists' heated propaganda – William Lloyd Garrison wanted slave states to be flung out of the Union – the more moderate states like Kentucky and Virginia would in due course have emancipated their slaves peacefully.

Mrs Stowe's form of abolition, however, was only marginally political. Her impetus, focus and drive were whole-heartedly religious. If Henry had made lead bullets to kill men, Harriet was about to create a silver bullet to pierce the heart of the evil thing itself.

One more personage had to be met by Harriet before she could begin melting and moulding her silver. She already had 'Simon Legree' from Louisiana, the 'Shelbys' from Kentucky, 'Miss Ophelia' from Connecticut, 'Topsy' from Calvin's memories of his youth in Natick, and many clerical models from Ohio, especially the Rev. John Rankin who would keep a lantern shining in his window all night to guide fugitive slaves across the river. Now, early in 1851,

LIBERTY LINE.
NEW ARRANGEMENT---NIGHT AND DAY.

The improved and splendid Locomotives, Clarkson and Lundy, with their trains fitted up in the best style of accommodation for passengers, will run their regular trips during the present season, between the borders of the Patriarchal Dominion and Libertyville, Upper Canada. Gentlemen and Ladies, who may wish to improve their health or circumstances, by a northern tour, are respectfully invited to give us their patronage.

SEATS FREE, *irrespective of color.*

Necessary Clothing furnished gratuitously to such as have *"fallen among thieves."*

"Hide the outcasts—let the oppressed go free."—*Bible.*

☞For seats apply at any of the trap doors, or to the conductor of the train.

J. CROSS, *Proprietor.*

N. B. For the special benefit of Pro-Slavery Police Officers, an extra heavy wagon for Texas, will be furnished, whenever it may be necessary, in which they will be forwarded as dead freight, to the "Valley of Rascals," always at the risk of the owners.

☞Extra Overcoats provided for such of them as are afflicted with protracted *chilly-phobia.*

In 1844 it was still possible to advertise the 'Underground Railroad'.

she met her major model for Uncle Tom himself, probably in Boston with her brother Edward. This was the Rev. ('Father') Josiah Henson, a Negro who had had both shoulders broken on a plantation in youth and an ear sliced off when he objected to an overseer's approaches to his wife; he was converted to Christianity, forgave his enemies, escaped by the underground railroad to Canada and founded a co-operative in 1841 for fugitive slaves at Dawn. He was to show the co-operative's products at the Crystal Palace Exhibition in 1851, and have an audience at Windsor with Queen Victoria herself.

With Henson's evidence to support what Harriet called her own 'most horrible vivid imagination' she had now only to sit down and write *Uncle Tom's Cabin*. But to sit down and write was not easy. She had six children (there was now another Charley, her last baby) and she does not seem to have got that room of her own until quite late in her career as a writer. We can imagine her scribbling *Uncle Tom* in the kitchen or on the back steps; or being summoned from her bedroom after only a few minutes' peace by the fish man, an apple seller, an agent, a friend, or other domestic demands. Yet it was a happy time – perhaps the happiest two years of Harriet's long life.

How did the miracle happen? How did this little poverty-bound housewife whose personality was said to be 'invisible', succeed in selling nearly 300,000 copies of her book in America in the first year, and more than a million in England. *Uncle Tom's Cabin* had two potent spell-binding charms: the vitality of its characters and the red-hot conviction of a message that is stamped on the reader's consciousness as if with a branding-iron. In his brilliant piece on Harriet

Beecher Stowe in *Patriotic Gore*, the critic Edmund Wilson, after noting that the book was in 'eclipse', as mere outworn 'propaganda', in the United States (though not in Europe) by the end of the nineteenth century, writes:

Out of a background of undistinguished narrative, inelegantly and carelessly written, the characters leap into being with a vitality that is all the more striking for the ineptitude of the prose that presents them. ... The Shelbys and George Harris and Eliza, Aunt Chloe and Uncle Tom project themselves out of the void. They come before us, arguing and struggling like real people who cannot be quiet ... in a drama that demands to be played to the end.

Harriet, who had been studying Scott, landed herself with two complex inter-related plots, one based on Eliza and George Harris, the other on Uncle Tom. The scene opens with a cynical slave-dealer named Haley bargaining with Mr Shelby, a kindly Kentuckian, over the sale of his trusted slave Tom. Mr Shelby is in debt and must sell some of his 'living property'. He tries to persuade Haley that Tom alone, a paragon of reliability and religious fervour, will cover the whole of his master's debt. 'Yes, I consider religion a valeyable thing in a nigger', agrees Haley, 'when it's the genuine article, and no mistake', but – 'haven't you a boy or gal that you could throw in with Tom?' Shelby reluctantly 'throws in' a handsome four-year-old quadroon boy, Eliza Harris's adored son Harry; Haley suggests that a gift of earrings or a new gown to Eliza, Mrs Shelby's much-loved personal slave, will easily make up for Harry's loss: 'These critters an't like white folks, you know; they gets over things, only managed right.' But the spirited Eliza cannot be 'managed'. She and her husband George Harris, a young mulatto slave on a neighbouring plantation, conspire to escape by the 'underground', Eliza and little Harry joining up with George across the Ohio river.

At this point a vivid thread running through both *Uncle Tom* and *Dred* must be picked out, for Harriet wove it in from her own experience. Her aunt Mary Hubbard had married a Jamaican planter who turned out to possess a family already – mulattoes. Aunt Mary left him; but the story remained in Harriet's mind and, having given us the Harrises and Cassy in *Uncle Tom*, reached a tragic climax in the black and white half-brothers, Harry and Tom Gordon in *Dred*.

Eliza's escape over the frozen Ohio with Harry in her arms and Haley and his tracking dogs at her heels shows the pace of Harriet's narrative at its best:

Right on behind they came; and nerved with strength such as God gives only to the desperate, with one wild cry and flying leap, she vaulted sheer over the turbid current by the shore on to the raft of ice beyond ... the huge green fragment of ice on which she alighted pitched and creaked as her weight came on it, but she stayed there not a moment ... stumbling, leaping, slipping; springing upward again! Her shoes were gone – her stockings cut from her feet – while blood marked every step; but she saw nothing, felt nothing, till dimly, as in a dream, she saw the Ohio side, and a man helping her up the bank.

The man is a white farmer. 'I don't see no kind o' 'casion for me to be hunter and catcher fer other folks', he decides, thus breaking the 1850 Fugitive Slave

Law and allowing Eliza to continue on her perilous flight. We should note that a Quaker woman, who has lost her 'little Henry' and gives Eliza the pathetic baby clothes for Harry, is Mrs Stowe herself remembering the disposal of the first little Charley's things. As for Eliza's agony, Mrs Stowe was later to say that only after losing her own child did she fully understand the wickedness of tearing children from their slave mothers. The horrible irony of a Christian nation adopting this practice is brought out by Haley's friend Marks: 'If we could get a breed of gals that didn't care, now, for their young 'uns', says Marks, 'tell ye, I think 'twould be 'bout the greatest mod'n improvement I knows on.'

Meanwhile Uncle Tom is holding a prayer-meeting before he is sold down river: 'O Canaan, bright Canaan, I'm bound for the land of Canaan.' The description of his departure from his family and cabin might be a page from *Animal Farm*. 'Haley whipped up the horse, and with a steady, mournful look fixed to the last on the old place, Tom was whirled away.'

Tom's unexpectedly happy months with the St Clare family in New Orleans show how fair Mrs Stowe was resolved to be to the South. With the St Clares she pictured slavery at its best, according to plan: 'I shall show in the most lifelike and graphic manner possible slavery, its reverses, changes, the *best side* of the thing, and something *faintly approaching the worst.*'

When Eva St Clare returns home after an absence she embraces all the house slaves in turn; a form of contact which revolts her aunt from the North, Miss Ophelia. 'Well, you Southern children can do something that *I* couldn't.' And the dreadful Simon Legree, it has often been pointed out, was a Northerner from Vermont.

St Clare intends to give Tom his freedom after little Eva expires in a deathbed scene that Dickens himself might have envied. But St Clare is killed in a brawl and Eva's selfish mother (significantly a 'hypo') puts Tom up to auction in the slave-market.

Then begins the 'crucifixion' of Tom by Simon Legree. Tom rejects the favoured post of overseer on Legree's plantation since it would be at the cost of brutalizing and battering his fellow slaves. When the slave-girls Cassy and Emmeline run away, on Tom's advice, he obstinately refuses to tell the mad-dened, blood-thirsty Legree where they are hiding: 'I know, mas'r; but I can't tell anything. *I can die!*' He is accordingly beaten to death by two ferocious blacks on Legree's orders. Dying, he forgives all three – and thereby converts his two repentant black persecutors to Christianity.

Perhaps Harriet made an artistic mistake in arranging for this dual conversion. Fortunately she stopped short at a triple ceremony including Legree. She certainly erred in sending off the incorrigible 'Topsy', Miss Ophelia's personal slave, to preach to her heathen brethren in Africa. But it was no error on Harriet's part to create an Uncle Tom who took the tenets of Christianity – forgiveness, turning the other cheek and 'blessed are the meek' – in earnest.

It was vital that her Uncle Tom, her illiterate Negro, should be the only utterly committed male Christian in the story. All the white Christians are flawed in one way or another. On its deepest level the book is a basic, shattering

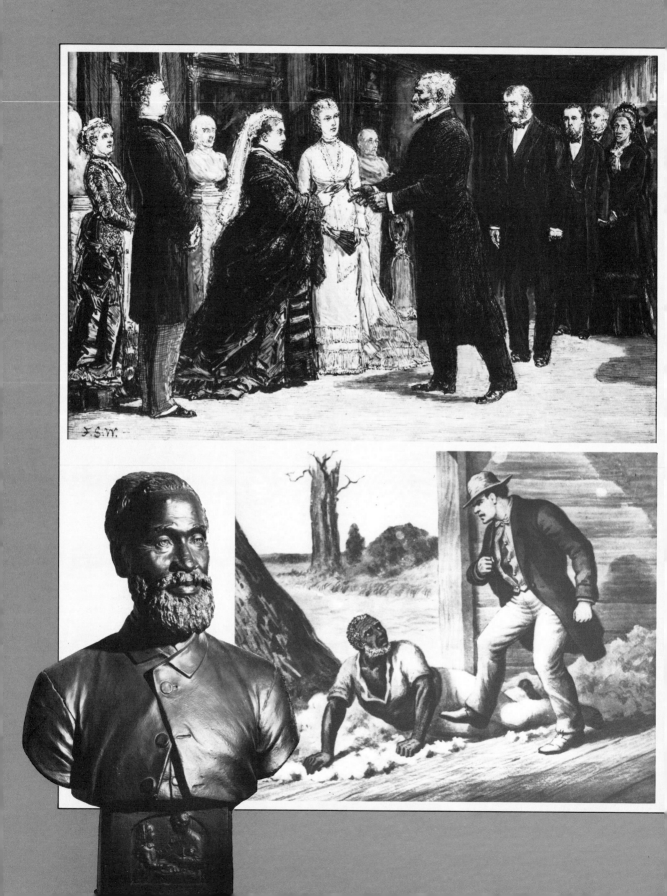

UNCLE TOM'S CABIN

UNCLE TOM & EVA·

TOPSY WITH MISS OPHELIA'S WARDROBE.

Harriet Beecher Stowe's model for Uncle Tom was 'Father' Josiah Henson *far left* who was received by Queen Victoria *above far left*. Uncle Tom was not only gentle with Little Eva *above left,* but took the Christian doctrine of 'turn the other cheek' to extreme lengths when he was killed *centre left*. Topsy *above*, however, when asked about the Creator answered, 'I spect I grow'd. Don't think nobody ever made me.' These characters and others burgeoned in Harriet's mind as she worked at her house in Maine *left*.

challenge to the Christianity which meant everything to Harriet Beecher Stowe. That challenge is thrown down through the institution of slavery. But the book's total message is of far more importance to Mrs Stowe than mere anti-slavery propaganda.

Through the black-white confrontation she epitomizes the whole idea of civilization's inexorable continuing choice between holiness and humbug. Even a minor character like the Negro Sam, who subtly impedes Haley's pursuit of Eliza, shows an understanding of the connection between the Bible and behaviour that is denied to most of the whites. 'Wal, missis,' Sam explains to Mrs Shelby, 'de Lord He preserves his own. Lizy's done gone over the river into 'Hio, as 'markably as if de Lord took her over in a chariot of fire and two hosses.'

Mrs Stowe is well aware that Tom's purely passive resistance can never be the human norm. 'Such a fellow as Tom, here,' says St Clare, 'is – is a moral miracle!' The normal human reactions to suffering are exemplified in Eliza's husband George Harris and Tom's wife Aunt Chloe. George believes in self-defence; he escapes with a gun and in fact shoots his pursuer in the legs. And when Tom parts from Chloe with the words 'Pray for them that 'spitefully use you', Chloe retorts, 'Pray for 'em! Lor, it's too tough! I can't pray for 'em.'

Nevertheless Tom must have the last word. 'It's natur, Chloe, and natur's strong, but the Lord's grace is stronger.' He has all along been in favour of Eliza running away from her lawful master. 'Let Eliza go – it's her right!' He agrees earlier with Aunt Chloe. 'I wouldn't be the one to say no – 'tan't in natur for her to stay. . . .' He is the spiritual exception who proves the human rule.

If Uncle Tom had upped and struck back, Legree might possibly have collapsed but the whole story would certainly have collapsed with him. This is proved by the contrasted spiritual and human origins of Harriet's inspiration.

She saw a vision of Uncle Tom's martyrdom in February 1851 just after receiving Communion at Brunswick Church. Harriet described her vision of Uncle Tom's death to her husband, who staunchly urged her, 'Hattie, you must go on. You must make up a story with this for the climax. The Lord intends it so.' For this reason Harriet was to say of *Uncle Tom's Cabin*, 'The Lord Himself wrote it' and 'it all came before me in visions. . . .'

Harriet's consistent story of her inspiration does not mean that she had a 'messianic delusion' as her otherwise sympathetic biographer Edward Wagenknecht suggests – unless of course all visions are messianic delusions, including Uncle Tom's own vision before he suffers martyrdom. During what might be called his agony in the plantation, he suddenly sees a vision of 'One crowned with thorns'; whereupon his own 'dread soul-crisis' is over. For though Legree has indeed bought him with gold, we are made to realize that Christ has bought him with blood.

Conversely, Eliza's escape was in no way visionary but probably inspired by

The popularity of *Uncle Tom's Cabin* was exploited by theatrical companies who continued to stage 'Uncle Tom' plays such as this one well into the next century. *Overleaf*: 'The Cotton Pickers' by Winslow Homer, 1876.

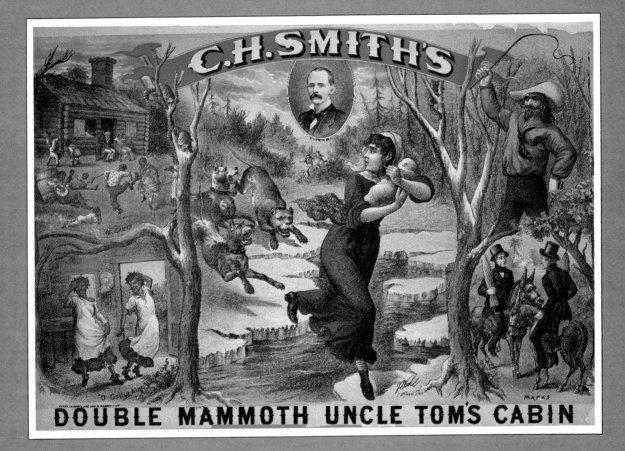

Harriet's down-to-earth conversations with the Rev. Josiah Henson. He is known to have regretted all his life advising a group of slaves *not* to run away, for they were subsequently sold down the river. Harriet's Uncle Tom had learned the lesson of 'Father' Henson.

The sensational success of her book in America caused the pirating of English and European editions. In 1853, the year after its publication, she and Calvin sailed to England on a combined promotional and sight-seeing tour.

Harriet was already aware of, and armoured against, stormy criticisms, especially from the pilloried Southern states: that she had purposely exaggerated the horrors; that plantation slaves were no worse off than English 'factory hands'; that in the words of Mr Jekyl in *Dred*, 'It pleased the Lord to foredoom the race of Ham'; that in any case Mrs Stowe had misrepresented and misquoted her opponents, both clerical and lay, especially a certain Rev. Joel Parker, who created a furore on the subject of a footnote in *Uncle Tom* offensive to himself. Harriet's most rabid critics declared that her descriptions of sexual assaults on slaves gave her obscene pleasure. Altogether she was a 'vile wretch in petticoats'.

Harriet Beecher Stowe in her prime could look after herself. Though she appeared to apologise to the Rev. Joel Parker she never corrected or cancelled the offending footnote. Nor did she fail to point out that all the horrors she had described could and did happen under slavery. By 1853 she had produced a best-selling *Key to Uncle Tom's Cabin*.

It was as an already famous and controversial figure that Harriet landed at Liverpool in April 1853. To hear her own language spoken in a foreign country gave her 'a strange, throbbing feeling'. But these feelings were nothing to the violent throbs that were to shake her as wave after wave of wild enthusiasm rolled over and around her; so overwhelmingly, indeed, that for a time she collapsed from physical and emotional exhaustion.

Of course the animosity of the Southern states found shrill echoes in English reviews: *The Times* attacked Mrs Stowe for making bad blood in her book and the *Spectator* denounced 'Tom-mania'.

Her unqualified admirers praised her in unison; Lord Palmerston read her book three times over for its statesmanship; the legal pundits Lords Denman and Cockburn extolled its services to humanity; the historian Macaulay acclaimed it as the most valuable addition that America had made to English literature; the Royal Academy showed 'Uncle Tom' paintings, and songwriters and playwrights crooned her theme. On the Continent Tolstoy invited *Uncle Tom* to share the throne of moral art with *A Tale of Two Cities* and *Les Misérables*, Heine compared it to the Bible and George Sand rapturously called its author a saint.

The beautiful and liberal Duchess of Sutherland became Harriet's patroness and Lord Shaftesbury, England's premier philanthropist, her patron. When he led her on to the platform at the annual festival of the British and Foreign Bible Society in Exeter Hall, the vast audience rose to its feet in homage.

Miniature of Lady Byron from Harrow School.

Invitations poured in from all over the United Kingdom. A meeting of celebrities at Stafford House, the Sutherlands' palatial London home, had already drafted an 'Affectionate Christian Address' against slavery, now to be presented to their 'Sisters' in America through Harriet Beecher Stowe, the greatest 'sister' in the world. The Stowes, however, were not received by Queen Victoria. But the omission was political not personal.

'I have heard from a high titled lady', wrote the American ambassador James Buchanan in November 1853, 'that the Queen had absolutely refused to see Mrs Stowe either at the Palace or the Duchess of Sutherland's. . . . She remarked very sensibly that American slavery was a question with which Great Britain had nothing to do.'

This report did less than justice to the Queen's personal feelings. Like virtually all the British reading public, Queen Victoria had devoured and become deeply involved in *Uncle Tom*.

What sort of impression did this most celebrated visitor make on England? Her own famous self-portrait speaks of 'a little bit of a woman, – somewhat more than forty – about as thin and dry as a pinch of snuff; never very much to look at in my best days, and looking like a used-up article now.' She kept up her modest Puritan image by not drinking wine in England or wearing the fashionable low-cut evening gowns; but she was pleased when the popular artist George Richmond produced a flattering portrait of her in crayon.

The poet Elizabeth Barrett Browning has left a tribute to Harriet's copious, dusky, wavy hair and freedom from 'rampant Americanisms'. But Mrs Browning found Harriet's mouth, from which issued such an unexpectedly pleasant low Yankee voice, neither frank nor sensitive enough for her taste. (This early criticism was to change into close friendship, when Harriet visited the Brownings' Italian home in 1860.)

By the time she had seen the best of Britain, in the form of the Scott country, the Shakespeare country and what she took to be Gray's country churchyard (though she wept in the wrong one), and the worst of Britain in the form of advertisements for London gin-palaces (as bad as 'slave-markets') and the railways ('such blind, confusing arrangements', she was to complain on her second visit) Calvin already itched for Andover and home. The Stowes had moved from Brunswick to Andover, Massachusetts, in 1852, where Calvin was Professor at the Seminary.

As the famous lady's husband, Calvin had had to answer for her at all public occasions; for a lady could not make an after-dinner speech. Calvin showed his New England spirit on one occasion when Lord Shaftesbury was denouncing slavery. If Britain would stop buying Southern cotton, retorted Calvin, slavery would peter out.

Harriet, however, had not seen nearly enough of this gloriously welcoming England, or of her new exciting friends. Her most interesting was George Eliot and her most precious Lady Byron. 'She is a noble, true woman', Harriet was to say of George Eliot apropos of her affair with George Lewes, 'and if anybody doesn't see it, so much the worse for *them*, and not her.' As for Byron's widow,

Harriet with her favourite brother Henry Ward Beecher.

Harriet was determined to meet this saintly character again when she, Harriet, returned for her second visit to England. Byron's poetry had given the young Harriet many wicked thrills, and now his widow gave her a 'strange mythological feeling' that demanded to be repeated and explored.

Harriet sailed again for England in 1856, finishing her second anti-slavery novel, *Dred: A Tale of the Great Dismal Swamp*, on board ship. It had only been published four weeks before 100,000 copies were spreading over England. 'After that who cares what critics say?' wrote Harriet. One of these copies was put into the hands of Queen Victoria by her private secretary, Colonel Grey, on 28 August at King's Cross station. Harriet was standing by her husband's side looking on.

The encounter had been 'accidental, done-on-purpose' according to Calvin, since it was now even more difficult for the Queen of England to meet such a notorious Northerner as Harriet Beecher Stowe. The Civil War was only five years away.

The discreet meeting took place when the Queen and Prince Albert happened to be standing at the window of the royal train, bound for Balmoral Castle, and the Stowes were on the platform, about to visit the Sutherlands at Dunrobin Castle. (Actually, Calvin made for home from Glasgow.) Calvin sent his account to a friend in Andover:

Yesterday, we had just the very pleasantest interview with the Queen that ever was. . . . The Queen seemed really delighted to see my wife. . . . She pointed us out to Prince Albert, who made two most gracious bows to my wife and two to me, while the four royal children stared their big blue eyes almost out of looking at the little authoress of *Uncle Tom's Cabin*. Colonel Grey handed the Queen, with my wife's compliments, a copy of the new book [*Dred*]. She took one volume herself and handed the other to Prince Albert, and they were soon both very busy reading. She is a real nice little body, with exceedingly pleasant manners.

The nice little body preferred *Dred* even to *Uncle Tom*, though there was not 'one good clergyman' in it, as the *Washington Independent* complained. But then the Queen herself did not consider most clergymen were specially 'good'. Nor did she subscribe to the criticism of Nassau Senior who found girls like Nina Gordon 'vulgar' and offensive to 'the taste of the best educated part of the English public'. Queen Victoria, though not perhaps 'best educated', criticized Nina's premature death rather than her 'vulgarity'. The Queen may also have noticed that there were no awkward comparisons drawn in *Dred*, as there had been in *Uncle Tom*, between the slaves in America and the Irish in the British Empire.

Queen Victoria kept Harriet in mind when they both returned from Scotland. Harriet was staying at Stoke Park near Windsor with the Laboucheres, friends she had met at Dunrobin. During her visit a royal invitation reached the Laboucheres for dinner at Windor Castle. There Queen Victoria questioned Lady Mary Labouchere closely about the Stowe family and *Dred*. The next day Harriet was exhilarated to meet the royal carriage while driving in Windsor Great Park. The Laboucheres drew to one side. The Queen bowed graciously. And the romantic Harriet remembered the occasion as 'one of the loveliest visits I have made'.

This delight in hobnobbing with the nobility and even royalty was to be criticized in Harriet, just as Uncle Tom's devotion to the whites was, and still is, severely censured. If Tom 'cringed', his creator 'grovelled'.

Having renewed her devotions to the languishing Lady Byron, Harriet was suddenly treated to a rivetting account of Lord Byron's incestuous love for his half-sister Augusta Leigh that had resulted in the birth of a daughter Medora. Lady Byron added that she had forgiven Augusta and befriended Medora. She asked Harriet if she should divulge the story in the interests of self-defence and truth.

Harriet's first reaction was to publish. But on discussing the matter all night with her sister Mrs Mary Perkins, who was also Lady Byron's guest, Harriet counselled her hostess to take no steps. Lady Byron should entrust the story to 'discreet friends' who would wait till the actors in the drama were all dead.

Harriet herself, alas, was not to follow her own wise advice. The 'facts' of Lady Byron's story remained vividly in her mind, unforgotten and unverified. If she had been able to research them as she had researched *Uncle Tom* and *Dred*, she would have found out that the last two alleged facts were untrue: Lady Byron neither forgave Augusta nor was loyal to Medora. And it has never been proved that Medora was Byron's child. The facts, however, mattered less to

Harriet than her own now proven friendship with the ill-used titled lady who had disclosed them, almost fainting as she spoke the word 'incest'. Harriet's farewell message to Lady Byron was a fitting commentary on her own infatuation. 'I left you', she wrote, 'with a strange throbbing feeling – you make me feel quite as I did years ago – a sort of girlishness quite odd for me.'

Lady Byron died in 1860 and nine years later Harriet appointed herself the 'discreet' friend, destined to reveal all. *Lady Byron Vindicated* (1870) created a sensation as great as *Uncle Tom*; indeed it is a wry tribute to Harriet's art that she wrote *two* of the most sensational books of her era. *Lady Byron Vindicated*, however, did her nothing but harm. The American magazine *Atlantic Monthly*, in which it was first serialized in 1869, lost 15,000 subscribers. One critic accused her of writing pornography. And among the angry readers of its English version in *Macmillan's Magazine* was Lady Byron's nearest surviving relative, her granddaughter Lady Anne Blunt, who spoke of 'the odious Stowe pamphlet'.

Meanwhile, before leaving for that last visit to England in 1856 Harriet had organized a monster petition against a proposal to extend slavery into the free states. Her brother Henry Ward Beecher was auctioning slaves from his pulpit in Brooklyn, in order to achieve their freedom. 'We shall see', said Harriet when they doubted her capacity to defeat the lawyers and politicians. 'We will see', said Henry when they mocked his holy auction; 'Pass the plate.' Someone else said that America was inhabited by saints, sinners and Beechers.

**The admiration and respect surrounding Uncle Tom's creator turned
to disgust when she exposed the Byron scandal.**

A   VOICE   FROM   THE   MIGHTY   DEAD.

SPIRIT OF BYRON :—"GRATUITOUS SLANDERER! WHOSE FAME WILL YOU BLAST NEXT FOR THE SAKE OF FILTHY LUCRE AND PUBLIC NOTORIETY!"
SHAKESPEARE to MILTON :—"HUMPH! OUR TURN MAY COME NEXT, JOHN, AS WE DID NOT LIVE HAPPILY WITH OUR WIVES!"
UNCLE TOM to EVA :—"LOR' A MUSSY, MISS EVA, AFTER PAINTING A NIGGER LIKE ME SO *WHITE*, HOW COULD SHE PAINT ONE OF HER OWN BRETHREN SO *BLACK!*"

John Brown's body, strung up after Harpers Ferry, combined with *Uncle Tom* and Henry Ward Beecher's auctions to help precipitate the Civil War. Harriet had little intrinsic interest in the Union. After the war had begun, she paid her celebrated visit to President Abraham Lincoln not to extol the Union but to make sure its victory would mean the extinction of slavery. 'I start for Washington tomorrow morning', she wrote to her friends the Fields, 'and mean to have a talk with "Father Abraham" himself. . . .' He is said to have greeted her with the words: 'So this is the little lady who caused this big war.'

Causing the war, however, was not her only feat. When she found that English sympathies were largely with the South (apart, paradoxically, from the Lancashire cotton-spinners who personally suffered unemployment from the war) Harriet lashed out at her second home: 'O, England, England! What, could ye not watch with us one hour – for the sake of the cause?' Exeter Hall was 'a humbug, a pious humbug', and Mrs Stowe hurled back the 'Affectionate Christian Address' of her English 'Sisters'. Nathaniel Hawthorne thought her furious exposure might make John Bull 'blush', even though he was a 'hardened and villainous hypocrite'.

Lincoln declared the emancipation of slaves on New Year's Day 1865. Harriet was one of the great throng in the Boston Music Hall. 'Mrs Stowe! Mrs Stowe! Mrs Stowe!' they trumpeted.

Her publication of the pleasant *Oldtown Folks* in 1870 had brought in more money, and after the Lady Byron débâcle of the same period she was glad to retire for the winters to Mandarin in Florida, where she had bought an estate. She divided her life between the pulpits of Hartford, both Episcopalian and Dissenting, and the oranges of Florida.

Calvin died in 1886, more 'hypo' than ever and weighing eighteen stone. As he lay moaning that the Lord had forgotten him, Harriet said breezily, 'Oh, no, He hasn't; cheer up! Your time will come soon.' There was a vein of irony, if not iron in the lady who caused the war.

As she grew older her writings at least went soft: 'Sunny Memories', 'Bright Ideas' and 'Little People' took the place of 'Dismal Swamps' and 'Life among the Lowly', the sub-titles of *Dred* and of *Uncle Tom*. She was cared for by her twin daughters, Hattie and Eliza, who never married. Her memory began to play her tricks. One day she clasped in her arms an elderly colonel believing him to be her long-lost son Fred who had been wounded in the war, had succumbed to alcoholism and then mysteriously vanished in San Francisco.

Her son Henry had been drowned before he could become 'converted'. This tragedy, following the similarly unsanctified drowning of her sister's fiancé Professor Fisher, finally emancipated Harriet from the slavery of the Calvinist belief in 'election'.

Like Florence Nightingale she had become a half-remembered legend before she died, aged eighty-five, on 1 July 1896. To the two most distinguished friends of her last years she showed that the prose style of her letters, at any rate, had not suffered from the ills of dotage. In her very last year she whimsically described the signs of her second childhood: 'My mental condition might be called nomadic.' Her way of life was nomadic too: 'rambling about the neighbourhood and calling upon my friends' – Mark Twain was one of those Hartford neighbours into whose house she would wander, drift around and patter out again.

A letter to her distinguished friend Dr Oliver Wendell Holmes exquisitely pictures the calm listlessness of old age: 'My brain is tired out . . . and now I rest me, like a moored boat, rising and falling on the water, with loosened cordage and flapping sail.'

In the preface to her memoirs (written under her supervision by her son Charley) she ended with a quotation from *The Pilgrim's Progress*: 'My sword I give to him that shall succeed me in my pilgrimage. . . .'

Many were to take up the sword and some were to turn it against her politically. The religious message of *Uncle Tom's Cabin* was to be derided as a sell-out, a betrayal of the Negro cause; at best 'period trash' that had served its purpose and was no longer in print in America during the two world wars.

Harriet's sword had indeed been beaten, not into a respectable ploughshare but into a vast pulp of 'Uncle Tom Literature', which touched bottom with an immensely long-running play in which Tom, now a 'nigger minstrel', did his shuffle between acts. In this respect, those people were right who felt that Mrs Stowe's black hero had shuffled off his responsibilities.

So much for Harriet's sword. What of her pen? It is hard to think of anyone to whom she could have bequeathed that magical instrument. Perhaps the German writer Erich Maria Remarque achieved a comparable miracle with his *All Quiet on the Western Front* and George Orwell with *Animal Farm,* novels that made the civilized world as nauseated with war and Stalinism respectively as *Uncle Tom* had made it with slavery.

In some ways she was a woman of commonplace, or at least ordinary tastes and feelings. She fell for things because they were fashionable, like phrenology and spiritualism. She built for herself a monstrosity of a house in Hartford which she could not keep up and had to sell. Her Puritanism was not flawless either. She posed as a teetotaller in England but in middle life found she required wine at 11 a.m. or even after breakfast at home, to get her through the writing day. On one hot afternoon she passed out at a friend's after too strong a draught of claret cup. Her hooped skirt flew up, revealing that she wore white stockings, flowered garters and little elastic-sided boots. When the friend tried to pull down the hoop for the sake of propriety, Harriet groaned and said, 'I won't be any properer than I have a mind to be.'

She was not an excessively good mother, at one point bewailing the fact that writing to her grown-up children interrupted her creative energies. Though she was a born writer, yeasty with ideas and fluent as a dissenting preacher, she rose only once out of the rut – but then into the empyrean. As Edmund Wilson wittily suggested, *Uncle Tom* might well have been written by God, since all the succeeding nine novels were so evidently the unaided work of Mrs Stowe.

There was something else besides *Uncle Tom*, however, that makes Mrs Stowe a candidate for greatness, alongside her Victorian 'sisters' on both sides of the Atlantic. After a shaky start she developed strong feelings for the rights of women. 'Yes, the day is now come, thank God,' she wrote in *My Wife and I*, 'when a woman as well as a man can have some other career besides that of the heart.' And why not 'a woman president as well as a woman queen of England?' Only because, said Harriet, a female candidate for the presidency would have to be 'a brazen tramp of a woman' to stand all the dirt the press would throw at her.

Her disastrous championship of Lady Byron was due partly to the adored one being a woman unjustly treated by men. The debasement of slave *women*, whether as mothers bereft of their children or as their owners' mistresses, was particularly repugnant to her. The aim of *Uncle Tom*, she wrote, was to show that Jesus Christ had 'a mother's love for the poor and lowly'. Elsewhere she noted that 'lacking mortal father, Jesus was absolutely his mother's boy'. Harriet expressed a feminist wish that Mary had shared more in her son's ministry. However, there was in Him 'more of the pure feminine element than in any other man'. Edward Wagenknecht calls attention to a feminine element that commentators have claimed to see in Uncle Tom himself. Personally I find him sexless rather than feminine. I believe in him but not in his cabin or the domestic life that Harriet portrayed there. The feminine aspect of God was boldly stated in *Oldtown Folks*: 'All that there is in the best fathers and best mothers *must* be in him.'

Soon Harriet Stowe was writing to George Eliot that emancipation of the slaves must be followed by the emancipation of women. She believed that women were more loyal than men. In *Uncle Tom* the sturdiest pleas for abolition all come from women, especially Aunt Chloe with her 'obstinate sense of justice'. The Negress Milly in *Dred*, who rescues abandoned children, puts the best multi-racial case to be found in the Stowe *oeuvre*: 'I don't make no distinction of colour, I don't believe in dem; white children, when dey 'haves themselves, is just as good as black, and I love 'em just as well.' Nina puts the most aggressive point for sex equality: she won't be told not to read Byron's *Don Juan* by men who read it themselves; her aim being 'to put down these men, and stand up for my sex.'

At the end of the day, however, Mrs Stowe's feminism is not quite whole-hearted. She quarrelled with two of the outstanding American suffragists, Mrs Elizabeth Cady Stanton and Dr Victoria Woodhull, because they helped to expose Henry Ward Beecher's alleged amours. In Harriet's pungent phrase they were 'the free love roost of harpies generally'. Both were caricatured in *My Wife and I*, Stanton as the absurd Mrs Cerulean and Woodhull as the brash and sexy Miss Audacia Dangyereyes. There is quite a funny scene between the hero and Miss Audacia when she claims her 'rights', to smoke, drink, come up into his room and invite him into hers. 'Say, will you come round?' But this predecessor of Mae West does not really make Mrs Stowe laugh.

To all of this *Uncle Tom's Cabin* is the final reply, the unique answer. A small-town housewife Harriet may have been, but it was her pen that at one miraculous stroke signed the order of release for more than slaves, and issued the passes to freedom.

MARY KINGSLEY

1862–1900

No Victorian woman had a more extraordinary character than Mary Kingsley, or led a stranger life than hers during the few years that were at her own disposal. Her sexual urges were so completely repressed that she sincerely believed she had never had any. 'I have never been in love, nor has any one ever been in love with me', she wrote to Stephen Gwynn her friend and biographer. In fact, what D. H. Lawrence was to call the dark forces were all there, but transferred to 'darkest Africa' – its black peoples, impenetrable equatorial forests and sunless lagoons.

Yet her attitude was strictly rational, being that of an anthropologist, explorer and author of a unique travel book. Unlike Annie Besant, she did not exemplify in herself all the threads of Victorian life; she crossed them. The thread of respectability tangled with the thread of bohemianism, patriotism with an itch to get out of England, imperialism with a loathing for all its official instruments except the armed forces, belief in the Divine Christ with contempt for Christian missionaries, deep melancholy with an almost music-hall humour, a resolve to achieve as much as any living male in her own field with a refusal to support campaigns for women's rights.

Mary Henrietta Kingsley was born in London on 13 October 1862, the only daughter of Dr George Kingsley and niece of the Rev. Charles Kingsley who wrote *Westward Ho!* and *The Water Babies*. Henry Kingsley, another uncle, was also a novelist. Mary's eldest uncle, Gerald, had died as captain of a fever-stricken gun-boat, the last man to expire after eighteen hideous stagnant months at sea. In Coleridge's *Ancient Mariner* a similar situation was described:

> I looked upon the rotting sea,
> And drew my eyes away;
> I looked upon the rotting deck,
> And there the dead men lay.

Mary was later to apply two other lines of the poem to her own West African mangrove swamps: 'Yes, slimy things did crawl with legs/Upon the slimy sea.' Indeed the *Ancient Mariner* seems to have run in her head. During a lecture she quoted from it again – 'The moving Moon went up the sky/And no where did abide' – and was convulsed with merriment when a patronizing reporter advised her to stick to prose, which was readable, while 'her' poetry was unfortunate.

Mary and her younger brother Charles spent their childhood in a cottage with a long garden at Highgate, North London. Nothing much is known of her mother Mary Bailey except that she had delicate health, was armed with revolvers and kept dogs – the last two items to deal with possible robbers attacking from the Highgate hinterland. Young Mary was allowed to keep fighting cocks. Her interest in them was focused on their beautiful ferocity and her own power of subduing it.

Her scientist father abominated the cocks' crowing or any other loud noise that aroused his violent temper. However, he spent months on end away from home indulging his wanderlust. When he returned for brief spells he taught Mary much, from swear words to science. One day he picked up his struggling daughter and shouted to Mrs Kingsley, 'Where does this child get its language from?' 'Not from me', replied his wife. Did young Mary at least learn from Mrs Kingsley to drop her h's? Gwynn, who knew Mary well, said she nearly always dropped them, a curious contrast with her cultivated voice. Her biographers have suggested that she picked up this habit from her mother.

George Kingsley was a true scholar if an erratic one. Mary enjoyed the freedom of his library, where she fell in love with *The English Mechanic, Solar Physics* and many volumes on anthropology, especially 'sacrificial rites'. Like most scientifically-minded children, she tried to make gunpowder and succeeded in blowing a tub of manure on to a line of clean washing. Books on buccaneers exerted special charm, for she knew that her ancestors on Papa's side had been soldiers, sailors, slavers and planters.

She had one bitter grievance. Her father never sent her to school or paid for her to be taught anything professionally except German, to help him in his own scientific researches. When the family moved to Cambridge to be near her brother Charles at Christ's College, Mary wept to discover her ignorance. A Cambridge don compared Mary's knowledge of chemistry to a mere alchemist's.

Her father and his friends were none the less a growing inspiration in her life. According to her memoir of George Kingsley she was the 'underworker' to this 'many-sided' man and the doer of 'odd jobs' for him. 'I have always been a doer of odd jobs', she was to write, '– and lived in the joys, sorrows, and worries of other people.' Her domestic odd jobs included unremitting housework. While Papa was travelling and Charley wielding his pen to no great effect but at considerable cost, Mary was dusting; and dusting in an atmosphere of social seclusion, for Mrs Kingsley was soon too ill to entertain. Nevertheless Mary's intellect and vitality were such that with training, she could have obtained a Cambridge degree – if Cambridge had given women the chance.

At thirty Mary had changed little from the pale, thin, blue-eyed girl she had been at sixteen. With fair hair and quiet domestic habits, she was reserved, a somewhat unfeminine, gawky young woman, still dedicated to serving her father and brother, and concealing an interior sadness. It is ironic that within a few months of her thirtieth birthday, men would be serving *her*. In 1892 her father and mother died within six weeks of one another. Suddenly this withdrawn Lady of Shalott, who had hitherto seen life only in the mirror of other people's minds, found the mirror had cracked from side to side and she was out alone in the world.

Whenever her brother Charley needed her to housekeep for him, she would oblige. But by 1893 he had gone out East. Mary felt totally unwanted. Her melancholy intensified and she wondered if the last odd job for her to do, the last tidying up, the last dusting operation would be to tidy herself away and return to dust: 'Dead tired and feeling no one had need of me any more', she wrote afterwards, '. . . I went down to West Africa to die.' West Africa was the legendary 'White Man's Grave' so that the final odd job should not be too onerous.

She chose West Africa, the cheapest tropic available, because she had some tidying-up jobs to do for her beloved father before the grave claimed her, that dilettante scholar having left much of his tropical research unfinished. Two academic friends, Dr Günter of the British Museum and Dr Guillard of Cambridge advised her to concentrate on 'fish and fetish', assisting her with collecting cases, bottles and spirits.

In August 1893 she boarded a battered old cargo-boat, the *Lagos*, with her eccentric luggage: one black bag, one portmanteau and one long waterproof carrier containing boots, blankets, books and one pair of trousers borrowed from Charley. Her friends had advised her to wear entirely male attire. She declined. With a naturally unfeminine appearance, she took care not to emphasize it with masculine clothes. Her strong black skirts – always the same, always serviceable – were to prove her salvation. Once she was to crash 15 feet down into a game-pit and but for the thick folds of her skirt would have been 'done for' on its spikes.

Captain Murray of the *Lagos* found her eccentric in more than luggage – and completely irresistible. She found him the best instructor she could have chosen and his old steamer the best transport. She made him teach her navigation, 'trade English' and the lore of 'the Coast'. His crew of rough seamen showed her how everything worked in the engine-room and galley, and she became a familiar sight popping up from some part of the ship banned to passengers, with the words, 'It's only me'. Her nickname was soon 'Only Me', the two words aptly covering her remarkable combination of humility and cheek.

As they approached the notorious coast of West Africa, Mary had two memorable experiences. Wisps of hot peculiar air from the mud-flats caused her a rare moment of doubt: could she actually land? (Evil smells in themselves were then supposed to carry malaria.) The other experience was of her first tornado. Its beauty and terror inspired her with one of her magnificent purple passages. After describing the three separate thunderstorms which converged in the tornado, she added: 'While in between these phenomena wandered strange, wild winds, made out of lost souls frightened and wailing to be let back into Hell, or taken care of by someone.'

It is not difficult to detect Mary's own identification with those lost winds. Indeed she was to describe herself as having a closer relationship with 'non-human things' than people. This was the result of her upbringing and she never really changed, despite her subsequent fame. 'I am no more a human being than a gust of wind is. . . .'

Her first journey to West Africa passed as quickly as the wind – August 1893 to the beginning of 1894 – but she learned a great deal from it. Most important was her high estimation of the traders. Known to the Colonial Office as 'palm oil ruffians', the traders seemed to Mary Kingsley to be the spiritual descendants of Drake's merchant adventurers – 'of such is the kingdom of England.' Indeed she became a bit of a merchant herself, going out with £300 and augmenting it by small deals in rubber and ivory. She enjoyed haggling. In her eyes the traders were *carrying* Britain's flag rather than *following* it according to the accepted slogan, 'Trade follows the flag.' Far from blaming the French or Germans for competing in the 'Scramble for Africa', she admired their zeal. But she wanted her own country to have a fair share. Like her father, she believed Britain to be a colonizing power 'by divine right'. Unlike her father, she saw that 'right' in danger of abrogation unless Britain fulfilled the one essential condition: to understand the Africans. This the government officials failed to do.

Thanks to the traders, Mary learned to communicate with Africans even when no interpreter was available. In most African villages there were a few men whose commerce had put them in direct touch with white men. Mary evidently fell for their 'trade English', introducing many phrases such as 'for one' (exactly), 'one time' (at once) or 'plenty' (very) into her writings. When lost in her canoe she once spent the night with four 'plenty' rough characters rather than look for a government vessel. The traders told her all about the food she would soon be eating in African huts: plantain, yams, maize, fish, snails, snakes, maggots and the eternal manioc, their bread. They also enumerated the agues and fevers she would face: kraw-kraw, Portuguese itch, Guinea worm, smallpox. Despite her apparent death-wish, she rigorously obeyed certain rules of hygiene. 'Unboiled water was my *Ibet* (taboo)', and the first thing she did on arriving at any new village was to order her African courier to make tea. It was a trader who told her to get to know the Wesleyans before any other missionaries: 'they are the only people on the Coast who have got a hearse with feathers.'

The missionaries, of whatever faith, compared ill in Mary's opinion with the traders. The missionaries' language might be respectable, but they used it to smear the traders as purveyors of 'poisonous' gin and rum to the Africans. Mary was soon to find that the gin sold in West Africa contained no more poisons than that sold in London, and if the Africans were prevented by government or missionaries from buying it, they would produce a far more deadly brew at home. She herself came to believe that the awful climate made some spirituous liquors almost a necessity, and finally came down on the side of the drink-trade as against temperance missionaries by comparing drunkenness in West Africa and South London: 'In the whole of West Africa, in one week, there is not one quarter the amount of drunkenness you can see any Saturday night you choose in a couple of hours in the Vauxhall Road.'

On her first visit she met at least two white missionaries whom she unreservedly admired. One was Dr Mary Slessor, a redoubtable little Scots spinster whose character was as strong as her own. Dr Slessor entirely dominated an isolated mission at Okyon in Calabar. After staying with her twice Mary Kingsley wrote: 'The sort of man Miss Slessor represents is rare.' Understanding tribal customs, Dr Slessor was able to rescue and take to her compound many slave women and children, especially twins, who would otherwise have been killed. Denis Kempe was the second missionary. He and his wife put up Mary in 1893 and he was to become her personal father confessor. Dr Nassau of the US Presbyterian mission in Gabon and Batanga was later to become another revered friend.

Mary landed in the enveloping vapours of Sierra Leone during the wet season, determined to enjoy the spirit of the place and 'help it on' instead of opposing it, however unprepossessing it might appear. For that reason she did not appreciate the westernized Africans of Freetown, flaunting their 'second-hand rubbishy white culture', but was enthralled by the Coast as she travelled southwards to Portuguese St Paul de Loanda in Angola, and then back again.

In one village there was a sudden invasion of dreaded driver ants. A wild rush of everyone including Mary from the huts was followed by frantic shrieks for some left-behind object: 'Where him live?' 'In him far corner for floor!' Clearly the rescue of a luckless black baby was to be Mary's odd job for the day. 'Although not a family man myself', she wrote, 'the idea of that innocent perishing in such an appalling manner roused me to action. . . .' Dashing into the hut she seized the small black thing already swarming with ants and handed him to his distraught father – who plunged him into a water-butt and held him under with a hoe. 'Him' was a ham.

Mary succumbed to the charm of the Coast and wrote in her *Travels*: 'I saw more than enough during that voyage to make me recognize that there was any

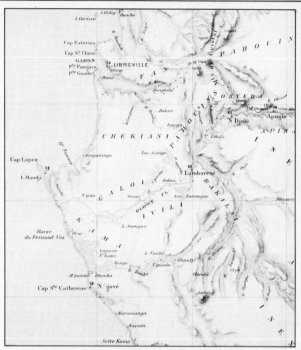

Nineteenth-century Sierra Leone. *Above right*:
contemporary map of the area Mary Kingsley
explored. *Above*: her battle with the Ogowé rapids.
Right: a member of a female secret society.
Opposite left: Fan women. *Opposite right*: a leopard
trapped. *Opposite below*: a trading station.

amount of work for me worth doing down there.' ('Down there' was Africa, 'up here' England.) 'So I warned the Coast I was coming back again and the Coast did not believe me. . . .' Her work was not only to augment her zoological collection but to study pure Africans. And the purest Negro, the one almost untouched alike by officials, missionaries and traders, was the cannibal.

Out to see Africans 'at their wildest and worst', Mary began her second, much longer voyage late in December 1894. She travelled with Lady Macdonald, wife of the Commissioner for the Oil River Protectorate, staying under the Macdonalds' roof from January till May 1895. With them she visited the island of Fernando Po. The 'Fanny Po' ladies, with their touch of Spanish blood, were considered the handsomest in West Africa, though Mary preferred the 'sable' Igalwas of the mainland. The Bubis on the island, however, taught her some lessons. She sadly asked one hunter why he trapped animals instead of shooting them clean. He replied that a gun made a 'nize' and would attract thieves. 'But traps can be robbed.' 'No, sah, them bian [charm] he look after them traps, he fit to make man who go tief swell up and bust.'

Mary felt constricted by even lovely islands and longed for the great landmass of her dreams. Her aim was to sail up the River Ogowé by steamer, or by canoe when she reached the rapids, returning to the town of Lambaréné and so across country to the River Rembwé and Libreville on the coast. 'Across country' meant penetrating unknown territory inhabited by tribes whose reputation at least was only too well-known. They went by a name that today sounds deceptively agreeable, the Fans.

Mary landed in Gabon, French Congo, on 20 May 1895. '*Vive la France!*' she cried as the Customs allowed her to take in her bottling spirit duty free, since it was for science. '*Vive la France*' was about all the French Mary knew. Her father, like most of the Kingsleys, was 'Teuton' in sympathy and did not have her taught what happened to be the main language of tropical Africa. Her enthusiasm for *la France* subsided when the French Customs wanted to charge her fifteen shillings for her revolver. She relinquished it, preferring a bowie knife for emergencies. Afterwards she believed that part of her prestige among Africans was due to her never having ordered a man, however menacing, to be shot. She learned to rely on other powers. As for hunting animals, 'I do not think it is ladylike to go shooting things with a gun.'

At Lambaréné on the Ogowé she found herself speaking up for missionaries, especially French missionaries' wives. Their devotion and courage were often underestimated at home. Moreover, these charming French families who entertained her on her way up the formidable Ogowé were the only missionaries who did not incur her censure by attacking polygamy. Polygamy was a hopelessly thorny question. 'The more wives the less work', Mary was told by African women; and what about the three years when an African mother was feeding her baby and did not sleep with her husband? 'We must attack

Natives in Victorian dress. Mary Kingsley wanted the Africans' beliefs and taboos to be respected, not replaced with 'second-hand rubbishy white culture'.

polygamy with the feeding bottle', an American missionary told Mary, and a gross or two of bottles were accordingly sent over to West Africa. But they did not take on, and the missionary returned to the States.

Mary arrived at Njole, ninety miles above Lambaréné, by the steamer *Mové*. But here the French officials said her journey had to stop. Ladies never faced the rapids. What about Mme Quinée? asked Mlle Kingsley, well-informed as ever. Ah, Mademoiselle, but she was with her *husband*, came the answer. But husbands were not among the essentials for explorers listed by the Royal Geographical Society, argued Mary. She got her way.

Nevertheless, the absence of a husband was to prove a perpetual difficulty with the tribes, and Mary finally gave up saying she did not possess one. 'I am looking for him', she would explain instead, pointing in the direction she wished to travel.

A planter helped her to assemble an African crew for her canoe, which she forced upstream against the rapids until she reached an utterly remote perilous 'heaven' on the upper Ogowé:

The moon was rising, illuminating the sky, [wrote Mary Kingsley] but not yet sending down her light on the foaming, flying Ogowé, in its deep ravine.... In the darkness round me flitted thousands of fireflies, and out and beyond this pool of utter night flew by unceasingly the white foam of the rapids; sound there was none save their thunder. The majesty and beauty of the scene fascinated me and I stood leaning my back against a rock pinnacle watching.

She had stolen out absolutely alone, leaving her crew of Africans fast asleep in camp.

Do not imagine it gave rise, in what I am pleased to call my mind, to those complicated, poetical reflections natural beauty seems to bring out in other people's minds. It never works that way with me; I just lose all sense of human individuality, all memory of human life, with its grief and worry and doubt, and become part of the atmosphere. If I have a heaven, that will be mine....

The journey upstream was dangerous enough, but steering a canoe down again after reaching the Alembe Falls, with the roaring river giving its ferocious 'tiger-like spring' among the rocks was a thousand times worse. 'Jump for bank, sah', Mbo the leader would shout to Mary each time they got jammed between boulders, and Mary would jump with half the crew on to a slippery crag while the other half dragged the canoe free. During one of the upsets a member of her crew of eight went missing until, amid the turmoil of waters, she heard an anguished mission-school voice howling out the hymn, '*Notre port est au ciel*'. She was able to take this African Lorelei off his lonely rock. Mary was to call their adventure, 'our knock-about farce before King Death'.

Back in Lambaréné at last, she resolved to become an expert canoeist on her own account. She began to tame her craft in slack water but was quickly whirled into the current at the risk of her life. 'You'll be drowned! Come back! Come back!' shouted the missionaries from the bank. But Mary paddled on. 'If you attend to advice in a crisis you're lost.' As for a steam-boat, she could honestly say, 'I would rather take a 200-ton vessel up a creek than write a book.'

Today she would no doubt have rounded the world on her own, catching rare fish as she went along. The haul she eventually presented to Dr Günter included two new species named after her: the *Ctenopoma kingsleyae* and the *Mormyrus kingsleyae*. Her proudest achievements in West Africa were to have pleased Dr Günter with her fish and to have learned to paddle her own Ogowé canoe as if she were an African – 'pace, style, steering and all, "All same for one"....'

After the rapids came the swamps. Following her adventures of June 1895, Mary explored the Ogowé delta, home of the tribes of Ouranogou. Her love of water and power of word-painting were again prominent. Above her in the green gloom rose countless thousands of grey trunks, 'as straight as ships' masts' (a nautical metaphor always seemed the best) and between them a mass of bush-ropes like serpents fixed for ever in some Homeric battle:

while beneath you and away into the shadowed vastness lay the stagnant currentless dark waters, making a floor for the forest, a floor whose face is like that of a mirror seen in gloom – dimly showing you the forms outside it, seeming to have in it images of unknown things.

Dawn has flushed a distant mountain peak amethyst, daffodil and rose, 'while night, accompanied by crocodiles, slides away down into the dark waters....' Mary has heard the swish of their tails all night and feels they may bring down her rickety hut on its fragile stilts while she sleeps.

In the delta she was offered the post of General to a village army which wished to snatch back one of their wives – 'the most precious woman of modern times' – who had eloped with 'a gentleman from another village', as Mary put it. (She never failed to refer to individual Africans as 'ladies' and

Ctenopoma kingsleyae. **One of the new species of fish that were discovered by Mary Kingsley and named after her.**

'gentlemen'.) Appointed arbitrator, since she declined to be General of a punitive expedition, Mary succeeded in preventing a Trojan war from breaking out over this black Helen. So far her odd jobs for Africans had included doctor, artisan, prophet, talisman and arbitrator.

An earlier legal success near Lambaréné emphasized how skilful she had become in the interpretation of African customs. She managed to rescue two Africans who had been condemned to death by the Igalwa tribe's secret society, the Ukukar. She later attributed her success to twenty-four hours' solid palaver and a bit of bribery. Never once did she threaten the Ukukar representative with an avenging government. Instead she showed her understanding of, and qualified sympathy with, the pagan mores – sympathy for which she was afterwards soundly berated by the local missionary, though not by his wife.

All Mary's skill and nerve were necessary as she vanished on 22 July into the Great Forest. Her object was to cut through the unexplored bush from the River Ogowé near Azingo to Agongo on the River Rembwé and so to Libreville on the coast. In her *Travels* she described this fabulous journey with some omissions (restored in her lectures), for she had learned a lesson from the experiences of her great predecessor, Paul Belloni du Chaillu. So incredible sounded his stories of gorillas and other notables, that many people refused to believe either in them or in his less spectacular tales. Mary at first suppressed her gorillas for the sake of scientific credibility.

She hired four armed Ajumbas, whom she named Grey Shirt, Singlet, Silence and Pagan (from the number of fetishes he carried). A timid Igalwa volunteered to come too. He was seeking work at John Holt's factory on the Rembwé but dared not travel alone through the sinister Fan country. 'All Fan now', said Singlet gloomily as they paddled up a tributary of the Ogowé, avoiding sandbanks strewn with parties of hippopotamuses and crocodiles. To divert their thoughts from Fans, Mary asked Pagan if there were gorillas and elephants as well? 'Plenty too much!' he said.

Their safety depended on Pagan's assurance that he had a trade friend in the Fan village of Mfetta on an island in Lake Ncovi. As they beached their canoe, 'a brown mass of naked humanity' came pouring down a steep cliff path to meet them. The Fans stood in silence twenty paces from Mary, each man with his gun and knife. There were no women. Then Pagan and Grey Shirt got out of the canoe and did their act, stretching out their arms towards the Fans and calling the name of their trade friend, 'Kiva – Kiva'. The Fans burst into angry discussion while Silence broke silence at last and whispered in Mary's ear, 'It would be bad palaver if Kiva no live for this place.' Mary stood up and casually climbed out of the boat giving the Fans the traditional greeting, 'Mboloani'. They grunted noncommittally; but at this moment a fine man decorated with a fragmentary loin-cloth, a strip of leopard skin and a bunch of leopard and wild-cat tails hanging from his shoulder, broke through the crowd. Pagan rushed forward. 'Don't you know me, my beloved Kiva?' The great man's arms were raised as close as possible to Pagan's without quite touching, and with this gesture of friendship ended the longest twenty minutes of Mary's life so far. Never had she seen such a set of 'wild, wicked-looking savages'.

Up in the village, in the palaver house, Mary began her favourite bargaining, this time for three Fan carriers to join the party, since she now had to proceed overland. Three was all she would take. If Fans outnumbered Ajumbas in these wilds, the cannibal Fans would neatly cut up and eat their companions, smoking any surplus meat. Mary had no wish to arrive smoked at Rembwé, 'even should my fragments be neat'. When she heard that the Fans' palaver might well last three weeks she said firmly, 'My price is for a start tomorrow . . . after that I go away.' Her toughness paid off and the three wealthiest cannibals in the village volunteered: 'beloved' Kiva, Fika and Wiki.

Kiva lent her his hut for the night. He also lent her his lice. Unable to sleep, she stole out, paddled a small Fan canoe to the mainland, hit upon a family of snoring hippopotamuses, paddled silently and swiftly away again, landed in a remote cove on the island, undressed and washed off the lice, dried on her cummerbund and glided back into her hut.

Their next Fan village was Efoua, where the inhabitants, though less villainous-looking than the Mfettas, still surrounded them with a menacing ring until Kiva was greeted by a friend. Assigned a chief's hut, Mary suffered this time from something worse than lice: the stench of human ears, toes, hands, 'and other things', tied up – neatly of course – in bags on the wall. Mary tipped them out into her sealskin cap and examined them before returning them to their bags.

From Efoua to Egaga was an exhausting journey which necessitated wading through the black 'batter-like' ooze of swamps. Mary took her turn as leader, since it was the leader's disagreeable duty to find a shallow enough passage for the others to walk through. Sometimes she would go in three or four times up to the neck in stinking slime before finding a passage. Mary despised the town whites who demanded litters and left all the dirty work to blacks.

At the end of her tether, she suddenly saw there was a swift river to be crossed at the bottom of a gully before entering Egaga. She had the choice of swimming against the fast current, for which by this time she was too weak, or walking along a slippery tree trunk high above the foam; which she did, to the cheers of her men below.

Egaga had the reputation of being the most evil of the Fan villages. Instead of merely hoping for the best, she boldly accused the Egaga chief of ruling over a 'thief town', and challenged him to prove this was not so by his hospitable treatment of her party. While expressing deep shock at such allegations against his 'highly respectable town', the chief showed no resentment but sat down and explained to Mary much arcane matter about law and fetish. He finally introduced her to his old mother who was dying of a poisonous fish bite but was restored by Condy's fluid and the lancet. That night, though pining for sleep, Mary had to rouse herself and settle a murderous feud between Kiva and his hosts. There was really nothing to choose between the Fans of 'thief town' and her own Fans. Nevertheless, with all their faults and fetishes they were steadily appealing to her more and more as 'an uncommon fine sort of human being'.

After an episode in the Fan village of Esoon she came to believe that women, who were fighting for their rights in England, already had 'power and position in Africa'. Her evidence rested on the action of four male Fans, complete with warpaint and sixteen spears, who went to consult a higher authority about Mary's arrival – their mother. With the help of this 'quiet old lady', Mary settled a feud between Esoon and Egaga.

Wild animals in the bush were a perpetual hazard that Mary faced with her usual unconcern. A gigantic roaring gorilla advanced upon her and two Fans near Esoon, and she had to wait till the appalling apparition was within a yard of her, since only one of the Fans' guns was serviceable, and that one must be sure of killing. The Fan shot him point-blank in the chest. Afterwards Mary enquired how gorillas themselves killed. For answer the Fans rushed her off to a newly dug grave in the bush, from which they exhumed a gorilla's recent victim. Mary recorded that it was death by a lethal clasp, the shoulder-blades being torn clean out. Except for their graceful trapeze-like action through the trees, Mary found gorillas irredeemably hideous. The terrifying beauty of leopards, however, held her awed and spellbound. As for crocodiles and hippopotamuses, she thought nothing of batting them on the snout with her paddle or umbrella when they got uncomfortably close. One crocodile actually got its feet over her canoe's side before she fetched it one. She narrates several unique adventures with leopards, the strangest when she liberated one from a snare. Unable to sleep for its cries, she went to its rescue. When it was at last free

it circled round her, sniffing instead of bolting as she had expected. 'Go home, you fool', she said firmly. It went; and out of a tree dropped a Fan hunter to worship this woman who had spoken to a leopard and been obeyed.

Mary Kingsley's attitude to fear is a subject which has exercised all her biographers. Some insist that she did not know what fear meant; others that she showed the true courage of someone who was often horribly alarmed. Certainly she dwells in her *Travels* on her 'nervous disposition'. On the other hand she was once asked by a friend if she did not feel frightened or at least flustered when she approached a

Reports of Mary's successful battle with the crocodile inspired this picture in the *Illustrated London News*.

cataract, say, and saw death staring into her face and shouting in her ear. She replied:

I have never felt that. I don't know what it is; I have an idea that if once I *did* feel so, I should collapse entirely. But whenever I have been in real danger, which simply needed every effort of every *bit* of me, I had a strong salt taste in my mouth. Whenever I feel *that*, I know I've got to take myself as seriously as I know how.

Rudyard Kipling, who knew her personally, wrote: 'Being human, she must have been afraid of something, but one never found out what it was.'

In the words that Sir Samuel Baker the explorer applied to his intrepid wife Florence, 'she was not a *screamer*.' It may be that Mary Kingsley deliberately built up the picture of 'a nervous sort of person' in order to mislead. For psychological reasons she insisted on maintaining a 'ladylike' rather than a 'mannish' image. And Victorian ladies were notoriously nervous. But she admitted to that 'salty taste' in her mouth and also to becoming 'preternaturally artful' in a moment of crisis. She rose to it and was more fully herself. One can call it courage, resourcefulness, a sense of challenge, love of danger, something that her ancestors felt in the line of battle, but not fear.

With her bottled fish and notes on fetishes she started home. But from the deck of the *Niger* off the coast of the German Cameroons, she faced what she called her 'great temptation' – and immediately succumbed. Her temptation had always been to climb the 13,760 feet of Mount Cameroon. Her ascent of 'the magnificent' mountain became a microcosm of all Mary's brilliance and oddity.

There were the special dangers of her chosen route. Sir Richard Burton, Gustav Mann the great German botanist and a third explorer had reached Mungo's summit before her. But all three chose the easier western face. She wrote proudly and significantly: 'I . . . am the third English man [*sic*] to have ascended the Peak and the first to have ascended it from the south-east.'

There was her success in getting all her Africans safely up and down, through the eerie, freezing bogs they feared and hated. Whenever she went off prospecting they panicked. 'My men, by now, have missed their "ma" and are yelling for her dismally', she wrote; and recorded afterwards with pleasure their saying, 'I was Father and Mother to them, and a very stern though kind set of parents I have been.' Africa satisfied all her instincts.

The sudden emergence of Victorian pruderies on the Throne of Wonder completes the collection of Mary's oddities. Staggering into kind Herr Leipert's station 2,500 feet up, mud-caked and splashed with blood on face and hands, she is offered 'an instant hot bath' which she instantly declines. 'Men can be trying! How in the world is any one going to take a bath in a house with no doors, and only very sketchy wooden window-shutters?' Yet this is the woman who had undressed on Lake Ncovi under who knows what wild eyes.

Mary had chosen the testing south-eastern face of Mount Cameroon to get a view of the mountain ranges behind the Sierra del Cristal, in order to plan her next expedition. But she was never to see West Africa again. It was partly because Charley failed to go abroad as planned; partly because of the political propaganda which suddenly swallowed up her last years.

On arriving home at the end of November 1895, Mary was content to housekeep for Charley in congested quarters at 100 Addison Road, West London, while she wrote up her African travels and gave lectures for a living. Her racy style – what she called her 'vulgarity' – her fondness for slang, her naturalness and the enormities which she was often forced to describe astounded the 'grim old budgeroons' (chapel deacons) in her audiences. Particularly as the farrago of melodrama and science issued from the mouth of a pale-faced woman in black silk who might have been a duke's housekeeper with the countenance of a Dürer madonna. Mary always stood rather woodenly, like a ship's figure-head, in her little round sealskin cap – perhaps the same into which she had poured those human mementoes at Efoua. The audiences wallowed and shuddered and packed the lecture halls. When Mary's *Travels in West Africa* were published in 1897 she became an immediate scientific sensation as well as a popular one. Famous people trooped up and down the echoing stone stairs of 100 Addison Road and later came to a house in Hammersmith.

In vain Mrs J. R. Green (wife of the historian) would plead with Mary to adapt her platform manner to her intellectual image and academic prestige. Mary explained: '... I do not want to be *anyone* and this laughable stuff is the thing – just as much as the Fetish is, etc.' When scientists came to her lectures expecting unnatural seriousness, 'all my innate vulgarity breaks out.'

It seems to me that Mary Kingsley's dropped h's were all part of the show. She picked up strong language from her father and probably strengthened the habit when consorting as 'one of them' with the traders on the Coast. As she made the traders her small offerings of ivory and rubber it must have been another of her 'big temptations' to say as they did, ''Ow much?' Later it would have become part of the complicated bravado that is still common today, especially among the young.

Mary made her enemies. Her self-appointed mission to explain the West African to the English attached to her the unfair reputation of a pro-cannibalist. While going into her many fascinating and complex expositions of tribal law, it is possible to pick out a single simple theme: that all the African customs, however abhorrent, had a point, usually based on fear. Take funeral rites; a Nigerian's wealth consisted in wives and slaves. If a chief's wives and slaves died with him, they were less likely to 'put bush in his chop' (poison in his food). If he arrived in the underworld attended by no ritually slain wives and slaves, but only by palm oil and rolls of crimson velvet, he might be mistaken for a slave turning up with stolen goods; whereupon he would be returned to earth at his reincarnation as a real slave. No doubt the African 'forest-mind' was in fearful confusion of 'stupidity and crime'; 'but when you get to see – well! As in the other forests – you see things well worth seeing.' Mary insisted that the African must be respected as a human being and enabled to retain his self-respect.

Fan warriors *above right* and Fan villagers *below right* from photographs Mary Kingsley used to illustrate her *Travels in West Africa*. Cannibals they may have been, but she respected them as 'uncommon fine' human beings.

220

If in the eyes of her traducers Miss Kingsley was pro-cannibal she must also be anti-missionary. This accusation had more substance. Her father had brought her up as a non-believer from her earliest childhood. She particularly deplored the way Christian missionaries removed the restraints of tribal fetishes without putting anything firm in their place. To teach converts a hymn about forgiveness – 'A little talk with Jesus, Makes it right, All right' – simply encouraged them. To Mary, ju-ju was less anti-social than the behaviour of African converts who began by keeping the new law but finally abandoned themselves to unrestrained sensuality. And she criticized the missionaries for turning all the West Africans into clerks, instead of teaching them agriculture and mechanics, at which they were hopelessly inept. Then there was the liquor question. Mary boldly revealed in her *Travels* how she herself had not hesitated, when hard-pressed, to pay off her Africans in rum.

At the same time, she was as likely to repudiate her admirers as her critics. When the *Daily Telegraph* congratulated Miss Kingsley on her ordeals in the 'Dark Continent', so 'manfully' born, as part of her strivings for the 'emancipation of the sex', she replied with derision. 'I do not relish being called a "new woman".' When not engaged in science, she did a lot of cooking and was tyrannized over by children. Just because she travelled, did this lay her open to the 'reproach' of being an emancipated woman? She knew hundreds of women who suffered far greater hardship than herself without ever leaving England. Her adventures were mere 'skylarks' and 'picnics'. She supported the Anthropological Society and the British Empire League, but when four members of the 'cause' – Votes for Women – came to canvass her she wrote to her friend John Holt, the shipping magnate, that the four had 'no good looks to spare' and anyway theirs was a minor cause. Mary first wanted to get Votes for Traders on a Council for African Affairs.

Nevertheless she stood up for women in a rather old-fashioned way. Parliament was unfit for them, she said, and they for Parliament, being too ill-informed; but they were more honest and 'unselfish than men and not an atom more fickle'. An Irish charlady of her acquaintance drank, worked harder than any African and was still fresh enough afterwards to 'knock some of the nonsense out of her husband's head' with the head of her broom. Conversely Mary Kingsley considered herself a typical woman and the Africans 'a female nation', though 'a great world race'. 'We', she said of the Africans and herself, 'dislike Mrs So and So because of her bonnet.' Perhaps her deepest feeling was that opinion on women's work remained in a 'morbid state'. She disliked the technique of those 'shrieking females and androgins [*sic*]' in their starched shirts and studs.

In 1897 a new quarrel blew up. In order to develop its West African 'estates' (as Joseph Chamberlain, the Colonial Secretary, called Britain's overseas possessions) the government needed to build more railways and to finance them

The Cameroons *above left* **were the scene of Mary Kingsley's great climb, and the Ogowé river** *below left* **taught her to handle an African canoe.**

and other improvements by means of a Hut-tax. Mary felt outraged, especially when the first imposition of the tax produced violence and bloodshed. Up till then Mary had admired Chamberlain for his drive. Now she called him 'pettifogging', and his whole colonial system a failure in a 'heart-breaking drizzling sort of way'. Hell was paved with good intentions and ignorance about West Africa. The government, in its abysmal unconcern with tribal law, had failed to understand that to the West Africans a tax on property (huts) meant that the property so taxed was no longer their own. The Hut-tax was thus a breach of faith, thundered Mary Kingsley, since Britain was bound by treaty not to dispossess the West Africans of their homes. 'West Africa today is just a quarry of paving-stones for Hell, and those stones are cemented in places with men's blood mixed with wasted gold.'

She got as far as persuading the government to set up a committee of enquiry on the Hut-tax; but its chairman, her friend Sir Denis Chalmers, believed that his report would be ignored. He died, thought Mary, of a broken heart.

Her heart too was broken, and her body racked by chest pains, probably a result of overwork, over-lecturing and frustration. For she still could not return to her beloved West Africa. In 1899 she published her *African Studies*, and in the same year George Kingsley's unfinished *Notes on Sport and Travel*, which Charley was supposed to have edited but had left to her. Yet Charley lingered on in England, wasting *her* life. Mary believed that her campaigns against the Hut-tax and for West Africa had failed. And if these had failed, what else remained? There was also an unrequited love, which did its destructive work.

A distinguished Jewish bachelor of her own age became Mary's close friend in 1899. Major (later Sir) Matthew Nathan was a civil servant, secretary of the Colonial Defence Committee, who had served with the Royal Engineers in Sierra Leone. He and Mary saw eye to eye over all things African except repeal of the Hut-tax – and this was the apple of her eye. How easy it would have been to repudiate her African friends and please her English ones.

But if I did once [she wrote to Nathan] I could not look you in the face again, and I must be able to – it is the only thing worth having living or dead. I have never done one thing in my life that I cannot face you with. I never shall. If you did not exist I should not be dishonourable, I should just be hard and I should not care. There is no mortal reason why you should care one way or the other what I am . . . I am of no account to you and I know it.

Nathan had been refused by Lytton Strachey's sister Dorothy five years earlier, and so perhaps his heart was broken too.

To all but her special intimates she was still the gayest, most amusing, light-hearted person they knew despite her possessing 'a brain masculine in its strength'. Like Harriet Beecher Stowe, she could look far from plain at parties when smartly dressed and animated. 'Who is that?' an artist once asked Stephen Gwynn. 'Mary Kingsley.' 'But you said she was plain! She is the most beautiful person here.' Yet the few who understood her best, like Gwynn, knew how to interpret the fact that she was now continually quoting the end of a favourite sea-shanty, 'Goodbye and fare you well. . . .'

Sir Matthew Nathan, whom Mary Kingsley loved.

The Boer War broke out in October 1899. Mary showed signs of unease about her beloved Empire's moral position. Nevertheless she volunteered to serve as a nurse. But it seemed that even the War Office did not want her.

Then at the beginning of 1900 the War Office found it had miscalculated and sent out Mary Kingsley after all. She delivered her last lecture in England at the Imperial Institute on 12 February, defending for just one more time the 'merchant adventurers of England' and 'the true Negro' of Africa. Even her slave-trading forebears got a good word, for was it not through their enterprises that the Negro had been civilized in the United States? Mary's heart sometimes overleapt her logic. She ended her lecture in words she had used so often before, 'Goodbye and fare you well', adding 'for I am homeward bound'. Was it a presentiment of death or did she mean that Africa was home?

She embarked on a troopship during the first week in March 1900 and on arrival in South Africa was posted to the Palace Hospital, Simonstown, where Boer prisoners of war were dying of enteric, in much the same squalor as Miss Nightingale had found at that 'giant's palace', the Turkish Barrack Hospital, Scutari. 'Five and six jaws a night have I had of late to tie up', she wrote, 'DAMN the *Haute Politique.*' Yet she was almost happy. 'I am down in the ruck of life again', she wrote to Mrs Green. 'All this work here, the stench, the washing, the enemas, the bed pans, the blood, is my world. Not London Society, politics, that gateway into which I so strangely wandered, into which I don't care a hairpin if I never wander again.' But within two months Miss Kingsley, according to Dr Carre the medical officer, changed 'a mortuary into a sanitorium'. She guided huge delirious Boers back to their beds and held them there until their ravings ceased with death or sleep. Their passionate fevered cries of 'Ons Land, ons Land!' – *our* land – touched her. She none the less believed that Britain should annexe South Africa, perhaps for the sake of the blacks. If this was her reason, she had foresight.

In the early summer the sanitorium she had helped to create became her own mortuary. She caught the fever and died of heart failure after an emergency operation for perforation of the bowel on 3 June 1900. Her last wishes were to die alone like an animal and to be buried at sea. So the nurses left her until she was unconscious, and her country gave her a military and naval funeral, carrying her coffin on a gun-carriage to the pier and committing it to the ocean from a torpedo-boat off Cape Point.

It was said that no woman had ever had such an honourable death. But had any woman ever had such a life? And all of it packed into the brief eight years between her parents' death and her own. Although she believed that she would be ignored, her lesson on ethnology has been learned. A medal for research was instituted at the Liverpool School of Tropical Medicine in her memory, as was the African Society and its *Journal.* The oft-quoted tribute of her friend Sir George Goldie – 'She had the brain of a man and the heart of a woman' – is generally taken to mean that Mary Kingsley had the best of both worlds. If that was indeed its meaning, it is a far from adequate summing-up of an unprecedented character.

In one sense she had the worst of both worlds. Victorian duty towards a father and a brother prevented her from forming a love-relationship of her own until it was too late. Added to these family stresses was her own ambivalence about the sexes. In the same breath she would apply to herself the terms 'a woman roustabout' and 'a scientific man'. It is truer to say that she had the brain and heart of a great human being. Beyond the mask of her gaiety and the reality of her griefs, lay the classic spectacle of genius liberating itself in spite of all.

JAMES BARRY

c. 1795–1865

This chapter must be something of a postscript. We have seen the Brontës limited to dreaming feminine dreams, George Eliot precariously living on both sides of the Establishment divide, Miss Nightingale wrestling with God and man for her vocation, Mrs Butler fighting alongside God for women beyond the pale, Miss Terry choosing the only profession in which women could do what they liked, Mrs Besant fighting alongside men for women, Miss Kingsley packing her life into the only eight years untrammelled by her family, Mrs Stowe fighting for slave-women at the moment when she was most enslaved by her own family. Now comes the strangest figure of them all. An eminent surgeon in the fighting forces who went through life as a normal man, but whom nobody in fact considered normal. James Barry may possibly have been 'intersex' but is far more likely to have been a woman. She was a woman for whom we have three different dates of birth, several suggestions for fathers, two possible mothers – and a very firm reason for her entering the British Army Medical Department.

Dr James Barry was one of the many nineteenth-century women whose vocation was to be a doctor. No women, however, were officially permitted to qualify until the last quarter of the century. Yet here was the extraordinary Barry taking her degree at Edinburgh University over sixty years before the breakthrough. Indeed she was not strictly a Victorian, being forty at the Queen's accession; but it was the Victorians who realized this early 'doctor's dilemma'.

Barry herself juggled with her dates of birth in order to further her secret vocational plans. At Edinburgh she was regarded as unusually young for a student, even in those days when there was no official lower age-limit on entry; indeed she was to give the year of her birth as 'about 1799'. This would have made her only ten years old when she registered in the autumn of 1809. She chose such a preposterously late date because she was on the horns of a dilemma. Being a young girl, her appearance matched the facts of her femininity but violently contradicted the myth of her masculinity. She was pale and delicate-looking though healthy, scarcely five-foot tall (about the same size as little Harriet Beecher Stowe and Queen Victoria) with high cheek-bones, tiny hands and feet, a shrill voice and extremely large blue eyes, sandy curls and 'a long Ciceronian nose' that was perhaps her only 'masculine' feature. To pass off this childish figure as a youth of fourteen or fifteen would have been tricky. To sign on as a boy of ten was most unusual but just possible; and the pretence of extreme youth would help to explain her girlish traits. The most recent and lively of Barry's biographers, June Rose, accepts Barry's date of 1799, referring to her more than once as this 'little girl'. I prefer, however, the date of 1795 which was indicated on the army list when her age was given as eighteen in 1813. The earlier date is also supported by her death certificate (age 'about 70') and her gravestone ('Aged 71').

Thanks to the researches of Isobel Rae, her first biographer, Barry's ancestry has been established as far as possible. She came of an Irish Catholic family, her grandfather being John Barry, a Cork shipbuilder, and her grandmother Juliana Reardon. Young Barry claimed as 'my uncle' the shipbuilder's son, eccentric bachelor and impoverished painter James Barry, RA; and as 'my aunt' Mary Anne Bulkley, née Barry, the painter's sister. If Mrs Bulkley was indeed young Barry's aunt (and not her mother) her father must have been either the painter himself – and this is not impossible – or else one of Mary Anne's 'wild brothers', of whom nothing else is known except that one was called Redmond.

Concentrating first upon her undoubted blood relationship to the painter, we find that her grandfather John Barry and his son James Barry had known the great Irishman Edmund Burke, James being Burke's close friend and a follower of Mary Wollstonecraft. James and Mary believed intensely in female education. Like young Barry, the painter was small of stature, hot of temper and an addict of fruit and bread. (Dr Barry, as we shall see, had a withering tongue and a vegetarian diet.) There was one pronounced difference, though, between the elder and younger Barrys: the painter was as dirty and unkempt as a beggar, the

It is impossible to identify Dr Barry's parents, but it has been suggested that her father was either James Barry RA *left* or General Francisco Miranda *right*.

doctor elegant and meticulous. With his interest in bluestockings, the painter would have had every reason to encourage his niece in the pursuit of her chosen profession, one closed to women.

Two letters to the elder James Barry have been unearthed from his sister Mrs Bulkley; dated 1804 and 1805 respectively, they implore her brother to help her in a situation of dire poverty. The first, written from Cork, describes the financial troubles of her husband (a grocer). A year later she has been turned out of house and home by her bankrupt husband and their married son, and has arrived in England with two daughters, Margaret aged fifteen and a much younger one whose name is not given. This may be 'James Barry' the younger. Mrs Bulkley, though in reality her mother, becomes her 'aunt', lest anyone in Edinburgh should turn up the fact that the two children whom Mrs Bulkley brought to England were both *daughters*.

If the painter had no money to spare, he did at least give his sister valuable introductions before he died in 1806: they were to his own patrons, the Earl of Buchan and General Francisco Miranda the exiled Venezuelan patriot and revolutionary. Buchan held the same revolutionary ideas on female education as old Barry, while Miranda contributed the library in which young Barry began her self-education. Struck by the child's absorption in science, the two revolutionaries put their heads together. She should take her degree, become an army doctor, serve in Caracas when Miranda returned to Venezuela, and be damned to a world which was as hostile to revolutionaries as it was to women.

The Edinburgh plan worked. 'Aunt' Bulkley took Barry north and stayed with her in lodgings. Barry worked hard at all the regular studies and also took two optional subjects, one being midwifery. In 1810 she was able to thank General Miranda for enquiring of her 'inestimable friend Dr Fryer' about her success. (Dr Fryer was the Duke of Sussex's physician.) But, she added, would Miranda please not tell 'Lord B' or anyone else about her friendship with her 'cousin', Mrs Bulkley's daughter. (This was probably Barry's sister Margaret; but since Barry was posing as a boy, such a friendship, if it were talked about, might cause difficulties.)

Six months later Mrs Bulkley had returned to London and Buchan was thanking the distinguished scholar Dr Robert Anderson for consenting to take 'poor Barry' as a boarder. Buchan's excuse for recommending Barry was 'the friendship which subsisted between Barry's uncle and myself and other circumstances' – a tantalizing phrase.

Young Barry succeeded by keeping herself to herself. She became intimate with only one student, a certain John Jobson, who understood that Mrs Bulkley was Barry's *mother*. He never suspected, however, that his friend was a girl. But he was puzzled by Barry's nervousness about crossing the rough quarters of the town and offered to teach her boxing. Jobson failed, for Barry would never hit out but kept her arms across her chest to protect it. (This supports the view that Barry had reached puberty, and was not an undeveloped girl of ten or eleven.) Jobson also recalled the long overcoat she wrapped around herself instead of wearing the usual short shooting-jacket.

By the autumn of 1811 she was preparing her thesis, a study of *Hernia Cruralis* (hernia of the groin) to be written in Latin and defended orally before the examiners. If Barry had ever been a schoolboy, Latin would have presented no difficulty, as she was extremely bright; but in her unprecedented position she needed special coaching, and her patron Lord Buchan again wrote to Dr Robert Anderson asking him to supervise her Latin. It was Buchan also who successfully intervened when the Senate objected to her youth. She boldly prefaced her *Hernia* with a quotation from the Latin poet Menander: 'Do not consider my youth, but consider whether I show a man's wisdom.' The quotation was ironic in two respects: Barry was not as young as she looked, being about seventeen; and she showed the wisdom of a *woman*. She dedicated the thesis to her two patrons, David Erskine Steuart, Lord Buchan '*Viro optimo ac dignissimo*', and General Francisco de Miranda. In her thanks to the latter she emphasized his '*curam paternam*' (paternal care). She was expecting to join him on his staff in South America, whither he had returned in 1811. Barry could not know that the Spanish were to imprison him during the very year she qualified so successfully as a doctor, 1812. Miranda died four years later. Dr Barry was always to fight for the human rights of prisoners. The man to whom she owed 'paternal care' may even have been her father. If so her mother, whoever she was, had shared the General's favours with Empress Catherine the Great and the polymath Mme de Staël. When Barry wrote her full name, 'James Miranda Steuart Barry' in her text-books, the Miranda was a man's name.

She spent a highly successful year in London studying surgery under the famous Sir Astley Cooper at Guy's, and as a pupil-dresser at St Thomas's, the

**A reconstruction of a typical operating theatre in the early nineteenth century.
It was in such a room that Barry mastered the techniques of surgery.**

two 'United' hospitals in Southwark High Street. A close view of operations, a table in the crowded dissecting room and a private bedroom were all available to Barry, through her specialist duties, as well as the usual experience of 'walking the wards'. Sir Astley Cooper was in the habit of telling his students to cultivate the heart of a lion and the hand of a 'lady'. Barry had both.

After Barry's death, a banker named Andrew Smith Mitchie revealed an alleged romance between her and his great-uncle Sir Andrew Smith. Little Barry was said to have followed him to Edinburgh dressed as a boy, but, on being rejected, banished him from her memory by joining the army. Romantic literature is full of Violas and Kaleds, girl-lovers disguised as pages, and the *Dictionary of National Biography* has given some life to the Andrew Smith legend: 'The motive of her singular conduct is stated to have been love for an army surgeon.' All we know for certain is that Barry and her Edinburgh colleague Jobson joined the army at Chatham in June 1813 and Barry went on to be appointed hospital-assistant at Plymouth on 5 July.

The initial difficulty of passing the physical fitness test at Chatham was not as crushing as it might seem. There was no actual necessity to undress. Examinations even of sick patients were frequently made beneath the clothes both in military and civil life. This cursory procedure was the more likely to be adopted in Barry's case because of the great demand for army doctors with first rate degrees and warm recommendations. (Lord Buchan may well have sent along a laudatory note.) If Barry could not conceal her beardless chin, woman's voice and lack of Adam's apple (except by a very high collar which she consistently wore), she could probably get away with baring nothing but her teeth.

It is significant that the *Lancet* of 1895, exactly thirty years after Barry's death, ran a correspondence on her sex. The editor introduced it with a list of eighteenth-century women who were known to have entered the fighting forces and not been discovered. In the nineteenth century the *Rocky Mountain News* wrote of a female 'Mountain Charley' who enlisted in the Wisconsin Infantry, while the *Colorado Transcript* described another 'Mountain Charley' serving in the Iowa cavalry in the Civil War. She was wounded but made her two doctors promise not to reveal her sex.

Barry wisely applied for the post of staff-surgeon, rather than regimental surgeon. As a staff officer, even on the lowest grade, she would have more privacy than in a regiment, as well as a chance later on to serve in one of the numerous garrisons abroad. Accordingly she was posted as hospital-assistant – the very bottom rung of the Army Medical Department's ladder – to the Plymouth garrison. But there the Medical Officer, Dr Skey, objected to her 'childish' appearance. However, on referring to 'the authorities' Dr Skey was warned 'that it was not desirable to agitate the question'. Since Skey himself had taken his degree at Edinburgh, we can guess that one of those pro-Barry 'authorities' was the Scottish laird, Buchan; especially as Buchan later admitted that he had recommended 'poor James Barry' to Skey.

The next two years passed uneventfully for Barry chiefly at Plymouth, though there were breaks at 'Chelsea' – presumably the Royal Hospital – and Stoke Park, the property of the Duchess of Beaufort. Then on 7 December 1815, some six months after Waterloo, Barry was gazetted assistant-surgeon to the forces, and in 1816 sent to the garrison of Cape Colony.

Before we launch 'poor Barry' on her long sea-voyage to Cape Town (she was always an appalling sailor) it is interesting to consider why Buchan referred to his protégée as 'poor'. Was it because her family were literally poverty-stricken? Because she was an orphan? Illegitimate? A pitiably under-developed man? A woman in disguise? At any rate in two out of three of Buchan's surviving letters she was 'poor' Barry.

'Cape Town is a tolerably extensive place', wrote the Count de Las Cases, who was to meet Barry there in 1817, 'and is built in a style of beauty and regularity.' Staff-surgeon James Barry had taken lodgings at 12 Heerengracht (now Adderley Street) near the bridge over the canal of that name. The Governor was none other than Lord Charles Somerset, son of the Duchess of Beaufort.

Barry promptly and even ostentatiously joined the gay circle around the handsome, widowed, 49-year-old Governor. With her dazzling scarlet uniform, its shoulders so obviously padded that the Cape coloureds called her 'the Kapok Doctor', her plumed hat, unwieldy sword, three-inch false soles and high-heeled boots, she cut a strange figure, particularly as she was always accompanied by a Negro body-servant, 'black Sambo' or 'black John', and a small dog called Psyche. She had a series of Psyches and one slept on her bed, no doubt guarding the secret of a bedroom that none was allowed to enter.

Out hunting, racing or dancing, Barry made a point of talking loudly, producing a stream of witticisms and partnering the prettiest girls. On the ballroom floor she flaunted her pea-green satin waistcoat and tight 'inexpressibles'. One lady who had been Barry's patient was to remember: 'It might

**A satirical print of 1832 criticizing the medical profession's
belief that doctors' careers were more important than patients' lives. It was
against this attitude that Barry fought so hard.**

have been a woman touching my head: the doctor's hands are so light.' She
believed his flirtatiousness to be 'one of the many affectations designed to avert
suspicion. He had a winning way with women. . . .'

Barry's medical brilliance and panache, however, were not affectations. She
had become the Somerset family's personal physician by the end of her second
year at the Cape. The oddness of her powerful personality is vividly described
by Napoleon's friend Las Cases who, together with his young son Emmanuel,
was virtually a prisoner of the English in the town's old castle. Both were sick,
and Dr Barry was sent by the Governor to attend them. 'I furnish him with the
best medical attention', wrote Somerset eagerly to the Colonial Secretary in
London. Las Cases was astute and he wrote of Barry in his *Conversations*,
published only six years after they first met:

The grave Doctor . . . was a boy of eighteen, with the form, the manner, and the voice of
a woman. But Mr Barry (such was his name) was described to be an absolute phenomenon. I was informed that he had . . . saved the life of one of the Governor's daughters,
after she had been given up, which rendered him a sort of favourite in the family.

Barry also became 'a sort of favourite' with Count de Las Cases. 'I found his
company very agreeable', wrote the Count when Barry prescribed a sensible
cure for Emmanuel, consisting of exercise in the fresh air instead of confinement
in a dungeon. Prisoners could always count on Barry's concern.

Las Cases's enthusiasm for this unusual doctor was redoubled when Barry proposed that the two French prisoners should live at Newlands, the Governor's enchanting country house, while the Governor himself and his staff were away on tour. Somerset consented, to the amazement of Las Cases, who had heard that 'nothing but a dog or a horse could claim his attention'.

Dr Barry's personal influence over the Governor reached its zenith towards the end of 1818. In just over two years at the Cape she had acquired, through his introductions and her own cleverness, an interesting clientele. As the prison doctor, she visited sick Negroes in prison as assiduously as whites. She even talked to the blacks directly instead of through a white, a practice which the white settlers could not comprehend: 'Why do you ask blacks questions, while Christians are present to answer?'

Sir Hudson Lowe, the Governor of St Helena eighteen sailing days distant, was advised by Governor Somerset to send his sick wife to the medical phenomenon at Cape Town. Indeed, the dying Napoleon would often sip nothing but wine sent to him by Las Cases on Barry's recommendation.

One of Barry's most perceptive patients in the early days was Captain W. H. Dillon of the Royal Navy, whom she cured of an eye infection. Three points stood out in Dillon's mind: Barry would take no private fee; Barry's prescriptions differed totally from those of medical colleagues and were much less drastic (she always cleared away all medicines supplied by previous doctors); Barry was the subject of widespread and intriguing gossip. 'Many surmises were in circulation relating to him', wrote Dillon; 'from the awkwardness of his gait and the shape of his person it was the prevailing opinion that he was a female.' And this testimony to Barry's sex was published in 1856 while the doctor was still alive and practising. Dillon must have been pretty sure of his facts to take such a risk.

Yet another distinguished visitor to the Cape was Lord Albemarle, who at once noted the brilliant doctor's weak spot. 'There was a certain effeminacy in his manner which he seemed to be always striving to overcome.' One way of overcoming it was to take extreme umbrage at any slight; she is said to have slashed off the ear of a mocker with her sword. Dr Barry never suffered fools gladly. A parson once summoned her to pull out a tooth. She sent a blacksmith with pliers and the message that a donkey's tooth was to be extracted.

Her personal popularity with Lord Charles reached its peak when she saved his life, having diagnosed 'typhus with dysentery', contrary to other professional views. It was said afterwards that Dr Barry never co-operated with colleagues. If a patient recovered, all the credit was hers; if the patient died she had been called in too late. She was equally short with her patients, however exalted, when she thought they were fussing. Lord Charles was said to have asked for a prescription which Barry considered unnecessary. 'Prescribe for yourself!' Whereupon he picked up the saucy kitten by the scruff of her slender neck and put her out of the window.

Within a year Lord Charles was finding her still 'the best of physicians' but also 'most wayward of men'. There are two possible reasons for the cooling.

The Governor and the doctor were both autocrats and they clashed. They may also have been lovers and the doctor foolish enough to become pregnant. Towards the end of 1819 Barry was sent to Mauritius for two months to help in an outbreak of cholera; and after that Somerset went home on leave, not returning until November 1821.

June Rose makes the ingenious supposition that Barry really sailed so far away (over 2,000 miles) in order to have a baby. And the gossip of many years later does report that Barry once had a son who died young. That Lord Charles was the father is not actually suggested by June Rose; but he is the most likely candidate, particularly as Barry was jealous of his women friends. 'Oh, I say Cloete, that's a nice Dutch filly the Governor has got hold of', Barry once burst out to Major Josiah Cloete, a military colleague. 'Retract your vile expression, you infernal little cad', retorted Cloete according to his own story; adding that he pulled Barry's 'long ugly nose'. Barry promptly challenged him to a duel with pistols. Fortunately the only result was that they became fast friends. If Barry was taking an unjustifiable risk of getting wounded and found out, she was also strengthening her rather frail reputation for 'manliness'.

Lord Charles Somerset returned to the Cape accompanied by a second wife. Perhaps he now felt safe enough to give his dynamic little protégée promotion. On 18 March 1822 Dr Barry was appointed to the responsible civil post of Medical Inspector for Cape Colony, and also became Director of the Vaccine Board. Her salary was much increased. Luckily for her own future she decided to remain in the army on half-pay instead of resigning as Lord Charles advised. Within eighteen months the outcasts of the Colony were much better off, and the Colonial Medical Inspector's prospects much worse. By 1825 this extraordinary CMI had had six major clashes.

Her first row broke out over the inspection of drugs, one of her duties being to issue licences for imports and sales. She refused to allow the practice of medicine to be debased by unqualified persons, as was then the custom. 'Apothecaries were practising medicine', she complained, 'physicians were keeping shop and shopkeepers were selling drugs.'

She was soon boasting that pedlars and quacks, who had been accustomed to 'puff off' their miraculous skills were no longer able to sell remedies worse than the disease. A 'Memorial' from the drug merchants to the Governor was rejected. One up to Barry. But she had made enemies.

These became personalized over the second, 'Leisching' row. The Leischings were a fine 'patriarchal' Cape family according to Las Cases, and they were bitterly insulted when Dr Barry refused Leisching junior an apothecary's licence on the recommendation of his father, who, though allowed to call himself a doctor, was not in fact qualified. Again Barry was putting principle above the usual, more lax practice. The row swelled to huge proportions involving the Cape's Colonial Secretary, Sir Richard Plasket. Plasket, wrote Las Cases, was like an encyclopedia whose pages had been bound up in the wrong order. Whether wrong or not this time, Plasket said Barry was 'impertinent' and heading for a 'scrape'.

The CMI's 'long Ciceronian nose' was still poking into shady corners. A third storm blew up over the treatment of lepers, mostly black, in the Colony. Barry demanded a complete change in general outlook, from the traditional attitude that they were 'criminals' to a belief that they were 'unfortunates'. Though improvements were made, Barry was branded as a troublemaker.

Her fourth assault was on the civil prison – *tronk* – and Robben Island, the convicts' prison. In the *tronk* she found men lying with fractured limbs, no beds, no blankets. On one official visit she had been accompanied by the highly respected Judge Kekewich. The judge, she reported to Governor Somerset, had walked out in 'disgust'. Disgust was to be one of the CMI's favourite words. She was becoming a positive nuisance to the Governor. All the more striking that a fifth hurricane should blow up in which she and the Governor were involved together.

A violent sensation was caused on 1 July 1824 by a placard stuck on the bridge over the Heerengracht Canal alleging an immoral relationship between Somerset and Barry. It was quickly torn down, but not before its contents (in Dutch) were circulated in various garbled versions. A copy was made for the court, one dreadful word, which the clerk could not spell, being left out.

Life was hard on Barry. To be born a woman – bad enough – and then to be accused of sodomy.... In the House of Commons they would impute to Lord Charles 'an unspeakable atrocity with his reputed son, the household physician'.

On top of this sensation occurred a new and final row over the *tronk*. Barry had refused to certify as insane a drunken sailor named Smith, who had broken into the Fiscal's house. However, Barry admitted that Smith's shocking ill-treatment in the *tronk* may in the end have driven him mad. In an official report

she gave her scornful tongue full rein. She was summoned by written message to the civil court but tore up the paper and threw it in the messenger's hat. Rumour added that she next sheared off someone's finger – and no doubt threw it into the hat also. When she eventually showed up in court she stubbornly refused to answer any questions. This deadlock was broken by an urgent call for the doctor's services by one of the Somerset ladies who at the critical moment 'providentially' fell sick. Nevertheless Barry was given a prison sentence.

An inmate of a lunatic asylum. Such treatment of mental patients was just one of the practices that disgusted Barry.

Meanwhile Somerset himself was under an official cloud. His increasingly autocratic rule had riled an influx of new 'Albany' settlers at the Cape. Somerset lost part of his empire and was forced to govern the remaining part through a council. At the same time Barry, though her prison sentence was suspended, found her office of Colonial Medical Inspector abolished – knocked away from under her feet; she was offered a position as a member of a new committee. Barry resigned her civil post.

As for her own future, she was partially exonerated by two commissioners who examined at length 'The Case of Dr Barry'. Her 'integrity and zeal', they reported, were undeniable; but her fine qualities were counterbalanced by her improprieties. These included her having appealed over the heads of her Cape Town enemies to the authorities in London; and having commented on one of the Fiscal's observations with a 'hoarse whistle'. It was with a reputation for brilliance, bravado and the bullying of local authorities that she took up her next employment, as assistant staff-surgeon in Mauritius. But before she left the Cape she was to enjoy a startling personal and professional success that still has its echo in South African history.

An urgent call reached her in 1826 to attend Mrs Thomas Munnik who was dying in childbirth. With characteristic decision, Barry immediately performed a Caesarian section. Success depended on speed. Thanks to those small sensitive woman's hands she had made the incision, lifted out the baby and sewn up the mother (all without an anaesthetic) in a matter of minutes. Both mother and child survived, making this the first completely successful Caesarian in South Africa, and only the second throughout the western world. At Barry's request the baby boy became her godson, James Barry Munnik. Among his descendants was a South African Prime Minister, James Barry Munnik Hertzog. And today the Munnik family are more convinced than ever that the benefactor of their line was a woman.

Hardly had Dr Barry arrived in Mauritius in October 1829 before she was at loggerheads with the Governor Sir Charles Colville. This hero of the Peninsular War appointed a Dr Shanks to the post of senior staff-surgeon. Shanks had worked in Mauritius for eleven years, Barry for two months. Barry none the less claimed her right of seniority on the army list and was not easily appeased. She finally took French leave from Mauritius, explaining in later years that she had been 'recalled' to London in 1829 because of Lord Charles Somerset's sudden grave illness. But when Sir James McGrigor, head of the whole Army Medical Department, demanded to know why she had come home, Barry is said to have quipped, 'to get a hair-cut'. After nursing Somerset through the crisis, she stayed in England looking after him and his family until he finally died in February 1831. Barry had witnessed his will and followed his funeral in a mourning coach.

On Mauritius, as at the Cape, Barry's sex had become a subject for more than suspicion. A midwife who had looked after one of Dr Barry's patients at Cape Town arrived at Mauritius with an interesting story. In a moment of emergency the nurse had rushed into Barry's bedroom to ask for help. (The doctor was sleeping in the house.) Barry flew into a rage and the nurse was hounded from the Cape because, she said, 'Dr Barry is and was a woman'.

Somerset's death (two years after Buchan's) left Barry for the first time without patronage. In no way subdued, she reached Jamaica in June 1831 for her much-delayed next posting. Because of its climate it was known like Sierra Leone as the White Man's Grave. But the white woman knew how to preserve her health. By now a confirmed teetotaller and strict vegetarian, Barry did not run the risk of tainted meat and always carefully washed away the 'animalculae' before eating her fruit. She was to need her health, for at the end of her first year the Jamaica garrison was ordered to put down a Negro rising.

Only a dozen or so white planters were killed, but the state of the troops, rushed in to support the Jamaican planters, was frightful. They dropped in scores from 'yellow fever' (tropical jaundice caused by mosquitoes). Their condition had always been bad – no proper diet and too much rum – and now their sufferings were appalling. Barry's work was unceasing.

Nevertheless she preserved her characteristic mixture of cool detachment, bombastic self-assurance and conversation, a colleague remarked, 'at an intellectual level one did not generally find in an officer's mess'. But at the end of four years, and even after a long leave, she looked desiccated. It was said that her sandy curls were now dyed.

In St Helena, for which she set out on 18 April 1836, opportunity again beckoned – for change and challenge. As Principal Medical Officer on the island, she was making herself felt within a few weeks of her arrival. Though the military hospital was well run and hygienic, she reported to McGrigor in London that conditions in the civil hospital were utterly 'confused and disgusting'. Barry urged that new buildings were needed for those casualties peculiar to every system, women and maniacs.

Women were particularly badly treated on St Helena. The East India Company had handed over the island to the Crown and had left behind hundreds of female paupers. In words that Josephine Butler was to echo, Barry described to McGrigor how these unfortunates 'were obliged to resort to prostitution for their support'. And she took action that Florence Nightingale was to repeat on a far grander scale. She introduced female nursing at least for female patients. 'I have engaged a respectable woman of colour as matron.' The circumstances, Barry added, in which male attendants looked after syphilitic female patients were 'disgusting'.

Nursing was one thing. But Dr Barry also attacked the Assistant Commissary General. This gentleman had been accustomed to supply only the military hospital, not the civilian one, and also to bend the rules by supplying the military hospital with only essentials instead of covering all requirements. Barry argued that a change in policy would save expense and greatly benefit the patients.

Nineteenth-century surgeon's instruments. Few other surgeons of the time were as skilled as Dr Barry whose successful caesarian section made medical history.

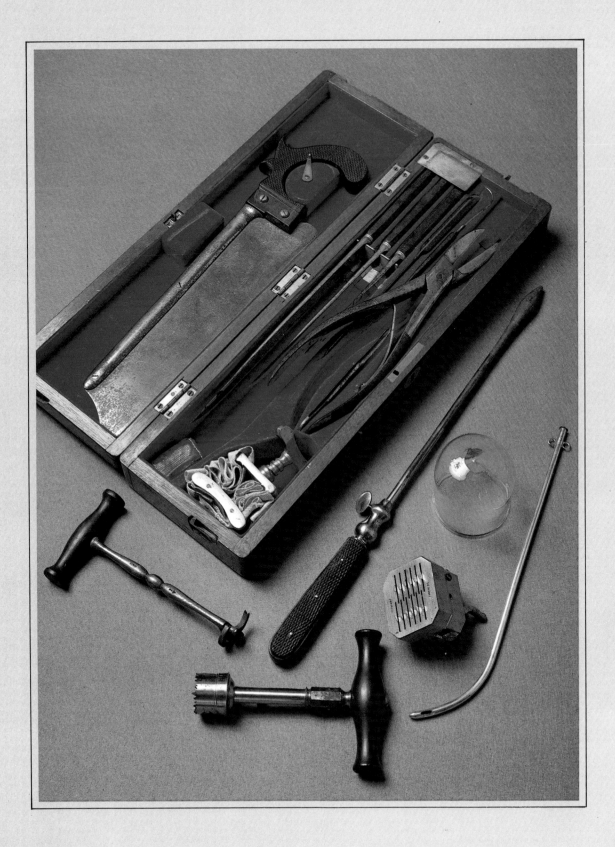

R Power
Operated on July 28th
Drew this Aug 11th 1817

The Commissary refused point blank on both counts. Barry then went straight over his head to the top, as was her wont, and as Florence Nightingale was to do likewise though with infinitely more diplomacy. Barry's letter to the War Office of 14 November 1836 spoke of 'the total absence of all rational objections on the part of the Commissary'. But the question no longer turned on female rationality but on male protocol.

On 13 November 1836 Barry was in her bath when her black servant announced the arrival of the Town Major. She put on her dressing-gown. '. . . I am sorry, Barry, I have bad news for you. . . . I am come to put you in arrest.' Barry stared, as if at a madman. Did the General know? He did not. Barry immediately set out for the General's house but was rearrested on the way by order of the Governor.

Court-martialled for 'conduct unbecoming an Officer and a Gentleman', she conducted her own defence. But her reputation was lowered. Two more years of well-justified but high-handed action lowered it still further with the authorities. In 1838, for reasons that have apparently been suppressed, she was sent home under arrest pending a Court of Inquiry. Early one morning the clip-clop of a small pony's hooves down the street drew several pairs of eyes to the slits in their venetian blinds.

Then came the Principal Medical Officer [wrote one of these observers] looking faded and crestfallen. He was in plain clothes. He had shrunk away wonderfully. His blue jacket hung loosely about him and his white trousers were a world too wide. The veil garnishing his broad straw hat covered his face and he carried the inevitable umbrella over his head so that it saved him from the general gaze. . . .

The Court of Inquiry in London could hardly avoid commending Barry for her zeal, especially towards what she herself called 'the poor coloured part of the community'. But she was demoted from Principal Medical Officer to a staff-surgeon on her subsequent appointment to the Windward and Leeward Islands in November 1838.

Despite their romantic name, the islands were reputed to be another tropical 'Abode of Death'. Here Dr Barry was to wrestle with death – her own and others' – for the next six years. This time she herself only just survived a lethal dose of yellow fever at Trinidad in 1844; worse still, the suspicions of her sex were at last confirmed by two young colleagues, thanks to her complete prostration on a sick-bed.

Barry was by now PMO once more. Fearing that death might be imminent, she broke her rule about doctors and sent for one, a responsible physician named Dr Connor. He was given instructions that were to be long remembered: no visitors while the patient lived and after death the body was not to be 'inspected or disturbed . . . but to be buried immediately with his clothes on.' Though 'he' did not die, the PMO's secret was disinterred none the less. Barry's youthful assistant surgeon felt it his duty to break the strict orders against visitors and pay

Even when anaesthetics were available many doctors preferred to work on conscious patients, as in this operation. Dr Hall believed the knife was a 'stimulant'.

a call on the PMO. He persuaded a friend to go along with him, left the friend on the veranda and entered Barry's bedroom. In a few minutes the sentinel was being summoned excitedly to the bedroom. The assistant-surgeon flung back the bed clothes and exclaimed, 'See, Barry is a woman!' Barry awoke. At first dazed, she made the two young intruders swear 'not to disclose her secret as long as she lived'. In 1881, however, a Colonel Rogers wrote a fictional account of Barry entitled *A Modern Sphinx*. Then the watcher on the balcony told Rogers his story, and how he had known the secret of the Sphinx's sex for close on forty years.

Barry was now due for sick-leave. She had behind her a record of devoted service in the islands. One of her reports, commissioned by the War Office, on the prevalence of *delirium tremens*, bears the stamp of a sane, compassionate and entertaining mind. The only effective treatment of *delirium tremens* in the West Indies, she suggested, was to send the patient elsewhere. As one of her own patients himself said: 'The weather is always too hot, rum always too cheap, and a man always too dry.'

The War Office report on Barry for almost the whole of 1846 was terse. 'At Home – sick.' Then in November of that year she took up the position of PMO, Malta. Efficiency and dedication earned her warm thanks from Wellington. Had the old man been told that he was not only thanking but promoting to the rank of Deputy Inspector-General of Hospitals a *woman*, he might well have repeated his own epigram: 'If you believe that, you'll believe anything.'

After Malta came Corfu. Another pleasant change which, however, did not save Barry from the crustiness of middle age; there is a story of her scolding the soldiers she cared for: 'Dirty beasts! Dirty beasts! Go and clean yourselves.'

As well as her black servant and black dog her 'family' now included a white servant named Thomas Salter of the 48th Foot, a cat and a parrot. In the West Indies she had included a goat too to make sure of pure milk. Mr Salter was to tell his grandson that he never suspected Barry of being a woman, though he was surprised by her refined hands and high collars.

By 1852 Wellington was dead and Lord Fitzroy Somerset, brother of Lord Charles, had become Lord Raglan and succeeded to the post of Commander-in-Chief. Two years later Raglan was left to handle a disastrous war which even Queen Victoria called 'unnecessary'. Barry served Raglan manfully in Corfu by receiving, at her own suggestion, several hundreds of his sick and wounded there and returning them to the battlefield in double quick time – though not without the expected rows.

Active service in the Crimea had been Barry's original ambition, but there was no room at Scutari for another Inspector-General. So she took her leave there in 1855, probably from April to June. Although she could not fight the Russians, she did manage to come to blows with Florence Nightingale. The incident was described years later in a letter from Miss Nightingale to her great-nephew Sir Harry Verney:

I never had such a blackguard rating in my life – I who have had more than any woman – than from Barry sitting on his horse while I was crossing the hospital square with only

Sketch of Dr Barry walking with her cat in Corfu, attributed to Edward Lear.

my cap on in the sun. He kept me standing in the midst of a crowd of soldiers, commissariats, servants, camp followers, etc., every one of whom behaved like a gentleman during the scolding I received while he behaved like a brute. After she was dead I was told she was a woman. I should say she was the most hardened creature I have ever met throughout the army.

Hardened Barry may have been but she still had human feelings of loyalty and jealousy. Jealousy of this woman, Miss Nightingale, would have been only natural. She had the ear of the War Office as Barry never had. And she was a fortunate woman who had been able to outwit the men publicly, while Barry had been forced to do it *sub rosa*. When the famous Royal Commission on the Health of the Army was later appointed, Barry commiserated with Sir John Hall on his not being a commissioner. Dr Sutherland, Miss Nightingale's favourite, would be 'worse than nothing'.

Inspector-General Barry's next and last post was also in a sense 'worse than nothing'. She was sent to Canada, a frail little tropical creature suddenly condemned to icy snows unknown even in the Scotland of her youth. She wrapped herself in long musk-ox furs and wore patent leather boots and 'long-fingered white gloves'. Her wig – they had said it was a wig for some time – had faded from red to flaxen. But her temper still flamed. She flew about visiting widely separated and ice-bound hospitals, sometimes thrown to the bottom of her sleigh as it bounded and bumped over ruts in the road. Her furious screams on these occasions were like 'the squall of an angry seagull'. But she was still a reformer and one of her most welcome reforms echoed, and perhaps copied, Miss Nightingale's activities at Scutari. Barry criticized the hospital meat in Quebec for being always boiled. Like Miss Nightingale she suggested 'the cheering change of a roast'.

Barry also campaigned for separate married quarters, to save wives from the 'disgusting language of a Barrack Room'. The soldiers' straw mattresses were disgusting too, and mattresses of hair or feathers would be more 'genial'.

Nothing could make the climate genial, however, and after relentless attacks of bronchitis Barry was sent home on sick leave in May 1859. Dr G. W. Campbell who attended her that spring in Canada was afterwards hard put to it to explain away his ignorance of her sex. He put it down to her bedroom being 'always in almost total darkness', and to his reluctance to examine her. 'If I had not stood in some awe of Inspector-General Barry's rank', he would tell his students at McGill in after years, well, ah, um, confound it, he might have spotted this 'crucial point'.

When Barry arrived home, 'meagre' and still dizzy from sea-sickness on 26 May, she was immediately summoned before a medical board conducted by three brash young doctors, all strangers to her 'peculiarities'. The three forthwith invalided her out of the army on half pay. It was a bitter blow. She tried to make the War Office change its mind, sending them her *cursus honorum* which has proved most useful to her biographers, even though certain items such as demotions and court-martials were omitted. But it did not sway the War Office. She also longed in vain to be honoured by Her Majesty.

Dr Barry in Jamaica *c.* **1856 with her black servant and Psyche.**
The doctor had a particular fondness for pets and kept a succession of Psyches.

She became ever more querulous in the last six years of her life. Nevertheless there were happy moments. While on holiday in Jamaica she made friends with the McCrindles, owners of a drug store, and left them a gold ring engraved with the words, 'Sacred to the Memory of Marion'. Had it belonged to Barry's mother, Mary Anne Bulkley? She also wanted to adopt the McCrindles' baby daughter. Fortunately this pathetic attempt at a feminine interest in her life failed, since Barry caught the prevalent diarrhoea and dysentery, which raged in the London district of Marylebone where she lived, and died on 25 July 1865.

'In my end is my beginning.' The woman who was called to lay her out, Mrs Sally Bishop, was the first to announce that Barry had been a woman not a man. With the excuse that Barry's landlady had denied her the perks of her profession, Mrs Bishop sailed up to the Army Agents and demanded to see the doctor who had attended Barry in her last illness, Staff-Surgeon Major D. R. McKinnon. In her rage Mrs Bishop accused McKinnon of being 'a pretty doctor, not to recognize a woman's corpse when he saw it.' McKinnon retorted that it was none of his business whether Dr Barry was male or female – 'and that I thought it as likely he might be neither, viz. an imperfectly developed man.' But Mrs Bishop was not to be put off.

She then said that she had examined the body and that it was a perfect female and farther that there were marks of her having had a child when very young. I then enquired how have you formed this conclusion? The woman pointing to the lower part of her stomach, said, 'From marks here, I am a married woman, and the mother of nine children. I ought to know.'

The marks were the *striae gravidarum* or scars of pregnancy. These marks are sometimes seen on people who have become obese, without being pregnant. But that was never the case with Barry.

Apart from Mrs Bishop's macabre but eventful visit to Barry's lodgings at 14 Margaret Street, Marylebone, it was rumoured that two very grand footmen (or alternatively, a nobleman's valet) also paid a visit after Barry's death. They were said to have taken away the Psyche of the moment, a diamond ring given to Barry by the Archduke Maximillian as a reward for curing a member of his crew at Corfu, and last but not least a mysterious 'black box' with which Barry had always travelled. 'Black John' her servant was returned to Jamaica.

Mrs Bishop's story could not fail to find its way into the clubs and provincial papers – but not into the London press. One can only assume that the Establishment – medical, military and political – wanted the story to lapse. Yet it persisted. Indeed the Registrar-General was soon asking Major McKinnon to give him the details, purely for his own interest.

This time McKinnon opened up a little. He told the Registrar the facts about Mrs Bishop already narrated. Though he had known Barry well in the West Indies and England, he had never once suspected her of being a woman. But he could hardly deny Mrs Bishop's story, not having examined the corpse himself. That was not his business. He was there only to certify death.

No one ever did deny the story. Professor Kirby, a South African who has written and lectured on Dr Barry, argues that this was because it was regarded as 'quite unimportant'. More likely it was both too important and also undeniable. When Barry died in 1865 the importance of women's rights, especially as physicians and surgeons, was reaching a new dynamic stage. To have it proved that one of the most successful army doctors of the period – a medical major-general – had been after all a woman, was not at all what the Establishment wanted. It would be better to let the whole thing drop; especially as every new item published on the subject pointed one way.

There was the Saunders *News Letter* in Dublin of 14 August 1865 which considered Barry's womanhood 'indubitable' because of her 'feeble proportions', squeaking voice and argumentativeness. The *Whitehaven News*, a Cumberland paper, published testimony in the same month to 'that extraordinary person ... always suspected of being a female'. (Barry had stayed with Lord Lonsdale at Lowther Castle, Cumberland.) On 26 August the *Medical Times and Gazette* noted that Barry's 'declining years were comforted by the cat, dog and parrot, so dear to elderly women, especially single ones'.

True, Edward Bradford, Deputy Inspector-General of Hospitals, wrote in September that the Barry stories were 'too absurd to be gravely refuted', and proceeded to refute them gravely. June Rose called this 'a military splutter'.

Then, less than two years later, Charles Dickens's magazine *All the Year Round*, revived the whole subject in vivid if inaccurate detail with a piece on Barry called, 'A Mystery Still'. Her sex at least no longer seemed a mystery.

Correspondence in the *Lancet* in 1895 produced several new tributes to Barry's 'peculiarities' from old comrades. A man signing himself 'Captain' referred to the general view that Barry was a hermaphrodite, but as 'Captain' himself did not believe in hermaphrodites he considered Barry a woman. 'A. M. S.' had often seen the doctor while on leave in London, where she was considered a woman by 'common repute'. And a woman writer in *Notes and Queries* signing herself 'R.A.' (possibly Lady Butler RA) recalled having once met 'the crotchety doctor' at a country house and described his tiny hands, flaxen wig, ashen complexion and wizened features. But he could speak 'well and wittily' in his high querulous voice. Colonel Rogers contributed three letters altogether, of which the second told how he himself had shared a cabin with Barry in 1857 – at least they shared it except at stated times, when Barry would say to Rogers, 'Now then, youngster, clear out of my cabin while I dress.'

The renewed Barry interest in the 1890s caused the astute Rogers to bring out a cheap edition of his *Modern Sphinx*. In 1903 a Colonel Battie, in charge of archives at the Army Medical Department, decided not to have Barry's papers destroyed since the doctor possessed the unique interest of being a woman.

What was this unique interest? Perhaps the sex problem should be finally got out of the way. Today the medical profession no longer recognizes the term hermaphrodite, which indeed evokes an impossible concept: a perfect male, the

Dr Barry's flamboyant signature ends innumerable letters of complaint that she or her suffering patients were being badly treated by the authorities.

god Hermes, combined with a perfect female, the goddess Aphrodite. Instead the term 'intersex' is used, implying that the subject is a mixture of both sexes.

Mrs Bishop, however, specifically described Dr Barry as having been 'a perfect female', while the nurse at the Cape and the young surgeon in Trinidad, who each claimed to have seen her unclothed, proclaimed her a woman.

Even Professor Kirby (a musicologist who, like many other learned men, enjoyed occasional excursions into pastures new) had to sum up Barry's masculinity, as he saw it, in a thoroughly unconvincing manner:

For although Dr Barry [he wrote] was *essentially* male in character, he undoubtedly possessed *external* characters that were sufficiently feminine in appearance to deceive the average person who happened to see him either partially or fully clothed. . . . I therefore consider that Dr James Barry was *definitely* male, though one who was unfortunately feminine in *external* appearance. [My italics.]

Professor Kirby blurs and begs the question with his choice of words like *essentially* and *definitely* to contrast with *external*. The most one can concede to those who still uphold the male Barry theory is that Barry's parents may not have been able at first to be sure of 'poor Barry's' sex. Her extraordinary Victorian career, however, makes it certain that if she had been born 'intersex' in the twentieth century, she would have gone to a surgeon as clever as herself to have removed inessential vestiges of masculinity and receive the final touches to her womanhood.

More important than the minutiae of Barry's sexual predicament is the light that her story throws on ideas of femininity. Her best and worst qualities were taken to be typically female: her compassion, common sense and concern for the weak, marred by her 'unreasoning impulsiveness', aggressiveness and generally bossy behaviour. On the other hand, the fact that she did not 'blench' while duelling with Cloete suggested to Professor Kirby that she must have been a man. Courage is not considered to be a female virtue. Again, Barry's decisiveness in performing difficult operations was cited in the press as one of her special gifts. In my youth however (a century later) it was often said that women could never succeed as surgeons because of their anxious indecision.

Barry's 'curious fondness' for pets was said to be another quality of 'elderly females', as we saw. That was surely because the Victorian system produced more lonely, companionless women than men. Today the elderly male is just as likely to take his dog, if not his cat, parrot and goat for a walk.

All the eleven women portrayed here might have been complete casualties of the nineteenth-century ethos, but miraculously were not. No century officially held out a more boring ideal for women than did the nineteenth. Woman was to be the masterpiece of a 'good man', her husband, father or brother. But these Victorian Pygmalions were too pompous and tyrannical for the idea to take root. The best of them backed out. With their support, women seized the marble and carved out the portrait themselves. It was happening among working-women as well as intellectuals, wherever a woman decided to be her own image-maker. The difference was that these eleven did it so marvellously well.

~~SELECT BIBLIOGRAPHY~~

ACTON, William, *Prostitution*, revised edition, London, 1870.

ANON, *The Ten Pleasures of Marriage*, 1682.

ASKWITH, Betty, *Two Victorian Families*, London, 1971.

BATTISCOMBE, Georgina, *Christina Rossetti*, British Council pamphlet, 1965.
The Reluctant Pioneer: The Life of Elizabeth Wordsworth, London, 1978.

BELL, E. Moberly, *Josephine Butler: Flame of Fire*, London, 1962.

BESANT, Annie, *An Autobiography*, London, 1893.

BIRD, Isabella, *A Lady's Life in the Rocky Mountains*, Edited, Daniel Boorstin, University of Oklahoma Press, 1960.

BLUNT, Wilfrid, *England's Michelangelo: A Biography of George Frederick Watts*, London, 1975.

BOCCACCIO, Giovanni, *De Claris Mulieribus*, c. 1356.

BRIGHT, Esther, *Old Memories and Letters of Annie Besant*, London, 1936.

BRONTË, Anne, *Agnes Grey*, London, 1847.
The Tenant of Wildfell Hall, 1848.

BRONTË, Charlotte, *Jane Eyre: An Autobiography*, London, 1847.
Shirley, 1849.
Villette, 1851.
The Professor, 1857.

BRONTË, Emily, *Wuthering Heights*, London, 1847.

BRONTËS, *Poems*, London, 1846.

BROWNING, Elizabeth Barrett, *Aurora Leigh*, London, 1856; recently reprinted (The Women's Press) 1978.

BUTLER, A. S. G., *Portrait of Josephine Butler*, London 1954.

BUTT, G. Baseden, *Madame Blavatsky*, (Theosophical Press) London, 1925.

BYATT, A. S., Introduction and Notes to *The Mill on the Floss,* London, 1960; republished (Penguin), 1979, 1980.

CAMPBELL, Olive, *Mary Kingsley: A Victorian in the Jungle*, London, 1957.

CECIL, David, *Early Victorian Novelists,* London, 1934; recently reprinted, 1980.

COBBETT, William, *Advice to Young Men and (Incidentally) to Young Women*, London, 1829.

CRAIG, Edward Gordon, *Ellen Terry and Her Secret Self*, London, 1931.

CROSS, J. W., *George Eliot's Life*, London, 1887.

DISRAELI, Benjamin and Sarah, *A Year at Hartlebury*, London, 1834.

EDEN, Emily, *The Semi-attached Couple and The Semi-detached House*, London, 1860 and 1859; reprinted (Virago), 1979.

ELIOT, George, *Scenes of Clerical Life,* London, 1858.
Adam Bede, 1859.
The Mill on the Floss, 1860.
Silas Marner, 1861.
Romola, 1862–3.
Felix Holt, 1866.
Middlemarch, 1871–2.
Daniel Deronda, 1876.

FABER, Geoffrey, *Jowett: A Portrait with Background*, London, 1925.

FAWCETT, Dame Millicent Garrett and TURNER, E. M., *Josephine Butler: Her Work and Principles*, London, 1927.

FREETHOUGHT PUBLISHING COMPANY, *The Queen v. Charles Bradlaugh and Annie Besant*, London, 1877.

FULFORD, Roger, *Votes for Women*, London, 1957.

GASKELL, Elizabeth, *Life of Charlotte Brontë*, London, 1862.

GÉRIN, Winifred, *Anne Brontë,* London, 1959.
Branwell Brontë, 1961.

Charlotte Brontë: The Evolution of Genius, Oxford University Press, 1967.

Emily Brontë: A Biography, Oxford University Press, 1971.

Elizabeth Gaskell, Oxford University Press, 1976.

GREER, Germaine, *The Obstacle Race*, London, 1979.

GWYNN, Stephen, *Life of Mary Kingsley*, London, 1932.

HAIGHT, Gordon, S., *George Eliot: A Biography*, Oxford University Press, 1968.

The George Eliot Letters (edited), Yale University Press, 1954–1978.

HOWARD, Cecil, *Mary Kingsley*, London, 1957.

HUDSON, J. C., *The Parent's Handbook*, London, 1842.

KAZANTZIS, Judith, *Women in Revolt*, London (Jackdaws), 1968.

LANE, Margaret, *The Brontë Story: A Reconsideration of Mrs Gaskell's Life of Charlotte Brontë*, London, 1953.

The Drug-like Brontë Dream, London, 1980.

LAS CASES, Count de, *Conversations of Napoleon at Saint Helena*, London, 1824.

LEAVIS, F. R., *The Great Tradition*, London, 1948, reprinted 1977.

MACKENZIE, N. and J., *The First Fabians*, London, 1977.

MANDER, Rosalie, *Mrs Browning: The Story of Elizabeth Barrett*, London, 1980.

MANVELL, Roger, *Ellen Terry*, London, 1968.

The Trial of Annie Besant and Charles Bradlaugh, London, 1976.

MARTINEAU, Harriet, *Autobiography*, London, 1857 and 1877.

MILL, J. S., *The Subjection of Women*, London, 1869.

MINUTES OF THE SELECT COMMITTEE ON THE CONTAGIOUS DISEASES ACTS, May, 1882.

MICHELL, Juliet and OAKLEY, Ann, *The Rights and Wrongs of Women*, London, 1976.

MOERS, Ellen, *Literary Women*, London, 1977.

MOUNTAIN CHARLEY: *The Adventures of Mrs E. J. Guerin, who was Thirteen Years in Male Attire*, Edited by Mazzulla and Kostka, University of Oklahoma Press, 1968.

NETHERCOT, Arthur H., *The First Five Lives of Annie Besant,* Chicago, 1960, London, 1961.

OLSEN, Tillie, *Silences*, London (Virago), 1980.

Tell Me a Riddle, London, 1964.

PETERS, Margot, *Bernard Shaw and the Actresses*, New York, 1980.

The Unquiet Soul, London, 1975.

PETRIE, Glen, *A Singular Iniquity*, London, 1971.

PICKERING, Sir George, *The Creative Malady*, London, 1974.

RAE, Isobel, *The Strange Story of Dr James Barry*, London, 1958.

REDINGER, Ruby V., *George Eliot: The Emergent Self*, New York, 1975.

ROBERTSON, W. Graham, *Time Was*, London 1931; reprinted 1980.

ROSE, June, *The Perfect Gentleman: The Remarkable Life of Dr James Miranda Barry*, London, 1977.

ROWBOTHAM, Sheila, *Women, Resistance and Revolution*, London, 1972.

SHAW, George Bernard, *Mrs Warren's Profession*, London, 1893.

Arms and the Man, 1894.

You Never Can Tell, 1897.

Candida, 1895.

Captain Brassbound's Conversion, 1899.

SPRING-RICE, Margery and LLEWELLYN-DAVIES, M., *Maternity,* London, 1915; reprinted (Virago), 1978.

STENTON, Doris Mary, *The English Woman in History*, London, 1957.

STONE, Lawrence, *Family, Sex and Marriage in England, 1500–1800*, Oxford University Press, 1977.

STOWE, Harriet Beecher, *Uncle Tom's Cabin or Life among the Lowly*, New York, London, etc., 1852; recently reprinted London, 1979.

Dred: A Tale of the Great Dismal Swamp, 1856.

The Minister's Wooing, 1859.

Oldtown Folks, 1869.

My Wife and I, 1871.

STRACHEY, Lytton, *Eminent Victorians*, London, 1918; reprinted (Chatto & Windus), 1948.

STRACHEY, Ray, *The Cause*, London, 1928; reprinted (Virago), 1978.

ST JOHN, Christopher (editor), *Ellen Terry and Bernard Shaw: A Correspondence*, London, 1931.

TERRY, Ellen, *Memoirs*, London, 1933. (First published as *The Story of My Life*, London, 1908.)

WAGENKNECHT, Edward, *Harriet Beecher Stowe: The Known and the Unknown*, Oxford University Press, New York, 1965.

WATERSON, Merlin, *The Servants' Hall: A Domestic History of Erddig*, London, 1980.

WHEATLEY, Vera, *Life and Work of Harriet Martineau*, London, 1957.

WILDBLOOD, Peter, *Victorian Scandals*, London, 1976.

WILLIAMSON, Joseph, *Josephine Butler: The Forgotten Saint*, Beds., (Faith Press), 1977.

WILSON, Edmund, *Patriotic Gore*, London, 1962.

WILSON, Forrest, *Crusader in Crinoline: A Life of Harriet Beecher Stowe*, London, 1942.

WOLLSTONECRAFT, Mary, *A Vindication of the Rights of Woman,* London, 1792.

WOOLF, Virginia, *A Room of One's Own*, London, 1929.

WOODHAM-SMITH, Cecil, *Florence Nightingale*, London, 1950.

INDEX